143109

BCFTCS

£12.99

D0245577

CULTURE ON DISPLAY

BIRMIN

ISSUES in CULTURAL and MEDIA STUDIES

Series editor: Stuart Allan

Published titles

Media, Risk and Science
Stuart Allan

News Culture
Stuart Allan

Television, Globalization and Cultural Identities
Chris Barker

Cultures of Popular Music
Andy Bennett

Masculinities and Culture
John Beynon

Cinema and Cultural Modernity
Gill Branston

Critical Readings: Media and Gender
Cynthia Carter and Linda Steiner

Violence and the Media
Cynthia Carter and C. Kay Weaver

Ethnic Minorities and the Media
Simon Cottle

Moral Panics and the Media
Chas Critcher

Culture on Display
Bella Dicks

Modernity and Postmodern Culture
Jim McGuigan

Critical Readings: Media and Audiences
Virginia Nightingale and Karen Ross

Media and Audiences
Karen Ross and Virginia Nightingale

Sport, Culture and the Media 2nd edn
David Rowe

Critical Readings: Sport, Culture and the Media
David Rowe

Cities and Urban Cultures
Deborah Stevenson

Compassion, Morality and the Media
Keith Tester

CULTURE ON DISPLAY
THE PRODUCTION OF
CONTEMPORARY VISITABILITY

Bella Dicks

OPEN UNIVERSITY PRESS

Open University Press
McGraw-Hill Education
McGraw-Hill House
Shoppenhangers Road
Maidenhead, Berkshire
England SL6 2QL

email: enquiries@openup.co.uk
world wide web: www.openup.co.uk

First published 2003

Copyright © Bella Dicks, 2003

All rights reserved. Except for the quotation of short passages for the purpose of criticism and review, no part of this publication may be reproduced, stored in a retrieval system, or transmitted, in any form or by any means, electronic, mechanical, photocopying, recording or otherwise, without the prior written permission of the publisher or a licence from the Copyright Licensing Agency Limited. Details of such licences (for reprographic reproduction) may be obtained from the Copyright Licensing Agency Ltd of 90 Tottenham Court Road, London, W1T 4LP.

A catalogue record for this book is available from the British Library.

ISBN 0 335 20657 3 (pbk)   0 335 20658 1 (hbk)

Library of Congress Cataloging-in-Publication Data
CIP data applied for

Typeset by YHT Ltd, London
Printed in the UK by Bell & Bain Ltd, Glasgow

This book is dedicated to my parents, Margaret and Clement,
and to my youngest son, Jude.

B.C.F.T.C.S.
143109

CONTENTS

SERIES EDITOR'S FOREWORD

The image of the tourist is one which has long attracted scorn ('Of all noxious animals,' the English diarist Francis Kilvert wrote in 1870, 'the most noxious is a tourist'), yet one which many of us self-consciously embody, or otherwise have imposed upon us, from time to time. We know the rituals, how we are supposed to behave, and where we are expected to point our camera, if we want to try to capture the 'true essence' of the 'authentic' scene before us. And yet, in holding a camera to our eye, we also effect a sense of distance, ostensibly removing ourselves from our surroundings. It is as if we can glimpse – for a fleeting moment – a world somehow made strange by the very act of observation.

Culture on Display: The Production of Contemporary Visitability offers an array of fascinating insights into the key issues at stake here. Bella Dicks explores the ways in which public places are made to assume a visitor-friendly face, demonstrating that it is a complex process achieved primarily through various strategies of cultural display. Of particular significance, she argues, is the manner in which 'visitability' is defined. To be visitable, public places must be seen to be consumer-friendly, accessible, interactive, performative and safe. Dicks suggests that such a definition has profound implications for our sense of what counts as 'culture' in everyday contexts. Culture effectively becomes something to be handled, modelled, even simulated. It also becomes equated with the idea of the world as a mosaic of distinctively colourful, performable identities, the pleasurable experience of which is available for purchase. She proceeds to examine a number of display sites configuring culture in this way, including city spaces, heritage exhibitions, museums, theme parks and virtual destinations in cyberspace.

By situating these sites within their lived cultural contexts, she seeks to show how they have emerged in relation to contending social, economic, and political imperatives. *Culture on Display* thus succeeds in providing a welcomed reappraisal of what constitutes culture, not least due to Dicks's provocative inquiry into who has the power to display whose culture, in whose name, and in whose interest.

The *Issues in Cultural and Media Studies* series aims to facilitate a diverse range of critical investigations into pressing questions considered to be central to current thinking and research. In light of the remarkable speed at which the conceptual agendas of cultural and media studies are changing, the series is committed to contributing to what is an ongoing process of re-evaluation and critique. Each of the books is intended to provide a lively, innovative and comprehensive introduction to a specific topical issue from a fresh perspective. The reader is offered a thorough grounding in the most salient debates indicative of the book's subject, as well as important insights into how new modes of enquiry may be established for future explorations. Taken as a whole, then, the series is designed to cover the core components of cultural and media studies courses in an imaginatively distinctive and engaging manner.

Stuart Allan

INTRODUCTION
CULTURE AS SOMEWHERE TO GO

Places today have become exhibitions of themselves. Through heavy investment in architecture, art, design, exhibition space, landscaping and various kinds of redevelopment towns, cities and countryside proclaim their possession of various cultural values – such as unchanging nature, the historic past, the dynamic future, multiculturalism, fun and pleasure, bohemianism, artistic creativity or simply stylishness. These cultural values have come to be seen as a place's identity, the possession of which is key to the important task of attracting visitors. And this identity is expected to be easily accessed by those visitors or, to use a currently favoured term in urban design, to be *legible*. Places whose identity seems inaccessible, confusing or contradictory do not present themselves as destinations. They do not, in other words, seem visitable. An identity that is not pointed to in the form of well-restored or beautifully designed buildings, artworks, shopping plazas, streets, walkways or gardens does not compose itself into a view nor offer itself as an 'experience'. To avoid such a fate, places should 'make the most of themselves' – rather like the well-toned body promoted in healthy living magazines. In this way, they can find their niche in the new cultural economy of visitability.

In this book I argue that visitability is dependent on the display of culture, but culture defined in particular ways. I explore how culture comes to be produced in visitable form, and the implications this has for its representation. Culture is central to the production of visitability, for it enables a place to become somewhere to go. In the process, it becomes something for everyone to experience (and not just for the well-educated 'literati'). But if we can now talk of visiting culture, and if that takes the form of experiences and interactions as well as spectacles, the question remains of what it is that feeds these, what it is that provides their resources and symbolism. What is the 'culture' that is being reproduced in today's museums which deal in ways of life rather than detached objects; in ex-industrial space turned over to exhibitionary space in urban redevelopment schemes; in ordinary houses and workplaces that have been re-presented as heritage; in a countryside segmented into themes and embellished with artworks? Make-overs and reconstructions use technologies of interpretation, which 'deliver' cultural meanings into places. The aim is to create 'talking environments' that will address people as visitors and keep their attention. But what is it they are trying to say?

Objects, places and artefacts, it seems, are increasingly presented through the lens of their relationship to humans (Foucault 1970). In the process, they are (supposedly) made intelligible and accessible. Making environments communicate is not, of course, a new thing. The countryside has long been constituted as a 'view'. As the object of a romantic gaze it has traditionally been held up as an antidote to urban modernity – in such forms as managed landscapes, national parks and fenced-off 'wildernesses'. It has, accordingly, long functioned as a designated zone where the purity of nature can be sought out as an escape from city life. But now that the countryside has been appropriated as cultural space – an 'outlet' for art, education and leisure facilities – it is no longer seen as nature's exclusive domain. Instead, swathes of countryside are turned into destinations and serviced with car parks, visitor centres, signage and sculpture. It becomes a legible space – decked out with themes and images designed to address the visitor. The implications of such transformations, which seem to suggest a blurring between 'culture' and its erstwhile opposite – 'nature' – will be explored in the chapters that follow.

Bringing 'there' here

The ultimate example of the culturally embellished 'fantasy city' is Las Vegas, built in order to tempt travellers on the old highway from California to stop off and indulge in a spot of gambling. It now contains within it built simulations of New York City, the Egyptian sphinx and pyramids, a Roman villa, Hawaii, King Arthur's Camelot, Paris, Venice, the Arabian Nights, Italy's Lake Como, the Wild West and the French Riviera (Gottdiener 2001). Obvious Vegas companions are shopping mega-malls such as Canada's West Edmonton Mall and Minnesota's Mall of America, which are vast, themed buildings functioning as leisure destinations in their own right. Such malls strive to recreate the feel of a convivial and authentic city, with districts, streets, squares and walkways to stroll along. You can sit out under parasols just as you would in a Parisian café. One of the builders of Canada's West Edmonton Mall boasted at the opening ceremony: 'What we have done means you don't have to go to New York or Paris or Disneyland or Hawaii. WE have it all here for you in one place, in Edmonton, Alberta, Canada!' (quoted in Crawford 1992: 4). Malls, then, bring 'there' here. Museums and theme parks, of course, are the ultimate providers of distance (other peoples, other times, other places) in the here-and-now. Increasingly, they are trying to overcome the visitor's sense of that distance by adopting interactive, participatory strategies (Chapter 6). These allow the visitor directly to experience the reality of another time or place (just as the theme park allows direct habitation of a fantasy world).[1]

As this process of 'de-differentiation' has intensified, so culture has begun to move out of the self-contained, single-use museum, mall or theme park and into streets, urban shopping quarters and interactive, multi-purpose display venues (such as the new 'discovery' parks and centres of art and technology). New, hybrid exhibition-entertainment centres have appeared in cities, clothed in spectacular architecture, while urban streets have been redesigned to send out messages of sociability and fun (Hannigan 1998). Since the 1980s, transformations in the interiors and exteriors of buildings, in street furniture and artwork have been increasingly centred on the idea of design (see Julier 2000). As a result, urban space is becoming divided into design-conscious, specialized enclaves and zones of consumption, where theming, heritage, entertainment and public art are used to manufacture an ambience of multi-faceted cultural vitality (Zukin 1995). Typical projects include waterfront and canal-side redevelopments and the restoration of entire historic areas. The aim is to transform urban space into visitable space (Chapter 3).

Before the age of exhibition, whose beginnings can be traced back to the eighteenth century, viewing other cultures and ways of life used to involve quite arduous physical travel. This was an occupation reserved until the early twentieth century for the very wealthy (Urry 2002). An affordable and convenient alternative was provided by the rapid development of public museums and exhibitions in the late nineteenth century, which brought other cultures to the visitor's doorstep. The museum and gallery were increasingly joined throughout the twentieth century by other kinds of visitor-magnet: first, department stores, cinemas and exhibition centres of various kinds, then theme parks, heritage centres and shopping malls – themselves providing alternative ways of bringing 'there' here. Electronic media have further fed the desire for immediate representations of cultural difference – networked computers offer windows onto the 'live' world via screens sitting on the breakfast table or the mobile phone (Chapter 7).

Ironically, these various sites of display, which appear to obviate the need for travel, have developed in an era in which travel has become a mass activity – easy and affordable for large sections, at least, of the world's wealthier populations. What this suggests is that, rather than travelling to places in order to interact with the people who live there, visitors are travelling to places to interact with displays of those people (and of people who live elsewhere). In other words, the more people travel, the more they encounter their destination's culture in the form of visitable representations. So now, when they arrive at a place marked out as a destination, visitors expect to be offered interesting and condensed sites of cultural display that allow them to glimpse immediately the 'essence' of the local life-world. These may be seen as a prelude to or, perhaps more often, a substitute for venturing out into the disorganized spaces of that world themselves. As Kirshenblatt-Gimblett (1998: 9) puts it, in the political economy of cultural display, 'virtualities, even in the presence of actualities, show what otherwise cannot be seen. Tourists travel to actual destinations to experience virtual places.'

A short history of cultural display

Cultural display is not new. Culture first began to be displayed as a public, visitable space during the eighteenth century. This was when the modern usage of the word exhibition – showing for the public – developed. Until the late seventeenth century, exhibiting meant offering the sacred Host in mass, or goods for sale in markets, but not yet the exhibiting of art or culture (Ward 1996). Collections of antiquities and artworks, it should be said, did predate this, being amassed in Europe during the Renaissance. The Medici collection displayed in the Uffizi Gallery of Florence was a prominent example of an early public museum (Hooper-Greenhill 1992). However, as Bennett (1995) points out, most collections at this time were displayed to a small elite rather than to the general public – to visitors such as scholars, well-connected travellers and various members of the ruling strata.

During the eighteenth century, royal collections did start to be made public as a means of trying to legitimize monarchical power to an increasingly restless populace, through functioning as show-places for the wealth, taste, power and knowledge of princes and kings. It was not until the nineteenth century, however, that an important further shift occurred, in that collections of art and culture came to be displayed to a public reconceived as a citizenry rather than a subject people (Bennett 1988, 1995). This shift from monarchical to nation-state power (in Foucault's terms, from juridical to governmental power) required making people feel included in the nation's culture so they could see it as part of their own inheritance and identity (see also Duncan and Wallach 1980).

Cultural display was essential to the formation of this national citizenry. During the nineteenth century, distinctively modern ways of seeing the world came to be institutionalized, which involved apprehending the world as exhibition (see Mitchell 1988). This was evidenced in various new sites for display – from commodities to entire cities. Ordinary commodities such as (Huntley and Palmer's) biscuits and (Pears) soap were newly differentiated from each other by being branded and packaged, using imagery from the colonies of 'Darkest Africa'. Pictures of colonial conquest and cultural difference, of other places and people encoded as exotic and 'other', found their way into ordinary working-class households in the UK via match-boxes, cigarette packets, board games, toothpaste pots and chocolate bars (McClintock 1995). Mass-produced commodities thus functioned as everyday spectacles of racialized otherness.

Cities such as Paris were rebuilt so as to function as display-cases of modernity and Empire. Mitchell (1988) describes how pre-colonial Cairo, with its labyrinths of buildings, alleys and courtyards, refused to present itself as a view or a picture to visiting Europeans, who were consequently unable to make sense of it as a *whole*. Part of the 'civilizing' discourse of colonialism was to impose order and discipline by rebuilding the city so that it became a representation of something else: a display of political and cultural order. Thus, display was built into the very structure of the nineteenth century city. At the same time, culture was released from the confines of aristocratic private collections and drawing-rooms and brought into the public domain through the development of various visitable institutions dedicated to what Bennett (1988) calls the 'exhibitionary complex'. These included

history and natural science museums, dioramas and panoramas, national, and later, international exhibitions, arcades and department stores – which served as linked sites for the development and circulation of new disciplines (history, biology, art history, anthropology) and their discursive formations (the past, evolution, aesthetics, man), as well as for the development of new technologies of vision

(Bennett 1988: 73)

Indeed, the nineteenth century was quite unprecedented in its generation of new forms of public cultural spectacle oriented towards large numbers of visitors. It was a time, as Prosler (1996) points out, when the idea of 'the world' as a collection of sovereign states became familiarized through colonial discourse, and museums emerged as display-cases showing a world composed of inter-dependent but separate, hierarchically ordered 'peoples'. Museums allowed nationalist movements and governments to display the cultural patrimony of fledgling nations to publics who, for the first time, were being encouraged to recognize themselves as unified communities (Anderson 1991). In the second half of the nineteenth century, the advent of world expositions (discussed in Chapter 4) served a similar purpose. These represented the first large-scale exhibitionary alternative to museums, the first being London's Great International Exposition held at Crystal Palace in 1851. They were hosted by the colonial nation-states as a means of showing off to the world their colonial conquests, technological achievements and scientific knowledge.

This was the era when exhibition became bound up with values of public improvement. The great Victorian exhibitions of science and culture did not, Bennett (1988) argues, seek simply to impress or overawe their audiences with displays of political and economic power, but to turn the principle of progress into a publicly owned spectacle – so that onlookers felt not separated from, but embraced by and included in, its ambit. This was bound up with the project of popularizing the idea of nationhood. Yet it is also clear that museums rarely lived up to their missions to be vital and crowded meeting-places for the popular understanding of science or art. Throughout most of the twentieth century, culture on display for the public also demonstrated its stratification. As Ward (1996) points out, the nineteenth century spawned both public art museums as well as elite, invitation-only exhibition spaces mounted by artists and dealers in private houses. And, in spite of their proclaimed role as agents of public enlightenment, most museums were content to offer a minimum level of labelling and public information, and made few efforts to reach out to wider audiences. They were, to all intents and purposes, institutions catering to a small and well-educated section of the population (see Bourdieu and Darbel 1991). Culture was not opened up to wide public understanding through the museum, it was held up as something to be revered as part of the nation's patrimony.

It was not until the late twentieth century that another shift occurred, one that underlies the sites of cultural display this book describes. From the early 1980s on, we find that cultural display starts to become redirected at a truly mass audience. Museums begin deliberately to court the 'ordinary' visitor. New, 'living-history' sites arrive for the display of a more vivid and vernacular past. Culture is put on display in malls, streets and leisure-entertainment complexes; hybrid 'discovery' centres bring art, technology and science together; art itself moves into urban streets and the countryside. Town and city redevelopment zones drape cultural symbolism around shopping plazas, architecture and 'festival retailing' complexes. In short, culture moves outside of the walls of elite institutions and into the new, highly demarcated environments of visitable, consumerist space.

In many ways, the principle of cultural display identified by Bennett (1988) – that it makes people feel culturally knowledgeable and thereby cultured themselves – has not changed. However, from the late twentieth century on, the forms of cultural knowledge that museums and other sites of display reproduce have become more inclusive and less hierarchically ordered. Increasingly, cultural differences are seen in terms of 'lifestyle' rather than hierarchies of taste. People are invited to see these lifestyles as knowable and accessible, both through the exhibitionary gaze and also through purchase – in the form of souvenirs, restaurant meals, clothing, fashion and other commodities. Culture has in the process become more multifarious, more ordinary and more 'graspable'. In this sense, cultural display is increasingly geared towards the cultivation of the model consumer rather than the model citizen. Whether such developments will produce (or are designed to produce) a 'wide public understanding' of culture, however, is a matter of debate, and one that will be explored in the chapters that follow.

Characteristics of cultural display

These developments have not occurred in a vacuum. They are the result of the coming together of a number of different social forces and trends, the most significant of which will be discussed in the next chapter. For now, however, let's consider the general characteristics of cultural display – as it appears in many contemporary museums, theme parks, urban zones and tourism attractions today. Below, I enumerate a number of these, and identify some of the key questions they seem to pose. Of course, not all sites of cultural display have adopted these strategies, and many vary in the extent to which they have moved in the directions identified. Certainly, one would not expect to find many sites that managed to embody all of the trends specified. Nevertheless, they are suggested by an examination of current tendencies within cultural display today, and help explain its popularity both with planners and the public. I suggest 12 key points here, although others can no doubt add to the list.

1   Since the 1980s, visitability has become a key principle in the planning
     of public space. What I mean by this is the production or makeover of
     various kinds of spaces (physical or virtual), so that they actively call
     out to and invite the attention of visitors. As I have already suggested,
     this is not a new phenomenon. Visitability is predicated on the quin-
     tessentially modern idea of the touristic attitude – the desire to
     experience something different, something which is part of the lives of
     others but which can be related back to the self. Modernity both sti-
     mulates this quest for difference as well as claiming to satisfy it. In one
     sense, then, today's visitability is a manifestation of the *longue durée* of
     'modernization'. On the other hand, the particular proliferation of
     visitable culture over the past 20 or so years, utilizing distinctive forms
     of display (see below), is particularly striking. One of the questions that
     this book will address is the nature of the forms taken by the touristic
     imaginary today, and what they might suggest about how that ima-
     ginary is changing.

2   Cultural display promises, above all, the experience of meaningfulness.
     City enclaves decked out in cultural referents literally carve a human
     identity into their material structures. The countryside, marked out by
     ecological and artistic messages, seems to guarantee the indispensability
     of human life and creativity even to nature. Everywhere, we have made
     environments that communicate to us, that seem to show us their
     'human' faces. At least two questions arise from this. First, how far is
     this quest for meaning explained by a desire for authenticity? In an
     influential argument, MacCannell (1976, 1999) sees an insatiable and
     hopeless search for authenticity as the bed-rock of tourism – something
     which modernity has erased but is constantly driven to reconstruct (see
     Chapter 1). Others, however (e.g. Urry 2002), have questioned whe-
     ther, in today's postmodern consciousness of pastiche and marketized
     identities, authenticity is still a key determinant of the tourist gaze. This
     is a debate to be raised again in the pages to come. But, even if
     authenticity is indeed at the root of cultural display, a second question
     concerns how we should define it – in terms of older values such as
     nostalgia and escape, or some different urge which springs from our
     highly technological, mobile times?

3   Cultural display is going global. No longer confined to the European/
     North American/Australasian axis, the increasing reach of interna-
     tional tourism has sprouted far-flung display sites aimed both at the
     Western traveller, and, where indigenous tourist trades have developed
     (as in China and Japan), at their own domestic visitor market, too. The
     Pacific and south-east Asia are the two key areas of development here,

where 'ethnographic theme parks' are sprouting up in Fiji, Hawaii, Indonesia, China, Taiwan, Japan, Malaysia and elsewhere (Stanley 1998). Two questions arise from this. First, now that Westerners find *themselves* on display within cultures they had traditionally seen as the exhibits rather than the exhibitors, are we witnessing a reversal of the West's historic monopoly on displaying 'the other'? (See Hendry 2000). Secondly, it might seem as if we are seeing such a generalized diffusion of cultural display throughout the world that every place will eventually turn into a destination. Yet it is clear that only certain places are honey-pots for visitors; most remain off the tourist map altogether. What spatial inequalities persist, then, within the general trend towards enhanced visitability?

4   Technology is at the heart of contemporary cultural display. Technological enhancement enables culture to be reproduced as an exciting visitor destination, allowing it to be experienced rather than merely gazed at. Experimental digital environments are providing the push, here, towards forms of display which simulate culture rather than simply representing it (Chapter 7). Yet technology, whilst promising us ever more intense experiences of the world in its 'natural' state, inevitably takes us further away from it. This presents us with a conundrum. The more we crave greater reality and meaningfulness, the more they come to us in the form of simulations. Are such cravings the symptoms of our increasing alienation or do they suggest some deeper reworking of the technology-nature couplet? (see Harvey 1998).

5   Interactivity is a key feature of contemporary cultural display. Cutting-edge environments designed for visiting, such as the new museums and discovery centres, are not static, mute or left just to 'sit there'. Instead they address the onlooker incessantly, refusing to leave him/her alone, offering conversations, challenges, puzzles, push-button options, gadgetry, devices, noises, textures, movement. At open-air museums and theme parks, for example, we talk to characters, themes and stories that are embodied by moving, living people rather than being stuck on the wall as graphics or in glass cases as objects. By making visitors feel included, capable and empowered, interactivity offers itself as a bridge across the distance between visitors and the culture on display. It seems to ensure accessibility, and to encourage active, curiosity-based modes of informal learning. Yet, since the exercise of active choice is often equated with the selection of pre-programmed options, there remains a question-mark over the direction in which interactivity seems to be manoeuvring us. It is pertinent to consider where the appeal of interactivity lies, and what kind of experience it delivers for the visitor. If it

invites us to simply to *feel* more in control, what does this say about our contemporary relationship with technology and the representation of 'other' cultures?

6   Much contemporary cultural display has turned away from official, ceremonial and formal depictions to embrace instead the vernacular realm. 'Backstairs' society has gained popular new appeal, taking over from pomp and splendour (Urry 1990). This manifests itself in a pro- liferation of sites displaying 'ordinary people's' history – history from below – or manor houses which let the visitor behind the cordon into the kitchens, the bathrooms and the servants' quarters. It is not that the lives and possessions of the rich, powerful and famous have slipped from public view (as the cult of the celebrity clearly demonstrates); it is rather that they are re-presented for a gaze demanding access to their every corner and secret. How should we interpret this move centre- stage for the vernacular, everyday realm? The extent to which it represents an escalating prurience, a depoliticized 'taming' of class experiences into mere spectacle or, conversely, a more informal – even democratic – reconfiguration of the visitor gaze, is another question that we might want to consider.

7   Cultural display is adopting hybrid forms and bringing different kinds of visitor space together. As the principle of visitability has spread, we can see a blurring of exhibitionary space and other kinds of space, such as shops, urban streets, bars, restaurants, art galleries, filmic spectacles such as IMAX, as well as the countryside itself (see Craik 1997). The Pompidou Centre in Paris (the 'Beaubourg') was one of the first examples of a hybrid museum/shopping/leisure space, and Manches- ter's Urbis museum, opened in 2002, will not be the last. Other museums have begun to move beyond their own walls into less con- ventional exhibitionary spaces around the city (such as shopping malls and railway stations). Art has spilled out from the gallery onto streets, pavements, roundabouts and park benches (see Chapter 3). And 'cul- tural quarters' bring together various kinds of shopping, performance and exhibition venue. Although we still find bounded attractions in the form of theatres, art galleries and theme parks, in many environments we have become used to seeing display all around us. Baudrillard (1983) famously suggested that the true function of theme parks is to deliver 'reality energy' to the world outside by persuading us that is it 'really real'. When boundaries dissolve, does this project become redundant?

8   Cultural display gets people to spend money in concentrated geo- graphical areas. It offers visitors the chance to consume the

particularity of place within the globalized networks of the retailing, design, building, entertainment and other leisure-oriented industries. Underneath the proliferation of city enclaves rich with cultural references there lies a global system of shopping opportunities. Given this consumerist underpinning, are we to understand visitors' apparent hunger for cultural display simply as a desire to consume lifestyles and identities in 'thing-like form', a desire which is produced and maintained by the object-advertising system of globalized capitalism? Or is it the manifestation of a deeper fascination with the signs and imagery of cultural difference? Globalization has been theorized as a system producing both multiculturalism, on the one hand, and intensifying demands for ethnic 'purity' and cultural particularism on the other (see Robertson 1992). It is interesting to consider how the proliferation of cultural display relates to both of these. It is also pertinent to ask how the economics of consumerism, on the one hand, and this global cultural 'turn' on the other, are mutually implicated in cultural display strategies today.

9   In cultural display, the world appears in the form of replicas and models. Culture is packaged into views, walks, trails, wall-boards, little worlds and parks through techniques of encapsulation, simulation and miniaturization. Japan, for example, has a whole series of open-air *gaikoku mura* (foreign country villages) which put on display miniaturized versions of countries from the West. They seek to make visitors feel they have actually left Japan behind and entered the country featured. And theme parks are only the most obviously constructed examples of encapsulation. Virtual reality is the ultimate provider of a mobile perspective looking for the next shot of believable 'eye candy' (Chapter 7). Display thus allows us to see reality as it never could be seen in the life-world (Kirshenblatt-Gimblett 1998). It seems that an expectation of immediate, meaningful and vivid experience becomes common-place in tourism and visiting. We need to consider what the implications of this might be for the ways in which visitors come to 'know' the cultures they visit. And how might it shape, in turn, the ways in which the 'visited' respond to that expectation?

10   The careful construction of meaningfulness in visitor-hungry environments depends on techniques of 'interpretation'. Interpretation endows objects and places with symbols that make recognizable references to human lifestyles, giving them a human context which situates them in places, times, narratives or themes. Theming, in fact, is one technique of interpretation. For example, at Cardiff Bay, a dockside redevelopment zone in Wales which majors on cultural allusions, John

Masefield's poem, *Cargoes*, is used to knit together various aspects of the spatial environment into a maritime theme, at the same time as allowing the poem to reach a wide public audience (see Chapter 3). The object of interpretation is to produce environments that are both aesthetically attractive *and* redolent with meanings with which visitors are already familiar in their everyday lives. But this principle of meaningfulness and accessibility suggests there may be implications for the kinds of knowledge that come to be displayed in these highly visual, experience-centred environments. How might the preoccupation with recognizable human contexts work to produce particular definitions of culture as opposed to others, and how might it shape the kinds of knowledge that are put on display?

11 Cultural display draws on the principle of 'legibility'. City and countryside, museums and malls are being made user-friendly through the provision of carefully presented and targeted information – in the form of guides, tours, signage, zoning and waymarking. The idea is to build 'total' environments where every aspect is carefully signposted, planned and designed so as to avoid confusion, clutter and chaos. Cities – and the countryside – are thereby invited to act as nodes for the flow of intelligible information. This focus on communication seems to institute a model of order and control that goes far beyond the great city-building and landscaping visions of the nineteenth century. As a counter to these ordering trends, many have seen the real culture of cities as inevitably chaotic, disorderly and conflictual – aspects of human life which may be unwelcome in the totally mapped city (see, for example, Robins 1995). So the question arises of what kinds of information are being made legible and what kinds illegible: what does legibility illuminate and what does it obscure?

12 These tendencies towards easy accessibility and the ready provision of meaning do not go unchallenged, however, and it is important to register some of the opposing tendencies in cultural display today. Techniques of collage, pastiche, irony and fragmentation constitute a trend that differs from techniques of interpretation and theming. Self-consciously postmodernist approaches adopted in some recent museum exhibitions, for example, have displays that juxtapose different items together, quoting fragments of text and disjointed narratives (see Chapter 6). Rather than tying meaning down, such techniques seek to foreground, often through irony or aestheticization, the impossibility of objectivism and the constructedness of every 'finished' account. Interpretation, by contrast, seeks to make meaning explicit. What kind of representation of the world does each tend to produce? We might ask,

further, how these different strategies of display succeed in engaging the visitor with the politics, as well as the poetics, of cultural display.

The duality of cultural display

This last point about the politics of representation opens up the question of how public representations define people, places and their culture (see Lidchi 1997). This brings us to a core tension, as I see it, at the heart of cultural display. Heritage and ethnic[2] displays provide representations for tourists, consumers and visitors, but these representations also address those whose culture is on display. Through display sites, people can ensure their own traditions continue, ones which might otherwise be lost, by educating people about them (for example, Fijian students learn rope-making in the Polynesian Cultural Centre on Hawaii and visitors learn Welsh at the Museum of Welsh Life near Cardiff, in Wales.) There is a remarkable *potential* fit, indeed, between the agendas of the visited and the visitor. It is no coincidence that cultural display moved out of the glass case just as local communities discovered the value (both economic and social) of their own place-based cultures. Experience-led tourism takes visitors 'into' the environment (whether literally or virtually) rather than keeping them entirely apart. Such a movement inevitably has implications for how 'the visited' think about and, perhaps, capitalize on their own culture.

The question is whether, as in MacCannell's (1976, 1999) analysis, the only possible outcome is a descent into performing for the tourists traditions which are only being kept alive for them. Yet can the tourist's desire to get to 'know' the other – albeit within controlled settings – not also produce the space for an exchange of knowledge? I argue that experience-led tourism and public display, which may indeed be predicated on the commodification of culture, are not only about economic exchange. Visitability does deploy culture as consumable 'resources', but it is also underpinned by contemporary discourses of both popular pedagogy (such as 'active learning'), as well as multiculturalism, environmentalism and conservation. Display seeks to preserve culture as both spectacle and knowledge; it feeds both the eye and the brain. One could argue that the educational and conservationist function of cultural display merely provides a cloak for its 'true' function – that of providing a lure for consumers. But one could also see both sides as its equal constituents. Making something visitable and viewable extends its life both as exhibition for others and, arguably, as cultural/educational resource for the self.

Structure of the book

A book about cultural display potentially involves examining an almost infinite number of sites, for cultural display today appears everywhere and in many different guises. There are many sites of display which this book will of necessity neglect, such as domestic and personal sites of display (for example, the home, the garden and the body) and, indeed, the whole realm of human social behaviour – from gestures and modes of speech to leisure, work and family practices – which can also be said to display something about the cultural values and meanings that characterize people's lives. Neither does it discuss public means of display such as the mass media – film, television, video, radio, the press – or the performing arts, such as theatre, dance and music, and the literary arts – such as novels, poems and works of non-fiction. Cultural display is everywhere, but this book is concerned with only one of its current forms: the proliferating sites of display which turn culture into a visitable entity.

Chapter 1 attempts to place cultural display in a sociological context, by examining some of the more significant developments within late modernity that have helped to create the conditions for culture's conversion into visitor attractions. This account will of necessity be a selective and partial one, for, as I have already suggested, the rise of visitability can be seen as one of the defining features of modernity itself. However, the development which has, incontrovertibly, been most central to the proliferation of visitable culture has been the rise in tourism and the recent diversification of tourism practices. This topic is discussed in Chapter 2. Here the focus will be on the relationship between tourism, travel and the question of authenticity, seeking to illuminate the problematic nature of encounters between visitors and the visited.

In Chapter 3, I turn to the city. As tourist cities have developed, and the idea of urban 'strolling/consuming' has come again to the fore, cities have turned to culture as a central means of putting crowds back on the streets. In the process, the city's built forms have become re-oriented away from their nineteenth and early twentieth century use as display-cases of *order* to display-cases of *life* (both human and natural). These processes have not been confined to urban locations, but have also appeared in the country-side, where an earlier emphasis on romantic landscapes and wildernesses has been supplanted by different cultural referents, particularly those fusing the values of art, 'quirky' technology and environmentalism. Such strategies are discussed in Chapter 4, in the context of theming. This chapter seeks to show how theme parks are not mere playgrounds, lying apart from these other forms of display, but, in their use of technological simulacra of culture, help to propagate a general expectation of culture as something one can step into and directly 'inhabit'.

Chapters 5 and 6 discuss one of the most visible and influential aspects of the contemporary visitor gaze on culture – the turn to the past. This is discussed in the context of the 'salvage urge' in modernity, which produces local economic policies devoted to producing the past as heritage, i.e. as somewhere to go (Chapter 5). In the following chapter this same turn is examined through a discussion of contemporary exhibitionary strategies in museums. This focuses on the increasingly contested and problematic nature of the relationship they stage between visitor and 'the other'. This has resulted in a hybrid kind of museum space which seeks to exploit all the techniques available for inviting the visitor 'into' the exhibit and over-coming the awkwardness of this relationship. This aspiration, which seeks to wrap the visitor in cultural 'reality' without having to travel, is explored further in Chapter 7. Here, the ultimate immersive and mimetic technology – digital 'third nature' – is examined, and analysed as a symptom of the unending desire to access and to experience (but not, finally, to live in) other worlds.

Notes

1   Henri Lefebvre (1991) argued that there is always a tension between space as it is represented in organized and/or professional discourses (such as planning or architecture, for instance) and space as it is represented in its everyday usages (by groups of people inhabiting space in various ways). Cultural display invites people to explore space as an exhibition carefully constructed by planners (via facades, theming, public art, etc.), but cannot determine how they make sense or use of it (see Raban 1974). The task of describing how people do so is an important question, but not one that this book can address.

2   We should note that, although the word 'ethnic' refers to the characteristics of any group of people, including white, it is often a term used by dominant groups to refer only to minority cultures. It thus becomes a way for dominant groups to portray their own culture as 'standard' (see MacCannell 1999).

1 | A CULTURE OF DISPLAY

> The Europe one reads about in Arabic accounts was a place of discipline and visual arrangement, of silent gazes and strange simulations, of the organisation of everything and everything organised to represent, to recall like an exhibition some larger meaning. Outside the world exhibition, it follows paradoxically, one encountered not the real world but only further models and representations of the real. Beyond the exhibition and the department store, everywhere that non-European visitors went ... they found the techniques and sensation to be the same. Everything seemed to be set before one as though it were the model or the picture of something.
>
> (Mitchell 1988: 12)

In Mitchell's mid-nineteenth century, pre-colonial Cairo, the world of the modern 'exhibitionary complex' (Bennett 1995) had not yet arrived. There were no public museums, gardens, theatres, department stores, viewing stations, zoos or panoramas, boulevards or building facades. It was 'a place whose life was not yet lived as if the world were an exhibition' (Mitchell 1988: 22). The West, by contrast, was 'a place where one was continually pressed into service as a spectator by a world ordered so as to represent' (Mitchell 1988: 13). Mitchell's account of Egypt's colonization, and its inculcation into the world-as-exhibition, draws attention to the funda-mental importance of display to the imperial era foundations of modern, Western culture. The principle he identifies, that Westerners of the time experienced reality as that which can be exhibited, i.e. that which is readable as a view, or a representation of itself, laid the foundations of the culture of display in which we now live. It has become, arguably, such a taken-for-granted aspect of modern/postmodern times that it is striking to remember its novelty in the nineteenth century. In this chapter, I discuss today's culture of display in the context of the social and economic relations that appear to be encouraging its proliferation in new directions. In the first section, I look at transformations in both display and culture, each term in this book's title being equally important in understanding the roots of new exhibitionary forms. In the second, I examine the wider social and economic relations which have contributed to the diffusion of cultural display today.

Display

The first point to note is that display, as a feature of our contemporary environments, has become more prominent than ever. For example, when we visit places, we expect them to present us with readable views and vistas capturing the qualities promised by postcards and brochures. And, furnished with this exhibitionary imaginary, everyone becomes a tourist, mentally logging the environment they move through into signs and symbols. It is, therefore, unsurprising that public environments of all kinds are being constructed in response to this imaginary. As more and more space is turned over to viewability and visitability, an increasingly mundane expectation takes root – that the spaces we move through will address us, presenting us with a coherent and 'legible' set of symbols and messages and, in short, become 'talking environments'.

The world as exhibition drives nation-states, too. In relation to contemporary world expositions, Umberto Eco (1986) argues that 'the prestige game is won by the country that best tells what it does, independently of what it actually does' (1986: 296). This indicates the extent to which powers of display have become central to the global competition among places and corporations for economic success. This success is achieved through getting visitors to queue up, to marvel at what they see and then to get this reported so as to attract further visitors (see Harvey 1998). Similarly, Urry (2000: 151) notes the 'shift from public sphere to public stage', in which local, national and supra-national governments and agencies seek to promote their international image. This is achieved through hosting mega-events such as world cups, expos, olympics and city of culture years, and by engaging in media-focused public relations activity. It reflects what has now become a global culture of self-promotion.

These displays are no longer confined to galleries, museums or other dedicated exhibitionary venues. Forms of display today occupy visitable, material environments. Cultural meanings are literally written into landscapes, roads and streets, buildings, street furniture, seating, walls, screens, objects and artworks. Museums represent societies as walk-through exhibitions of material artefacts; heritage sites transform an entire historical era into a street with shops and cafés; shopping plazas and waterfronts claim to be cultural through giving space to artworks, exhibition-space and streets designed for strolling. Culture is thus inscribed onto physical surfaces as if, in the age of bytes and electronic images, we were afraid of losing it. The past, similarly, becomes incorporated into the built fabric of cities and towns, providing what Samuel (1998) calls 'memory places'. These 'do the memory work which in earlier times might have been performed by territorial belonging' (Samuel 1998: 39). The past seems more assured of a future, perhaps, when registered in ostensibly permanent structures.

Place-intensity

This point serves to underline the *placed* dimension of contemporary cultural display. Visitable sites of culture allow a representation of place-intensity. Stories and reconstructions of local places are arguably the central organizing concept in many of the new cultural and heritage centres (something which the literature on heritage neglected for some time, due to its focus on nation-state or post-colonial representation – e.g. Wright 1985; Coombes 1991; Delaney 1992). Such histories of the local often draw on the highly charged ideal of community (Dicks 1999). Cultural zones in cities and countryside, too, can be seen as providing a spectacular vision of place. Although themselves accused of contributing to a loss of place, such zones embody an attempt almost to force meaning and values onto places.

Indeed, we could see placed cultural display as an antidote to the proliferation of what Augé (1995) calls 'non-places' – places like airport departure lounges, motorways and service stations, cash-dispensers and supermarkets. He contrasts these with 'anthropological places' where rich layers of human meaning are built up through situated processes of historical memory and identity. Non-places of 'super-modernity' try to stand in for anthropological places by referencing local lifestyles. Cultural displays can be seen to do this same job of 'standing in'. Accordingly, they can be seen as a response to the perception of the dissolving link between cultures and places in globalized times, and its replacement with 'border' and hybrid cultures (Garcia Canclini 1992).

This ideal of the phenomenologically rich place suggests that places need to be marked out by offering visitable experiences of themselves. Plymouth Rock, for example, where the first pilgrims were supposed to have landed in America, was always a nondescript place which failed to provide any kind of exhibition of itself for expectant visitors. Now, however, the reconstructed village of Plimoth Plantation supplies the requisite, fully fleshed-out visitor experience, full of 'the sounds of life, laughter, songs and voices' from the year 1627, where visitors can talk to costumed pilgrims as they wander around (cited in Kirshenblatt-Gimblett 1998: 192). Similarly, Lands End, the bleak, southernmost tip of the British Isles, until recently lacked all but its famous signpost pointing to John O'Groats (the northernmost tip in Scotland). Now it has been equipped with shopping village, discovery trail and no fewer than five 'multi-sensory' walk-through experiences about topics such as air-sea rescue, piracy, shipwreck and 'the relentless sea' (see Lands End website).

Many of these display-sites occupy entire village-like material environments, with walk-through or ride-through reconstructions, strollable streets, parks, malls and squares. The screen-based or multi-media technology they use is always supplemented by the sheer physical presence of the built structures through which visitors move. In this they seem to go beyond the forms of mimesis offered by the camera lens. The camera, however, has been a fundamental precursor to these environments. It has helped to establish a culture of photographic effects in which perceptual limits are routinely transgressed and a modern subjectivity of disembodied vision is created (McQuire 1998). Photomimesis has taught us to accept that certain cinematographic signs stand for reality (Eco 1986). We also expect that these signs will be fully fleshed out and animated: not single objects in glass cases but scenes, landscapes, faces, groups of people. Through the lens, reality becomes a space which is vibrant, technicolour, multi-perspectival, densely textured, thoroughly perusable from every angle through the camera's movements.

Benjamin (1973) argued that it was only in the modern era of print, film and photographic technologies, the 'age of mechanical reproduction', that artworks finally completed their liberation from the ritualistic and cult practices within which they originally developed, and from which they continued to derive their 'aura' of artistic authenticity for many centuries. For Benjamin, the release of the artefact from historical aura opens up new horizons of social and political understanding:

> Our taverns and our metropolitan streets, our offices and furnished rooms, our railroad stations and our factories appeared to have us locked up hopelessly. Then came the film and burst this prison-world asunder by the dynamite of a tenth of a second, so that now, in the midst of its far-flung ruins and debris, we calmly and adventurously go travelling.
>
> (Benjamin 1973: 229).

Benjamin is drawing attention here to a new form of apprehending reality which allows us to overcome the limitations of embodied perspective – what Friedberg (1993: 3) has called the 'mobilised virtual gaze'. In particular, he points out how camera close-ups and detailed shots do not only 'make more precise what in any case was visible, though unclear'; rather, they restructure the subject's relation with reality itself (Benjamin 1973: 229–30).

The cultivation of this camera-centred perspective has, in the process, allowed us to consider a new kind of authenticity – one that is not dependent on aura but on mimesis, or the faithful reconstruction of reality. The camera suggests that views of life which are more extensive *and* detailed can be gained through its power than by the naked eye alone. This has inevitably left the traditional, glass-case museal display – where decontextualized objects reclining on baize cloth are arranged according to classificatory schema – looking rather bare and meaningless. In the camera age, I would argue, the ability of exhibited objects to conjure up *on their own* the times and places they are charged with representing is compromised by the availability of camera-based technologies that can recreate their entire environment in vivid detail.

Accordingly, object-focused public museums, which emerged at the same time as nascent technologies of photography, were soon left behind by the camera's mimetic language. By the arrival of the post-war television age, museums had come to seem dry and unappealing places. They could not compete with the screen's power to produce an exact copy of entire scenes. The camera, one could argue, has thus both created new possibilities for enhancing the display of objects and stimulated expectations for a level of realism objects cannot supply alone. In the process, the aura of the original object is recognized as needing a supplement. This supplement has appeared in the form of today's living history reconstructions, audio-visuals, interactive exhibits, scenic backdrops and animations, and so forth.

However, it is not that cinema or television have superseded the museum. On the contrary, museums promise to safeguard the aura of the original material artefact (not reducing this to electrons or bytes) as well as supplying a three-dimensional environment in which to situate it (although see Chapter 7 on virtual museums). The screen lacks these material effects. We could suggest that the cultural dominance of the camera also shows up the failings of its own mimetic powers, by feeding the desire for more and more reality. New forms of museal display step in to fill the gap created by this desire. Television, argues Huyssen (1995) helps to create a yearning for something it cannot satisfy: the experience of walking *through* past environments, handling three-dimensional objects and 'stepping into' the spectacle itself – talking to the people who live there, tasting their food, handling their merchandise, smelling their streets.

Museums allow us to walk through culture, even touch it. Accordingly, we can see the explosion in reconstructions and simulated environments as a kind of response to the televisual world of de-materialized, ephemeral signs. Whilst for many decades, in offering little more than labelled objects in glass cases and static dioramas, museums offered 'less' reality than television, new forms of cultural display adopted in many museums hold out the promise of offering more. They blend the three-dimensional advantages of simulated environments with the new multi-media electronic technologies to produce simulacra which allow the past to be consumed through all of the senses. The phenomenon of *living* history display – in which the visitor walks through reconstructed streets, climbs aboard refurbished old buses or trams, buys a ticket using period money, converses with real costumed people who speak in the language of the time, buys bread and cheese made in traditional dairies and bakehouses – epitomizes the fulfilment of the fantasy of total 3-D immersion.

Living history thus attempts to overcome the reality shortfalls inherent in both screen-mediated, electronic recordings (films, television and computer programs) as well as live, three-dimensional representations that occur on a stage or tableau (plays and other staged performances). The screen and stage hold the unfolding spectacle at a distance, thereby setting up a disjuncture – which they have to work hard to keep at bay – between the world on stage or screen versus the world of the viewer's squeaky seat. In screen technologies, the camera moves on the body's behalf, whilst the body stays static: one is left outside the scene. IMAX film technology responds to this shortfall by simulating motion and thus inducing the sense of travel (Acland 1998). In a museum, theme park or urban enclave, by contrast, the viewing subject is already mobile (on foot, on rides, on simulators, mini trains, 'time-cars', cable cars, and so forth): one is finally inside the scene. Similarly, computer-simulated virtual reality, whilst dematerializing this experience, constantly seeks to recreate it through the development of 3-D, kinetic and tactile technology. It thus, ironically, further draws attention to the allure of material, embodied experience (Chapter 7).

This is not to say, however, that the visitor to the living history site is thereby fooled by the simulation, or manipulated into believing the mimesis. Visitors to living history sites do not really believe that they have stepped back in time: they are surrounded by other visitors in jeans and trainers, and have constant reminders of their mundane present (the mobile phone's weight in the pocket; the feel of the polystyrene coffee cup; the distraction of thoughts about tonight's evening meal). Like the screen and stage, visitors still need willingly to suspend disbelief and to derive pleasure from apprehending – not the actual reality of the environment they are in – but the novel closeness of its approximation to that reality. Indeed, such environments can be seen as displaying their own constructedness, by showing off a hybridized conjunction of clever technological representations and reality (see Harvey 1998).

Such experiences are part of what Kirshenblatt-Gimblett (1998: 51) calls the 'museal effect', which both makes ordinary things seem special by placing them on display and makes the display become 'a model for experiencing life outside its walls'. She argues that, as exhibitions and museums multiplied through the nineteenth century, a new kind of social and anthropological self-consciousness – a certain stance of observation – began to creep in. People started to view their own habits and movements, the other people they passed on the street and the everyday environments they moved through, with a sense of detachment and constant cross-comparison. Everyday environments came to be seen as 'on view' and open to inspection and fascination, rather than simply being taken for granted (see Mitchell 1988). In the process, there was an increasing sensitization to small differences in lifestyles, an intensifying urge to differentiate between lifestyles and to assign them to different classifying categories.

'Reality TV' is where this desire can be satisfied today. Programmes like *Castaway*, *Big Brother*, *Survivor* and *I'm a Celebrity (Get Me Out of Here)* are game-shows which place the quotidian idiosyncrasies of other people (who are, simultaneously, like us and not like us), under the camera's microscopic eye. In the UK, historical re-enactments for television have recently gained tremendous popularity: highly successful series have included *The Victorian House*, *The Edwardian Country House* and *The 1940s House*, in which real people agree to live for an extended period in a house built and equipped to the standards of a previous era, and to submit to round-the-clock filming as they do so. *The Trench* meanwhile takes period discomfort a step further by re-enacting life in the First World War trenches in France.

Both 'reality TV' and museums put ordinary, everyday things on display within a setting which says 'here is something worth looking at'. This creates a spectacle out of other people's everyday lives and helps to fuel the appetite for further, ever more believable and vivid glimpses of other times and places. Further, we gain sight of a contrast between their lives and our own, which in turn allows us to see our own lives as 'other' – to 'pierce the membrane of our own quotidian world, allowing us for a brief moment to be spectators of ourselves' (Kirshenblatt-Gimblett 1998: 48). The ordinary and everyday becomes re-calibrated into the exotic and special by virtue of being on display. For example, *The Urban Dream Capsule*, a 'performance installation event' that originated in Melbourne in 1996 and subsequently visited Wellington, New Zealand, Montreal and London issues the following invitation:

> In a world where privacy is vanishing see what's in-store. Sealed into a shop window for a fortnight, four intrepid art-stronauts will transfer their entire lives to the high street in a 24 hours a day, non-stop incubation event. Without a curtain in sight, watch them eat, wash, cook, sleep and entertain. No one would have thought that life could be so interesting. Find out what it's like to go beyond the pane barrier and speak to them each day by phone, fax, email or web site, the addresses and numbers are on the windows.
>
> (from Urban Dream Capsule website)

Five actors lived for 16 days in four department store windows, transformed for the occasion into a bedroom with five bunk beds, a lounge/dining room/dance floor, a kitchen/telecommunications centre and the bathroom, complete with sink and shower. 'At no point in time were the blinds lowered, nor did the actors leave the windows. They ate, slept, bathed and performed under non-stop public scrutiny' (from *Urban Dream Capsule* website).

Similarly, there are many websites which allow subscribers to view video cam images of ordinary individuals' private and intimate lives. By no means are they all pornographic in content. There is often no sexual content or nudity at all; subscribers seem simply to crave routine access to the intimate physical space of another human being. Such sites represent either depressing prurience, suggests Tomlinson (1999: 169), or a desire for escape from 'the imposed emotional privacy of modern life'. No longer confined to participation in one's own intimate world, one can now pay for access to others'. Such access gives us, suggests Baudrillard (1994: 28), not the pleasures of secrecy or perversion, but a 'frisson of vertiginous and phony exactitude, a frisson of simultaneous distancing and magnification, of distortion of scale, of an excessive transparency'.

What spectators seem to be fascinated by is seeing the minute detail of others' lives unfolding as if they themselves were there. This experience – of seeing without being seen – is so familiar to our post-camera culture that it stimulates further desires, to get behind the screen and find other microscopic simulations of the everyday, but this time ones which are 3-D and material. In enclaves of wrap-around display or 'living history', a slice of life is taking place all around us – just as though we were not there. Yet we also know the environment is laid out *for* us and we can always catch the attention of the people there – rather than being ignored by them as on TV. Further, these 'little worlds' are safe and secure (Bennett 1995). They offer to satisfy the televisual itch to get closer to the 'otherness' of the past, but only through re-presenting it as 'same'.

Culture

This aspect of contemporary display is what we could call the allure of the microscopic everyday – a magnified view of ordinary life-detail. It is bound up with the idea that we can have access to others' intimate lives without fear of reprisal or danger. This brings me to the second aspect of contemporary cultural display to consider here – the new accessibility of culture. Museums are responding to the proliferation of display sites all over the city and, increasingly, the countryside, which are dedicated to making culture in some way more 'readable' and accessible – something that people can feel mastery over and 'relate to' in their own, everyday lives. This process is not taking place in a vacuum. Many of these display sites are reflecting the contemporary prominence of a particular definition of culture. On the one hand, this involves a broadening out of the term; in another sense, the meanings of culture are made quite narrow.

Subjects deemed worthy of display in today's expos, museums and cultural centres are not drawn exclusively or even predominantly from 'high' culture, but also from 'ordinary' or 'popular' culture. Everyday topics ranging from cultural identity to shopping have become routine material for museum exhibitions (see Macdonald 1998). City imagineers seek out and celebrate marginal, 'low' cultural forms, such as ethnic street festivals and working-class traditions, and plonk them down, centre-stage in the midst of urban cultural enclaves (Hubbard 1998). Huyssen (1986) argues that the polarization of culture through the 'great divide' between high and low began to disintegrate from the 1960s on. In the course of this fusion, culture has assumed a new visibility in all areas of social and economic life (Robertson 1992). Underlying this 'cultural turn' is the fact that culture is now seen as graspable and consumable in a way that it never was before. It thus becomes less over-awing, more fluid and manoeuvrable.

The world as cultural hierarchy

Here, we should pause briefly and define what we mean by 'culture' – a difficult task, as Raymond Williams (1981) reminds us. There are three principal ways in which the word 'culture' is commonly used today. Of these, two are identified usefully by Wallerstein (1990). First (in his 'usage 1'), culture refers to the differences *between* two or more social groups (the specific characteristics of one group against another), which may encompass character traits, behaviours, beliefs, values, customs, and so on. It is a relativist definition of culture in that it involves no hierarchical ordering. Let's call this the *anthropological* view of culture. In 'usage 2', by contrast, culture is used to specify the distribution of certain characteristics *within* groups. To this second usage belongs the traditional meaning of culture as creative excellence and the preserve of a minority, as does the phrase 'to be cultured' (used to distinguish those who are from those who are not). We could call this the *hierarchical* view of culture. This latter is specifically not a relativist usage, for it involves making ostensibly objective judgements about standards and values (especially in the field of aesthetics). It gives rise to debates about what qualifies as culture.

Both of these definitions of culture are potentially political and ideological: the anthropological view of culture allows groups to make claims to collective identity and unity (as in struggles to protect 'our' way of life), whilst the hierarchical view of culture allows an elite or minority to lay claim to prestige or power by reserving the term culture for itself (Wallerstein 1990). A third usage of the word culture is more politically neutral. It is one which Raymond Williams identifies in his essay 'The Analysis of Culture' (1961). As well as culture as the idea of excellence (the hierarchical view) and as a society's 'whole way of life' (the anthropological view, or what Williams calls the 'social' definition of culture), he observes that culture is also thought of as creative output in some kind of material or embodied form (such as artefacts, documents, works of art, performances and creative records). He calls this the 'documentary' definition of culture, in which culture is 'the body of intellectual and imaginative work, in which, in a detailed way, human thought and experience are variously recorded' (Williams 1961: 57). This usage sees culture in terms of cultural *products*, as opposed to cultural processes (van Maanen and Laurent 1993). Cultural products can be either hierarchically or anthropologically ordered: that is, they can be held to represent a whole way of life, or, conversely, a minority sensibility or talent.

Initially (i.e. from the late eighteenth century on), public museums tended to display culture both hierarchically and in the form of products or artefacts. Art galleries, for example, functioned as a means of marking out the 'superior' creative artworks and products from the rest – the ones that did not qualify for admission. Although ethnographic museums functioned differently, they still drew on hierarchical notions of culture. Rather than displaying, in Matthew Arnold's ([1869] 1932) phrase, 'the best that has been thought and said in the world', ethnographic museums utilized the documentary dimension of culture, by displaying the authentic object and document as *specimen*. Artefacts were seen as standing for an entire human culture, or, as one of anthropology's founding figures put it in 1871, 'that complex whole which includes knowledge, belief, art, moral law, custom, and any other capabilities and habits acquired by man as a member of society' (E.B. Tylor, *Primitive Culture*, cited in Burns 1999). However, these cultural 'wholes' were then ordered *within* the ethnographic museum into hierarchical classifications, such as via the doctrine of social Darwinism propagated by, among others, Herbert Spencer. Evolutionary classification enabled museums in colonial Europe and America to depict a world ordered along a continuum, from backward/primitive to more advanced/modern peoples.

The world as cultural mosaic

As the twentieth century progressed, these hierarchical orderings of culture came increasingly under attack, particularly the idea of the evolutionary ordering of peoples. Modern, professional anthropologists such as Franz Boas in the US embraced cultural relativism, in a perspective which sought to understand culture 'from the native point of view' (Ames 1992: 52). These anthropologists 'set off on a discovery of cultural uniqueness, identity and alternative paths of development' in which they depicted the world 'as the site of a diversity of cultures' – a 'cultural mosaic' (Kahn 1995: 99). In Dutch-colonial Indonesia, for example, this approach defined each of the island societies as culturally distinct and requiring study and policy formation on their own terms (see Kahn 1995: 81–100). This lead to the study and celebration of *adat* – the Indonesian term for indigenous custom – which was taken up enthusiastically by various indigenous associations as well as by Dutch colonial officers. This idea of a distinct cultural heritage located in a particular geographical territory has been central to many nationalist and indigenous movements. It is not, perhaps, surprising that Indonesia now has a well-established and extensive ethnographic theme park displaying the 'unity in diversity' of its various island identities, *Taman Mini Indonesia Indah* (Hendry 2000).

Ethnographic and history museums thus progressively abandoned the hierarchical ordering of culture, favouring instead the anthropological view that posited clear identities attached to different peoples. Art discourse has, arguably, held more tenaciously onto its hierarchical ordering, perhaps because art appears to be a metaphor for creative ability, and not, unlike the ethnographic artefact, a metonym for human life as such (see Bal 1996).

Since it concerns creative products, not people, its hierarchical ordering seems, perhaps, less contentious. However, we could actually see the whole of the history of modern art as a struggle to redefine and reclaim concepts of hierarchy, excellence and ability. This culminates in the current heated debates around the status of conceptual art and art installations, and whether these qualify as 'real' art. As we shall note in later chapters, art has increasingly moved outside of galleries and museums and been installed in streets and shopping malls, and galleries themselves have tried to appeal to a broader audience. Thus, while the discourse of art criticism continues to be structured by the hierarchical definition of culture, art has not been immune from the levelling influence of the anthropological tradition. The popularity and spread of 'ethnic art', or art tied to cultural identities, attests to this (Ames 1992; Ramirez 1996; and see Chapter 6).

It seems, then, that the currently dominant definition of culture has moved from the hierarchical to the anthropological definitional plane (or, as Mercer 1999 prefers to see it, from the aesthetic to the anthropological plane). The ascendancy of the anthropological view of culture has led to a widespread popularization of the 'cultural mosaic' – the idea that culture is something that 'belongs' to a place and a people, that it marks them out as special and distinct and that it can be discovered, described, documented and displayed. Ironically, anthropology itself has since moved on from its classic paradigms and abandoned the trope of the self-contained cultural island, embracing instead perspectives which see culture in less territorialized, more fluid and global terms (Clifford 1992). In addition, concepts such as multiculturalism have gone some way to undoing the link between culture and place, by seeing different cultures as belonging to the same nation-state or state-community. Yet the cultural mosaic definition still underpins multiculturalism, for the latter operates with the idea of clearly distinguished, homogeneous cultural identities, even though these are not necessarily tied to geographical territories (Welsch 1999).

Gupta and Ferguson (1992) suggest that popular ideas of culturally and ethnically distinct places have become even more salient as their actual lines of demarcation in a globalized world become more blurred. In popular display, certainly, the cultural mosaic imaginary remains predominant, both in its place-based and identity-based versions. The place-based version underpins the logic of visitability, for tourism works to cement and promote the idea of places having their 'own' cultural identities. By this logic, the world is divided into numerous 'destinations', all containing their own, particular cultural life-world (Kirshenblatt-Gimblett 1998). The identity-based version is also prevalent in the many references to cultural identity in theme parks, museums, heritage centres and urban design. Culture on display, then, is increasingly centred on the display of difference rather than hierarchies. And, as we have already seen in noting the proliferation of simulation and 'talking environments', the idea of culture is no longer confined to products. It has instead embraced ways-of-life, lifestyles and identities.

The global and the particular

It is clear that, whilst attention is now focused on the particularity of cultures and lifestyles, this phenomenon is dependent on a widespread recognition of globe-wide differences. As Kahn (1995: ix) puts it, 'it is now very difficult to travel very far in the world of the simulacrum without running into the signs of "cultural difference"' – such as so-called 'ethnic' restaurant meals and architectural styles, or travel brochures promising glimpses of 'indigenous life styles'. In the world as cultural mosaic, every-where is cultural and culture is everywhere, for every place and social group has its own special culture attached. This view is a product of globalization, in two senses. First, it is a response to it, in that it seeks to affirm the ongoing, local particularities of human life in the face of the ravages of high-tech, global systems (Robertson 1992). Large-scale, space-transcending information systems increasingly mediate our relationships with each other, making them more indirect (Morley and Robins 1995). Reactions to this propagate alternative visions of more close-knit, human scale, localized cultural identities, in communities which still remain culturally distinctive. The display of other, especially more traditional, cultures responds to (and stages) concerns about the dehumanizing effects of technology, whilst uti-lizing and displaying technology as the means of preserving those cultures. In a technologized world, technology appears simultaneously as aliena-tion's cause, symptom *and* solution.

Secondly, as Robertson (1992) further points out, cultural particularism is enabled by and is a product of globalization. Globalization has fostered awareness of a globe-wide system of cultural differences, which attunes us all to a conception of otherness defined in cultural terms. Thus we have 'the universalization of particularism' (Robertson 1992: 102) – a widespread awareness of the world as cultural mosaic. There is also a corresponding 'particularization of universalism' (Robertson 1992: 102) in that identity-awareness (particularism, or awareness of the cultural mosaic) is the pro-duct of an increasingly universalized set of ideas about what identity means. Claiming one's own identity-niche involves using a universal language of identity-claims. In this way, identity-claims proliferate under globalization, for more and more people throughout the world start to recognize and lay claim to their 'own' cultural identities. And those with access to exhibitionary resources (from media to museums) can circulate and market these through cultural display.

The uses of cultural particularism

The mobile gaze of the (post)modern consumer settles on a multitude of sites in the cultural mosaic – all of which it sees as non-mobile. Both 'exotic' cultures and the West's own 'indigenous' cultures (such as peasant and industrial working-class cultures) have all become objects of this gaze. Their interest lies precisely in their particularity, their fixity. Only certain kinds of cultural particularism are commonly revered, however, and it seems that a major criterion for reverence is being in a state of near or total eclipse. Islamic fundamentalism is a more contemporary source of anticonsumerist, anti-modernist critique. Revealingly, it is not afforded the West's wistful endorsement, no doubt because it appears more active, threatening and, certainly, more 'other'.

Fundamentalism of all kinds – whether religious, ethnic or nationalist – reminds us that cultural particularism is not merely an attribute of the mobile tourist gaze. It is also a powerful resource for various place-based, religious and ethnocentric claims to identity and autonomy, as evidenced in the rise of recent ethnic, nationalist and religious movements. Barber (1995) has argued that defensive forms of cultural particularism, including provincialism, parochialism and ethnic nationalism (what he terms *Jihad*) and global techno-capitalism (*McWorld*) only *seem* to be irrevocably opposed to each other. In fact, *Jihad* and McWorld are mutually dependent:

> McWorld cannot then do without Jihad: it needs cultural parochialism to feed its endless appetites. Yet neither can Jihad do without McWorld: for where would culture be without the commercial producers who market it and the information and communications systems that make it known?
>
> (Barber 1995: 155)

Cultural particularism is not only manifested in fundamentalist movements, however. It is also a resource for various levels of cultural awareness and claims to group identity. The kind of global culture described in Barber's notion of *Jihad vs. McWorld* glosses over the continued significance of *identity* (as opposed to parochialism) – something which is intimately bound up with the common historical memories and experiences of social groups in all parts of the world. As Smith (1990) argues:

> It is one thing to be able to package imagery and diffuse it through world-wide telecommunications networks. It is quite another to ensure that such images retain their power to move and inspire populations, who have for so long been divided by particular histories and cultures, which have mirrored and crystallised the experiences of historically separated social groups, whether classes or regions, religious congregations or ethnic communities.
>
> (Smith 1990: 179)

In other words, Smith is arguing that for images of culture to have any real significance, they have to mean something to actual social groups, rather than simply being either a defensive reaction to or a product of an overarching global consumerism. Cultural display invites both the consumer's gaze as well as the *self-gaze* of those who are exhibited, a gaze which is likely to be more critical and demanding.

Heritage, for example, can be seen both as the mobilization of identity for the tourist gaze and as the provision of a public platform for local memorialism. In the context of deindustrialization, for instance, industrial heritage provides an (alleged) economic alternative via the tourist industry, but it also allows ex-industrial workers to lay claim to public heritage in the form of *their own* lives and workplaces, as opposed to the traditional heritage fare of castles and cathedrals. This suggests the inherent duality of cultural display, mentioned in the last chapter. In both kinds of gaze (the local's and the tourist's, or the host's and the guest's), cultural display allows particular identities to be discovered, claimed and publicly affirmed.

Heritage projects constructed at the local level may thus allow the *possibility* of coordination between the uses of public display for local groups and those for tourists. However, whilst local groups are likely to want to recognize their own selves on display (with all the necessary complexity this entails), tourists may be expecting simply a reflection of received stereotypes about the other. This brings considerable potential for conflict and contestation, as I have shown elsewhere (Dicks 2000b). The co-existence of these two gazes does not, therefore, imply relations of equality between them. Those who gaze are likely to be more mobile, and have greater access to capital, than those who are gazed upon (see Chapter 2).

Particularism and authenticity

Underlying the rise in cultural particularism appears to lie a desire for the recovery of authenticity. This has been extensively theorized by MacCannell (1976, 1999). He argues that modernity itself generates its own guilt and regret for the pre-modern cultures and places it transforms, even destroys, in the name of progress. This results in the constant and accelerating creation of enclaves wherein cultures can be preserved, or, if it is already too late, reconstructed. For example, in the 1930s US, one arm of the New Deal instituted a radical programme of roadway construction, slum clearance and river dams, demolishing many historic environments and buildings in the process. Another arm, meanwhile, via the Historic Sites Act, was simultaneously cordoning off selected sites by embarking on a programme of preservation, archaeology and museum develop-ment (Wallace 1996). Economic development thus involved a binary trajectory of simultaneous clearance on the one hand and conservation on the other.

In MacCannell's (1976, 1999) argument, this contradictory trajectory turns these enclaves (whether national parks, historic towns or 'ethnic' communities) into exhibitions of themselves, for it marks them out as special and different. They are given protection (through planning and environmental regulations) and charged with displaying their own authenticity and difference from other places – places which have hope-lessly succumbed to modernity. In the process, they are made visitable, for they function as 'sights' which allow visitors to obtain reassurance about the survival of cultural and environmental diversity. Thus, modernity uses cultural display to fill a void that it has itself created.

These enclaves are preserved as 'stages' for cultural authenticity and cannot, by definition, be authentic themselves. This is because they survive only by virtue of the deliberate forbearance exercised by the forces of clearance. They are produced *by* modernization, not in opposition to it. The US in the twentieth century provides two paradigmatic examples of the interdependence of clearance and conservation. Henry Ford and John D. Rockefeller Jr were foundational American capitalists who, having built vast business empires out of industrial development, were hardly uncon-nected with the forces of clearance. Yet both were obsessed with preserving America's past. In their cases, however, mere preservation was not enough; complete reconstruction was needed. Each built vast visitor parks containing historic reconstructions costing millions of dollars: Greenfield Village, opened in 1929, and Colonial Williamsburg, completed in the mid-1930s. In this way, they provided Americans with visitable, three-dimensional snapshots of two very different versions of the American past (see Wallace 1996). In a succinct demonstration of the clearance/con-servation couplet, Williamsburg involved the restoration of 82 buildings, the reconstruction of a further 341 and the demolition of 720 built after the cut-off date selected by Rockefeller (the 1790s).

It is important to note that the creation of such enclaves is not only a Western phenomenon. The display of cultural particularism emerges, too, in those countries seen by the West as more 'traditional' – where it also, as in the West, draws on a critique of modernization. During the twentieth century, historians and other writers in Japan, Turkey, Mexico, Indonesia and Malaysia, for example, all 'discovered' and celebrated their own traditional village peasantries (Kahn 1995). They set these symbols to work as proof of their authentic national identities. Crucially, these writers were able to represent their countries as different from the West through the operation of what Kahn (1995) labels the 'trope of the demon commodity'. In other words, they played upon the idea that their own national identities were distinct from those of the colonial powers, through claiming that they were more natural, ancient and rooted in the earth. This is based on a discourse which critiques the commodified relations of the capitalist world. It sees these as artificial and homogenizing, and hence a threat to the survival of more authentic cultures.

The paradox, however, is that these discourses of authenticity arise within modernity itself, not outside. They are produced within the very flows and networks of meaning that characterize what Kahn (1995) calls 'techno-instrumental, consumerist modernism'. This means, among other things, that commodity-critiques are inevitably expressed from inside a world that is penetrated by relations of commodity exchange. Cultural particularism, manifested in the ubiquity of cultural display, as well as the 'critique of the demon commodity', have grown up within the decades that also saw the triumph of marketing and promotional discourse (Wernicke 1991). It is therefore not very convincing to see them as separate from those same developments. In other words, as MacCannell's analysis suggests, it is commodified consumer society itself which produces the desire for its own transcendence, to 'get beyond' the inauthentic relations of modern life. Hence, many sites of cultural display are also sites of commodity-exchange, such as theme parks, or have commodity-exchange as a key function, such as museums with cafés and shops. Further, places-with-identities are also promoted and marketed as such, thus becoming, in one sense, commodities themselves.

Consuming display

If cultural display is underpinned by the logic of a consumerist, marketized world, what does this mean for the kind of culture which is exhibited? It suggests, first, that display is oriented to visitors conceived as active consumers rather than as the passive recipients of authoritative knowledge

(Macdonald 1998). This has implications for the staging of exhibitions, namely the transition to modes of display that are more audience-inter-active and 'immersive' (discussed in Chapter 6). Secondly, it means that the exhibited culture is seen as something that visitors share, rather than something set apart from them. Culture can be about shopping, and shopping can be about culture.

In the process, culture becomes more embodied, more scenic. I mentioned above that exhibitions in museums have traditionally tended to display culture in terms of products (see Williams' third definition above) rather than processes (Richards 1996). The move to anthropological definitions of culture encourages a reinstatement of the life-worlds in which objects were used. Technology enables these to be represented in the form of visual, tactile and kinetic experiences. The problem, though, is that providing context in sensory mode, in the form of backdrops, virtual reality and reconstructions, is not the same as describing complex processes. Jordanova (1989: 26) points out, in this regard, that 'it is hard to convey a legal system in visual terms, but law is no less central to our historical understanding because of that'. In this sense, whilst culture on display comes more to reflect ways of life rather than 'the best that has been thought or said', it begins to resemble a sensory environment that can be viewed and walked through, leaving principles of abstract knowledge rather out in the cold.

Consumerism tends to turn particular cultures into quotations – that is, into samples and fragments – rather than allowing for the full expression of complex identities. There will always be a lack of fit between identity and the forms it takes as commodity, because identities are not transportable essences but constructs. These constructs take shape in response to locally and historically constituted centres of power and strategies of resistance (Ramirez 1996). The mainstream consumer market omnivorously seeks out symbols of ethnic and national identity, but since these take the form of consumable goods with 'image tags' (e.g. ethnic art, crafts, building-styles and restaurant meals), they become severed from the ways in which mar-ginalized groups on the ground use them to negotiate, resist or, indeed, assimilate powerful interests. Thus, the commodification of culture can turn it into essentialized images of 'otherness' seemingly frozen in time.

A further consequence of consumerism within cultural display is the contradiction between cultural particularism and standardization. Culture is displayed as unique and special, yet in forms which are market-produced. Disconcertingly, cultural distance becomes available through spatial proximity (via the Thai restaurant round the corner), heritage through the most up-to-date technology (via the multi-media interactive exhibit). Glo-balized markets are key to this contradiction. As Rojek (1993: 203) describes, 'when we fly to a resort in the tropics, in search of "a world which is the perfect antithesis of our own", we drive to the Hilton hotel in a Ford taxi, we lunch in a McDonalds' restaurant, check-in to a Sheraton hotel, watch CNN on the in-house cable channel and round off the day with a visit to the cinema to catch the latest thriller from Hollywood'.

This is not to suggest an inevitable superficiality to all forms of display, and it is important to distinguish between different sites and techniques. Theme parks and museums still rely on distinguishing themselves from each other in order to pull in their respective audiences (museums have a long way to go in shedding their dusty image before they become the Disney Worlds of tomorrow). Chapter 6 will examine, for example, some more experimental museal approaches that try to introduce complexity and contingency. Nevertheless, all sites of display are still inevitably situated within the relations of consumerism I have mentioned, and thus increasingly locate their modes of address within its coordinates. Interactivity, for example, has been theorized as a mode of address fully consonant with the kind of knowledge-power relations required by technological, consumerist capitalism (Barry 1998). Clearly, this opens up questions about how cultural and economic processes reinforce each other in the proliferation of display. The next section examines further the role of consumption in cultural display by looking at its economic uses.

The cultural economy of visitability

The first point to note is the fact that we live in a society dominated at many levels by the banal, routine ubiquity of exhibition and symbolic display. It is this penetration of the symbol into all areas of life that forms the wider social context for the acceleration of visitability discussed in this book. In their book *Economies of Signs and Space*, Lash and Urry (1994) argue that the much-used phrase the 'information society', by focusing narrowly on information-processing and computerized systems, fails to capture the non-cognitive, symbolic and aesthetic aspects of production and consumption in the contemporary period. They argue that it is the symbol, not the information byte, which has become the central resource of late-modern economies. This suggests that we are witnessing 'the colonisation of aesthetics by the market place' (Cooke 1990: 117). Through 'commodity aesthetics', products are differentiated from each other in terms of their form – namely style, design, packaging, advertising – rather than their content (Haug 1986; Fine and Leopold 1993). This economy of display also attaches itself to geographically located places and sites. Just as consumer goods need symbolic associations to become objects of desire, so places need clear cultural identities to become visitable.

Cultural display and economic development

Why has the production of visitability and its related technologies, such as exhibition and design, become so central to the activities of town and city planners? The waves of industrial closure in the manufacturing and extractive industries that characterized the last two decades of the twentieth century provide the key economic spur. In the accelerating rounds of post-1970s capital restructuring and accumulation, the decline of old industrial monopolies in the regions of Europe, North America and Australasia was accompanied by the need to create new competitive nuclei of local production and consumption (Massey 1984; Cooke 1989). Globalization has thereby heightened economic competition amongst localities, and set local governments the task of advertising their particular qualities in order to lure in capital investment (Robins 1991). Rather than weakening claims to place-identity, economic globalization makes them a central tool of policy intervention in local economic governance.

Cultural display has been a vital means of manufacturing and promoting this place-identity. As companies face increasing global competition, the need to find new markets and cut costs means that local variations become more rather than less important (Harvey 1989b). Such variations include local governmental regulation, institutional control, wage-levels, consumer habits, communications, land price, quality of life and – of key importance here – the aesthetics, image and cultural amenities of urban environments. Further, Harvey (1989b) also describes how nation-state governments have increasingly withdrawn from the attempt to buffer local areas against the deindustrialization, structural unemployment and fiscal austerity which hit local regions so hard in the late 1970s and 1980s. Local economic regeneration has thus been left to the local planning level. This has resulted in a rise in 'urban entrepreneurialism', in which local government has abandoned the earlier style of managerialist governance in favour of civic boosterism on a more intense scale than ever before.

Harvey (1989b) further notes that, of the options open to local governments for increasing their area's stakes in the market-place, the strategies seen as providing the best returns are those which will attract consumer spend that can be relatively confined to the locality in question. This means trying to lure in activities which will produce local concentrations of white-collar spend. Attracting visitors from outside, as well as companies whose employees will spend money in local leisure venues, is one part of the strategy. Providing the venues for that spend is the other – and this is where cultural display comes in. Gentrification strategies, waterfront and other property-based redevelopment projects, shopping centres and market places, festival retailing, urban spectacles, prestigious new museums, heritage, entertainment and tourism – these are all targeted at the creation of visitor space that will produce carefully sited pools of consumption.

Although established longest in the West, the use of culture in economic development is no longer a purely Western phenomenon. Japan and southeast Asia have become important players on the stage of international tourism and consumer-oriented cultural display. As Kong (2000) shows in the case of Singapore, the 1960s and 1970s were dominated by cultural policies geared towards nation-building, which were less directed at developing a distinctively Singaporean idiom than at keeping at bay the cultural values of the 'decadent West'. By the 1980s and 1990s, this policy had evolved to the point where the state began to recognize the global economic value of its cultural identity. This was impelled less by a policy of urban regeneration responding to economic restructuring (as has been the case in the West), than by a recognition that, as Singapore entered the global economy, it needed to attract global personnel with high technology skills, as well as tourists and business travellers. Thus, prestige cultural projects began to be actively pursued in the 1990s in order to create a lively urban setting with the requisite facilities for cultural consumption. Shenzen, China's economic development region bordering Hong Kong, is another key example of the strategic use of culture to attract highly qualified workers and visitors (see Chapter 4).

The examples of China and Singapore show that it is not only at the regional and local levels that cultural display is utilized for economic and political ends, but also at state level. There are a number of potential dimensions of state-interest in cultural display, such as for the improvement of the quality of life for citizens (and arguably thus for the containment of workers), for the pacification of internal cultural difference via state-sponsored 'national heritage', for the creation and/or shoring up of national identity, economic competitiveness and visibility on the international stage and for the straightforward economic benefits that cultural display can bring through tourism, consumer spend and the ability to attract foreign firms and skilled workers (see Kong 2000). States thus have an interest both in organizing international spectacles to vaunt their integration of cultural minorities, as well as in seeking to win the support of cultural groups by granting them 'the fantasy of self-display' on the national or global stage (Appadurai 1990: 304; see also Harvey 1996 on international expositions).

However, places themselves are divided into centres and peripheries, and not every area, region or nation-state can capitalize on cultural display. As Shields (1991) notes, marginal places carry all the stigma and invisibility that allow other places to bask in their own visibility and status. The cultural capital of cities, particularly in terms of their built environment, can be seen as the product of a global world-system in which resources become concentrated in key 'world cities', such as London, Los Angeles, New York and Tokyo (King 1990; Sassen 1994). Poorer cities, such as many of the vast and sprawling cities of the South, lack the foreign inward investment to create capital-intensive cultural mega-projects or zones of economic redevelopment. Thus, while cultural display is becoming global, it is very unevenly distributed.

Class and cosmopolitanism

Such political and economic factors help to explain why the growth of cultural display seems to have reached epidemic proportions in the decades since the 1970s. However, some of this recent proliferation is also connected to shifts in the relationship between social class and taste. What is significant here is the loosening of the bonds that historically tied culture to the intellectual class. Samuel (1994), for example, has suggested that the heritage boom may be explainable as a populist reclaiming of history by the working classes from the clutches of bourgeois institutions. This is because 'instead of heredity, [heritage] offers a sense of place' (Samuel 1994: 247). Rather than history taking the guise of codified knowledge in elite institutions, today's heritage-saturated, walk-through environments allow everyone to lay a claim to it. In this perspective, history is no longer seen as the exclusive preserve of an educated minority.

Others, too, have noted the fact that culture has slipped from the grasp of the intellectual class. Lash and Urry (1994) point to the increasing cultural dominance of a particular fraction of the middle class in Western societies that emerged in the 1980s – the 'service class'. This class does not possess land or capital, but occupies a social position that services capital. Its members are predominantly employed in the 'advanced services' sector (such as software, personal finance, education, health and welfare, business services, the culture industries), and have access to above-average leisure opportunities and disposable income. They are centrally concerned with symbolic work, both as producers (in information and symbol-related occupations in which human communication and knowledge of people's lifestyles is of crucial importance) and as consumers (being highly concerned with the symbolic value of the goods and services they purchase).

An example of the kind of effect the growth of this class has had on urban areas can be seen in the fact that, rather than living in new suburban estates outside the city, members of the service class are primarily 'gentrifiers' living in areas of the inner city. With their spending power artificially hiked by the removal of banking restrictions on personal borrowing from the 1980s on, they spend considerable amounts of money both on highly symbol-intensive domestic improvements and on lifestyle-related leisure services. In turn, all kinds of symbol-rich leisure venues and sites make their appearance in the city to cater for the expanded free time and consumerist attitudes that characterize this class. For example, the huge rise in popularity of eating out has transformed the restaurant sector since the 1980s, and made dining outlets highly symbol-competitive (Warde and Martens 2000). Although restaurant dining is by no means confined to the service class, it is the growth of this class, with its appetite for cuisines other than pie and chips on the one hand or traditional haute cuisine on the other, that has provided its mass clientele.

The work of Bourdieu (1984) helps to illuminate the nature of the service class commitment to symbol and sign, although he talks about the 'new petite bourgeoisie' rather than the service class. Whereas the old petite bourgeoisie aspired to self-denial, asceticism, deferred gratification, saving for a rainy day and self-improvement through anti-consumerism (emulating puritanical bourgeois values), the new petite bourgeoisie is committed to the values of consumption, display, spectacle, playfulness, aesthetics and 'living for the moment'. Borrowing from Bourdieu, Featherstone (1991) identifies a similar class fraction as the 'new cultural intermediaries' (NCI). Lacking the bourgeois sense of self-confidence, NCIs invest heavily in strategies for acquiring cultural capital through style-based consumption rather than through the cultivated 'habituses' of the bourgeois or the intellectual. They have access to jobs in the media, and are also, arguably, the principal addressees of contemporary media culture.

NCIs have contributed to the decline in hierarchical views of culture by applying cultivated judgments to culture not traditionally valued by intellectuals or the bourgeoisie (i.e. popular culture such as film, heritage, cartoons, TV). They have thus made it legitimate, worthy of serious comment and not simply dismissable by the intellectual class. The role of intellectuals, in the process, has become reduced to interpreting trends, rather than legislating on matters of taste (Bauman 1987). Above all, NCIs do not promote one particular style but a general attitude which sees style as all important. This fascination with the 'melting pot' of style is a key ingredient in the proliferation of cultural display today.

Exclusions and inequalities

The above analysis of class is not intended to suggest that cultural display belongs to the service class alone, nor that it is invisible or marginal to other class horizons. Rather, it shows that the expansion of this class in the West has provided a ready market for the culture-focused redevelopment of places and their reconstruction as zones of consumption. It also shows that images of consumerism – which represent the average Westerner as a fun-loving big-spender, cruising city bars and clubs and constantly nipping in and out of theme parks – are not universal, but constructed around class-based (and age-based) appeals. The flip-side to this image suggests that not everyone is connected up to these networks. Hannerz (1990) distinguishes between 'cosmopolitans' and locals, noting the emergence of a highly mobile class of culturally literate consumers who can navigate their way (literally and metaphorically) around global cultures. They are a minority, however, compared to the world's 'locals'. These latter, being largely confined to their immediate environment, are by necessity pre-occupied with it. And large sections of the global working class (such as those without work or in casual, intermittent employment) are non-participants in the games of lifestyle consumption and tourism. We can thus see that the culture of display is by no means universal or uniformly accessed.

This is the case within Western cultures as well as outside. Bauman (1987, 1998) discusses how consumerism in the West divides society into the consuming two-thirds (the seduced) and the state-dependent one-third (the repressed). Not everyone – women with children and those in other caring roles, for example – has access to the same leisure time and activities. Access to credit in the form of plastic and bank accounts is also highly stratified. Being unemployed, for example, does not exclude one altogether from a culture of buying things, but it certainly changes the experience of shopping. The interpretation of society in terms of a universal, opiate-like consumerism does ignore the experiences of many who are elderly, sick or disabled or on low incomes or benefits (Edwards 2000: 92). In terms of participating in the culture of city-strolling and visiting, many more individuals are excluded by virtue of being tied to home, or working long and/or unsocial hours. As Hannerz (1990) notes, not everyone has a chance to experience 'global interconnnected diversity' in the same way.

Although cultural display celebrates tradition and well-defined cultural identity, it does so through producing these *as* displays – aimed at mobile, (post)modern, gazing consumers. For world-inhabitants who are gazed upon, and the many more who are neither gazed upon nor mobile, the geographical fixity of being 'local', especially in places of economic decline or stagnation, is painfully underlined by the proliferation of sites displaying a spectacular 'elsewhere' (whether visible on the doorstep or via the media). Cultural display operates in a world of starkly unequal work and leisure opportunities. It feeds on identity, but only through the disjuncture between its own mobility (it can set itself up anywhere) and identity's fixity. As Bauman (1996: 24) comments, in economies demanding flexibility of workers yet denying them mobility, 'well-constructed and durable identity turns from an asset into a liability'. The assets of display are therefore the exclusions of 'progress'. Thus, although I have argued above that cultural display may help to revivify local identities, the current and future prospects for these identities depend on much more than either culture or display. Indeed, we should perhaps attend to Terry Eagleton's reminder:

> Men and women do not live by culture alone, the vast majority of them throughout history have been deprived of the chance of living by it at all, and those few who are fortunate enough to live by it now are able to do so because of the labour of those who do not.
>
> (Eagleton 1983: 214–15).

This divide is reflected, arguably, in the very constitution of the touristic imaginary, which sets up a disjunction between the minority who travel to gaze upon the culture of others, and the majority who stay put and have their culture either gazed upon or ignored. This problematic is the subject of the next chapter.

Further reading

Bennett, T. (1995) *The Birth of the Museum: History, Theory, Politics*. London: Routledge.

Kahn, J.S. (1995) *Culture, Multiculture, Postculture*. London: Sage.

Kirshenblatt-Gimblett, B. (1998) *Destination Culture: Tourism, Museums and Heritage*. Berkeley, LA: University of California Press.

Lash, S. and Urry, J. (1994) *Economies of Signs and Space*. London: Sage.

Mitchell, T. (1988) *Colonising Egypt*. Cambridge: Cambridge University Press.

Robertson, R. (1992) *Globalization: Social Theory and Global Culture*. London: Sage.

2 | VIEWS FROM THE HOTEL WINDOW

Touristic culture is more than the physical travel, it is the preparation of people to see other places as objects of tourism, and the preparation of those people and places to be seen. So, although most of us may not go to most of the places advertised ... the touristic gaze and imaginary shape and mediate our knowledge of and desires about the rest of the planet.

(Franklin and Crang 2001: 10)

Tourism turns culture into displayable objects and visitable places. Through travel programmes and documentaries on television, advertising, promotional brochures and films, tourism has generated a vast and continual flow of images and discourses about other cultures. Accordingly, tourism is crucial to the popularization and diffusion of an imaginary that views the world as display. That world is composed of a 'cultural mosaic' of familiar ethnic and cultural differences, all of which are thought of in visitable terms: they appear to reside 'in' places, which we come to think of as destinations. In this way, tourism helps to circulate a kind of 'National Geographic' perspective on the world, in which selected, highly demarcated cultural identities are expected to be on display in different places. It familiarizes us with certain cultural differences (such as Aboriginal versus white Australians), whilst ignoring or neglecting others (such as those among different Aboriginal groups). This perspective is structured by unequal cultural encounters between the ex-colonial centre and the ex-colonized periphery, whereby ' "foreign" populations have been compelled to be the subjects and subalterns of western empire, while, no less significantly, the West has come face to face with the "alien and exotic" culture of its "Other" ' (Robins 1991). This history grants tourism a particular set of unresolvable contradictions, which will be discussed below.

Tourism enables millions of people to gaze on other cultures at first hand. Herein, however, lies a further contradiction in touristic cultural display.

Whilst tourism delivers visitors to a huge range of different destinations quickly and easily, once there, they encounter local cultures more often in the form of representations than actualities. In tourist enclaves, historic city centres, museums, theme parks, festivals, heritage sites, monuments and exhibitions, local culture is displayed in its absence. Having arrived on its doorstep, visitors actually enter sites of display. In the days before mass travel, a small number of museums allowed non-mobile citizens a glimpse of distant worlds; now, a plethora of museal and other kinds of display offer highly mobile consumers simulacra of worlds that lie just outside their hotel window. Through these sites of display, culture is available in a highly condensed, vivid and concentrated form which works to 'reduce the amount of down time and dead space between high points' (Kirshenblatt-Gimblett 1998: 7). Sight-seeing often involves an endless and often frustrating search for cultural meaning, whereby places wherein its evidence is hard to locate, or which contain too much illegible or insignificant space, result in the equivalent of 'tourist hell' (Curtis and Pajackowska 1994: 206). To overcome this danger, sites of cultural display try to guarantee tourist paradise by offering high-density, compact, cultural capsules.

This raises a central question, which this chapter will explore: what is the relationship between this capsule, its visitors and the life-world it is orbiting? Since these capsules are increasingly technologized, in the sense that they depend on technologically enhanced representations (in the form of images, themes, spectacles, performances and other resources of display), the sense of intimacy they bring, of really 'knowing' the 'other', is an effect of the technology rather than an outcome of embodied social interaction across cultures. Thus, mass travel erodes cultural and geographical distance in the name of an easily attained intimacy with the 'other'. But such a contrived intimacy may have little to do with nearness in the sense of being actually 'touched' by difference and made to think things anew (see Robins and Webster 1999).

Tourism promises to supply comforts as well as attractions: attractions that are different to home life, comforts that replicate or surpass it. Tourism thus attempts to deliver both difference and sameness within the same package. It is this tension that grants tourism its core problematic. By offering the experience of 'otherness' within conditions of consumerism, security and accessibility, it acts as a mediating system that transforms this experience. Tourism produces interactions between the visitors and the visited which are always framed by the consciousness that one party is the spectator and the other the spectacle, and that one party has paid for something which the other is supposed to embody for free. This raises the possibility of mutual conflict and resentment. Of course, not all tourist encounters are as starkly counterposed as this might suggest, and the following discussion will show how important it is to keep in mind the variety of experiences which tourism encompasses. Nevertheless, these core tensions give rise to recurrent concerns around issues such as social inequalities, exploitation, commodification and authenticity (see, for example, Robinson 2001).

As Urry (1990) has pointed out, these encounters between visitors and 'other' cultures have historically depended on the construction of a predominantly visual appeal. The gaze on 'the other' is bound up in the West's historical privileging of 'seeing' as scientific observation, optical entertainment and aesthetic appreciation. This can be seen, for example, in the Victorian taste for landscape, photography and 'scenic tourism' (Crawshaw and Urry 1997). By the 1890s, people living in urban-industrial, technology-driven Europe and America already had a voracious appetite for visual spectacles delivered by a range of newly invented optical devices, such as panoramas and dioramas, magic lantern shows, stereoscopic displays and other more obscure, now forgotten devices (Hillis 1999). Now, as Urry (1990) argues, the objects deemed worthy of the tourist gaze have further diversified into highly differentiated visitor 'experiences'.

However, although tourist destinations are carefully constructed so as to attract different kinds of gaze, it is clear that the tourist experience itself does not take place on a purely visual plane. The clichéd image of busloads of Japanese tourists alighting onto pavements next to a series of pre-selected sights, taking pictures and then clambering back on board does not reflect the reality of many contemporary tourist demands. It seems that what tourists really want is to participate bodily in 'cultural encounters' rather than simply to gaze on sights (Franklin and Crang 2001). Franklin and Crang cite the work of Moeran (1983), who notes the emphasis in Japanese tourism brochures on offering real *contact* with local people, rather than clocking up sights and snapshots. Although the extent to which tourism can actually (or even tries to) offer 'real contact' is debatable, this nevertheless indicates an important departure in more recent forms of cultural display: the provision of sites and excursions offering multi-sensory interaction with and immersion in three-dimensional environments – real, artificial or virtual.

Culture and tourism

Contemporary tourism attractions are typically focused, then, on the experiential: destinations in which tourists can sample different socio-cultural realities. Tourism offers 'customised excursions into other cultures and places' (Craik 1997: 121), and tourists leave with the merchandizing, snapshots and souvenirs that epitomize and evidence the cultural identity they have 'visited'. Rather than 'dead' culture, in the form of stone monuments and empty palaces, tourists today are seeking 'live' culture, in the form of people and their 'colourful customs'. Culture has thus become central to tourism, just as tourism has to culture. Certain key historical transformations underlie this shift. I will mention three here, which have been crucial in bringing culture and tourism together.

1 Tourism as global

First, tourism has expanded and diversified into a huge global system. Already by 1992, tourism – as defined by the World Tourist Organisation (see below) – had become the world's largest industry in terms of nearly all the usual economic indicators, including employment, gross output and capital investment (Theobold 1994). Since then, international arrivals have continued to multiply year on year, and now number over 700 million every year (WTO website). They are expected to reach 1.6 billion by 2020, whilst in 1950 the figure was just 25 million (Urry 2002). Although Europe remains at the top of the league in terms of international arrivals, in 2003 Asia and the Pacific moved into second place, ahead of the Americas, for the first time. Arrivals in north-east Asia climbed particularly steeply, registering a 12 per cent increase, whilst south-east Asia saw a 4 per cent increase (WTO website). Japan and China – including Hong Kong and Macau – as well as Thailand, Singapore and Malaysia, have all become major destinations (although the SARS (severe acute respiratory syndrome) outbreak of 2003 caused a temporary dip in figures).

This global tourism system relies on high levels of standardization in infrastructure and facilities on the one hand, yet it also needs to be supplied with a highly diversified array of different holiday experiences on the other. These experiences have to lock into the multiple segments of today's consumer markets. Culture enables holidays to be packaged and promoted to match the fantasies and desires of every conceivable marketing niche. During the heyday of mass tourism in the decades immediately before and after the Second World War, holidays were more standardized and limited – both temporally and spatially – than they are now (see Urry 1990, 2002). People tended to holiday during the same two-week period at a handful of well-established local destinations. In the UK, these were typically seaside resorts or – from the 1950s onwards – holiday camps. The overseas tourism market remained underdeveloped, and thus travel and holidays played little part in stimulating widespread interest in other places and cultures. Once such interest had been stimulated, and had become, from the 1960s on, a mass rather than an elite phenomenon, cultural symbols became the daily currency of holiday companies' promotional campaigns.

2 Culture as ordinary

The second point to note about the tourism/culture couplet is that, as I discussed in Chapter 1, culture has become widely perceived as 'ordinary'. When the term culture was still predominantly thought of as high art, the preserve of a highly educated minority, the idea of acquainting oneself with it whilst on holiday sounded like rather hard work. And since holidays were by definition supposed to be the antithesis of work, culture in this traditional sense did not figure very prominently within them. The prospect of trudging around art galleries and museums seemed the very antithesis of ideals of escape, of ways of finding relaxation, fun and entertainment. But now, finding out about the history of US immigration while on a trip to New York, for example, no longer seems dull when available as an 'interactive experience' at Ellis Island. And the city's mercantile history can be enjoyably discovered through the shopping, eating and exhibitionary sites of Manhattan's rehabilitated South Street Seaport. Historic architecture ceases to be a tiring sight to gaze at, and becomes a lively environment to stroll through. Culture becomes simply an expected part of the trip.

Culture in tourism does not mean that holidaymakers are all earnestly engaged in the pursuit of historical and cross-cultural understanding for several weeks each year. Rather, they are lying on the beach, shopping, eating, drinking, relaxing and having fun, as they always have done. But culture is no longer seen as antithetical to these activities. Instead, tourism consumption in the form of sight-seeing, entertainment, shopping and eating are seen as ways of experiencing the identity of the place visited and, thus, of accessing its culture. At the same time, learning and education are no longer seen as antithetical to leisure in quite the stark terms they used to be (Urry 2002). Models of 'active learning', for example, include defining the subject matter in more thematic terms and delivering messages in lively, accessible forms that engage the learner through action and experience (Baldwin and Williams 1988). This model can be seen as consonant with the focus on interactivity, theming and 'hands-on' exhibits in many museums today.

The blurring of the boundary between education and entertainment is informed by the quasi-anthropological definition of culture discussed in the last chapter, which sees it in terms of ways of life lived in particular places. Thus, tourism is fundamental to the image of the world as cultural mosaic, organized around the belief that different places and groups of people (still) have their own characteristic cultures – embracing distinct values, connotations, imagery and traditions (see Agnew and Duncan 1989; Robins 1991). Culture in this sense has a quasi-ethnographic curiosity value: what is this place 'really' like? What is that group of people about? This curiosity fuels the culturalization of tourism. Culture in the more traditional, hierarchical sense of national state patrimony in art galleries and museums is still very much part of the sightseeing trail, but these sites have become more welcoming, more consumption-oriented, more design-led and style-conscious, less forbidding and institutional (see Chapter 6). Paris's Pompidou Centre (the Beaubourg) is a prime example. Here, you can shop, eat, stroll and people-watch, even if you do not venture into the art galleries themselves. Such venues have also benefited from the new popularity of experimental, must-see architecture, epitomized in several high-profile projects such as Bilbao's highly praised Guggenheim museum (Chapter 6).

3 Places as spectacle
The third point to note is the economic dimension of touristic place promotion. The cultural identities of places and localities, both urban and rural, have assumed a new prominence in economic development. In the post-1970s phase of capital restructuring which drastically reduced the West's monopoly on spaces of industrial production, large numbers of localities turned to consumption-oriented regeneration strategies, many with an eye to bringing in tourist spend (see Chapter 3). As place promotion has become a major force in local economic development, economies previously reliant on manufacturing production have turned their redundant industrial land over to real-estate development for leisure and services (Gold and Ward 1994). Localities now have to compete with each other for their share of shoppers, diners, drinkers and spectators. As more places become geared up for visitors through the construction of viewable and visitable environments, so more people find themselves living in areas dedicated to cultural display, and expect other places to offer it too.

Place-based regeneration strategies are not, however, confined to the West. Japan's industrial restructuring in the 1980s, which produced a shift from manufacturing to high-tech and service industries similar to that of Western societies, likewise stimulated a new emphasis on domestic leisure development. Moreover, less developed countries, too, have increasingly recognized the economic gains of attracting tourists from wealthier nations, who are now – thanks to the rapid development of highly organized travel infrastructures – more mobile and able to travel than ever before. In the process, poorer nations have entered the competition to attract visitors, a competition in which culture is seen as a major asset. South-east Asia, for example, has seen major new growth in international tourism receipts, with Japan providing aid, technical assistance and capital for tourism-related projects and also being the principal source of incoming tourists (Mackie 1992). Tourism in both the Caribbean islands and certain countries in Latin America has also recorded rapid growth (Harrison 1992). Culture has been central in each of these cases.

Economic development is not the only motivating factor in place-based cultural display. This period has also coincided with the appearance of various place-based claims to collective identity (nationalisms, regional-isms, ethnicities and other appeals to community). Many states and regions now find themselves having to make public gestures towards the values of cultural pluralism and multi-culturalism, even where relations of margin-alization and inequalities are, in reality, maintained (Kahn 1995). Tourist-oriented display can thus serve political, as well as economic, purposes. Where it is deployed to represent particular versions of collective identity in the public arena, it can perform valuable public relations work for nations, regions and, increasingly, corporations (Appadurai 1990).

Recognizing how public discourse about cultural pluralism and identity helps to popularize key place-myths also serves to illuminate the spatially uneven nature of cultural display. Some places are destinations or desti-nations-in-waiting; others are not. Localities blighted by the withdrawal of capital, where money has not been found for make-overs or mega-projects, remain invisible to the tourist gaze. In a different way, suburban areas primarily composed of residential estates are not usually oriented towards touristic viewing. Thus, as in any discussion of place-based spectacle, it is important to remember that one area's 'success' in constructing itself as a sight is another area's failure to compete in the visitor game in the first place. In Chapter 3, I show how two neighbouring ex-industrial areas of South Wales in the UK have been assigned two different fates: one embarking on a display-based road to renewal, the other left to relative decay and decline.

Tourists, visitors, travellers

All the sites of cultural display discussed in this book are potentially sites of tourism. They are spaces of consumption which aim to attract visitors, and tourists constitute a major category of visitors. However, it is difficult to define a particular type of consumer called 'the tourist', or to draw a clear dividing line between tourists and other kinds of visitors. Many sites of cultural display are visited both by local residents or workers, and by visitors from nearby catchment areas who have come for a day out. Tourists 'on holiday' might represent only one segment of their visitor base. The World Tourism Organisation in 1991 recommended that tourism be defined as:

> the activities of a person travelling to a place outside his or her usual environment for less than a specified period of time and whose main purpose of travel is other than the exercise of an activity remunerated from within the place visited...
> (World Tourism Organisation 1991, cited in Theobold 1994: 12)

This is a deliberately technical categorization, representing tourism in terms of the variables of function, space and time. It does not get us very far in understanding the varieties of cultural consumption in which different groups engage at sites of cultural display. Rather than trying to pin down visitor types, it is more meaningful to consider different kinds of visitor experience, and to recognize the increasing hybridization of these experiences. The same visitor may engage in activities of sight-seeing, carnival, shopping, strolling, adventure, physical exertion, spectator sports, sunbathing, and many others besides, both at different times in their lives and, potentially, within the boundaries of one trip. Work and leisure are increasingly combined; being on a work-related trip often includes leisure activities and sight-seeing. This chapter concentrates on the phenomenon of 'the holiday', i.e. the widespread practice of taking short periods of leave from work and routine and 'getting away', particularly to foreign destinations.

Tourism, inequalities and difference

If tourism is about 'getting away from it all', it is clear that not everyone is able to get away, and that not everyone is getting away from the same 'it'. Evidently, the 45 most highly developed countries in the world account for three-quarters of international tourism departures (Urry 2002: 5). This fact gives the spectacular growth in tourism a marked asymmetry, since by and large it is Europeans, North Americans, Australasians and the Japanese – the minority world – who are taking trips into the cultural mosaic of the less developed nations – the majority world. What they are getting away from are societies which are disproportionately affluent, consumerist, technologized, centralized and regulated. This inevitably shapes the kind of escape that is sought, and helps to project a particular set of expectations onto holiday destinations.

Differentiation is also apparent *within* societies, since different social groups, divided along the lines of class, ethnicity, gender and generation, are also getting away from different everyday realities. Accordingly, they are escaping to destinations required to play quite distinct roles in the imagination. The kinds of culture sought out within these tourism group-ings are similarly differentiated. If getting away involves a particular dynamic between ordinary self and fantasized self, then it is clear that the social spaces one inhabits at 'home' are part of the baggage one takes 'away'. The next section takes three key domains of social difference – class, gender and ethnicity – and considers how each works to produce the destination as a distinct object of desire.

Tourism, class and social stratification

Tourism is a system which is highly differentiated. Whereas some British people, it seems, can think of no better holiday destination to return to year on year than the Spanish resorts on the Costa Brava, others consider them the epitome of vulgarity and would rather spend a rainy week in Brighton than be forced to go there. Many writers have argued that selecting certain consumer goods and services over others is a prime means of commu-nicating social status and class position – and these arguments are eminently applicable to people's choice of leisure pursuits and holiday destinations. Douglas and Isherwood (1980), for example, in their book, *The World of Goods*, see activities such as travel as a form of commodity to which different social groups have both unequal access and aspiration. They argue that all goods, whether material or immaterial, carry social meanings – they 'make and maintain social relationships' by functioning as social markers. Holidays with a strong cultural element allow the profes-sional class to consume more 'informational' goods – something which is directly of value to them in their employment.

In Bourdieu's (1984) terms, one's preference for a particular holiday destination is not an attribute of one's individual tastes, but an expression of a social system of distinctions. These are propagated through the insti-tutions of society (such as school, the professions, the family) rather than within individual minds. Bourdieu argues that distinctions serve social purposes: they are ways of encoding, or making meaningful, social differ-ences such as class. He thus makes a fundamental break with the tradition of idealist aesthetics, which proposes that aesthetics is based on ideals such as quality, spirituality or equilibrium. Instead, 'taste is that which brings

together things and people that go together' (Bourdieu 1984: 241). Taste is
the result of a system whereby classes own different levels of 'cultural
capital', a system in which aesthetics is finely graded. In particular, the
higher the level of cultural capital one has, the more that aesthetic *form*
rather than content or function will be valued. Those who have completed a
higher education are more likely to embrace the 'Kantian aesthetic' –
foregoing the immediate, sensual pleasure of things (e.g. an easy read, a
soap opera, junk food or a fortnight at a beach resort), in favour of a
cultivated and abstracted stance that appreciates difficult, more formal
qualities that have to be deliberately sought out (e.g. poetry, haute cuisine,
an educational tour of cultural architecture or a hiking holiday to remote
and inaccessible places). This stance favours views that demand an appreciation of form and context (such as East European tower-blocks) rather
than subject (such as sunset beaches).

Accordingly, although the major determinant of a person's tastes and
preferences remains economic (what can I afford?) Bourdieu's analysis
shows that economic position alone is not a sufficient explanation. The
impoverished intellectual does not despise Torremolinos only because she
cannot afford to go there, but because she subscribes to a set of cultural
values that sees it as inauthentic, vulgar, standardized. Similarly, she
despises traditional bourgeois tastes for sumptuous interiors, stately homes
and formal gardens, because these conflict with the 'ascetic aesthetic' that
favours 'natural' materials, 'wild' landscapes and 'ostentatious poverty'
(Urry 2002). In this taste-culture, the more intellectual effort she has to
make to decode the destination, the more gratified she feels in having the
opportunity to exercise the discrimination afforded by her cultural capital.
In this way, she can come to see East European tower blocks as redolent
with culture. Featherstone (1991) adds, in his analysis of 'new cultural
intermediaries' (or NCIs – see Chapter 1), that intellectuals are increasingly
appropriating the NCI's populist cultural preferences, by adopting 'playful'
and ironic stances in relation to them. Thus, today's intellectual (who
would never call herself such) can enjoy both a culinary walking tour
through Crete and a weekend with 'the girls' in Blackpool.

Tourism, the gaze and gender

Just as class underpins the taste system of tourism, so gender can be said to
furnish some of its major coordinates. Key couplets underlying tourism,
such as safety/adventure, home/away, leisure/work and fixity/mobility, are
all enmeshed in the symbolic oppositions between the feminine and the
masculine realms. Home has different meanings for women than men, and

thus so does the idea of being away (Massey 1994). The ideal of travel, in which the mobile subject moves fearlessly and confidently through strange environments, looking at things detachedly as objects, rather than being looked at as an object, reflects the privileged position of the masculine standpoint. Jokinev and Veijola (1997) show how both modernity and postmodernity have been theorized through the idea of the subject's entry into a mobile, appropriating, restless and wandering mode of existence (see Simmel, Baudelaire, Benjamin and, more recently, Bauman). They point out that these appeals are predicated on devalued opposites which have traditionally been women's terrain – such as being stuck at home.

It is clear that placing the idea of the gaze at the very heart of the tourism system (see Urry 1990, 2002) tends to replicate this equation between travel and the freedom afforded by a masculinist perspective. It is an idea which adopts the perspective of the viewer, looking outwards towards a surrounding environment. It is a perspective which is in control. As a corrective to this one-way gaze, we need to consider the ways in which women tourists are caught up in various kinds of embodied self-display, which involve being the object of the gaze rather than the gazing subject. In Bali, for instance, female tourists' toplessness on the beach is an object of the gaze for fully dressed Balinese men (Picard 1996).

Being female further problematizes all the difficult self-other (wealthy/ poor; modern/traditional; familiar/exotic) relations that foreign travel sets into motion. Being a Westerner in an Arab culture may draw public attention; being a woman traveller in virtually every culture carries the added potential of sexual harassment. At the same time, men who travel do not encounter an undifferentiated category of 'locals' at their destination, but women and men, young and old, rich and poor. Women on the street may become part of the cultural 'sight' through the established, male right to gaze. On the other hand, women may be absent from the street, as in Goreme in Turkey, where Turkish women are kept hidden in their homes away from public view (Tucker 1997). However, Tucker also describes a female counter-gaze in operation here, where tourists blundering around the narrow streets provide the cloistered women with considerable amusement.

Women can also become part of the local 'entertainment' available for purchase. Thus, images of a country's 'attractions' may be styled around stereotypes about the sexual availability of its women, particularly through myths of exoticism in the East. Tourism in south-east Asia, especially in Thailand, South Korea and the Philippines, deliberately plays on exoticized images long in circulation in the West of passive, mysterious, silent and sexually available women. This has resulted in a high demand among male tourists and business travellers, from West *and* East, for so-called 'hospitality girls'. Other destinations offering the important cost differential of cheap sexual services include Africa, Latin America and the Caribbean (Hall 1992). This has grown up within societies which are characterized by stark sexual inequalities and divisions, and where the state has been willing, even eager, to promote and encourage the so-called hospitality industry as part of its tourism assets (Urry 2002). Such constructs cannot be understood outside of colonial and post-colonial myths of orientalism, but neither can they be located outside of an equally suffocating system of gender difference.

Tourism, orientalism and global inequalities

We have already noted how images of the 'world as cultural mosaic' are fundamental to the touristic imaginary (Chapter 1). Such images freeze cultures into unchanging essences, forever tied to one place and one time (Clifford 1992). Tourism was built out of the nineteenth century colonial powers' discovery of the appeal of 'pre-modern', traditional cultures, and has since provided a powerful economic incentive to keep them looking that way. Gregory (2001), for example, points to the stratified class relations of Western travel in the Orient during the imperial era. Today's tourist brochures advertising Nile river trips claim to transport visitors back to the same timeless 'elegance', advertising standards of service direct from 'another age' and thus reproducing the fantasy of experiencing colonial privileges without any of the insecurities and dangers of the historical period. Travel in the less developed, majority world thus furnishes a kind of utopia for the minority world. It offers the experience (through purchase) of living in a world where everything is laid on: the cleaning, the laundry service, the food court, the play areas, the sports facilities, the fun and entertainment. And yet, outside, the colourful, chaotic, pre-modern, traditional world endures.

Whilst many tourist destinations for relatively affluent Western and Japanese visitors are in the developing world, developing countries themselves produce few tourists (Harrison 1992). In many parts of Africa, Asia and the Indian subcontinent, travel is undertaken for utilitarian reasons rather than for leisure. First, travel is often a means to an end: a trip to see relatives, to seek work or to buy and exchange produce and livestock. Secondly, war-torn, environmentally degraded and economically impoverished regions produce motivations for escape quite different from those of the tourist. However, there are increasing numbers of locations in certain parts of the developing world where a small yet mobile and affluent middle class has developed which is eager and able to travel for leisure purposes. As Stanley (1998: 70) notes, the overwhelming majority of visitors to China's 'Folk Culture Villages' park is Chinese, comprising well-paid workers, officials and the military. They are novel participants in the touristic imaginary of self-display, and the parks afford them the opportunity of demonstrating their social distinction through exercising the mobile, leisured gaze of 'modernization'.

Hosts, guests and cultural imperialism

There are, it is clear, obvious inequalities between tourist-producing areas and many tourist-receiving areas. This is expressed not only in terms of indices of relative development, but also in terms of inequalities between urban and rural economies within the same country. These inequalities have attracted considerable attention in the literature on tourism. Anthropology has classically discussed the touristic experience in terms of a 'clash of two cultures' between the 'host' community and the 'guest' (see Smith 1989). The host community is held to be damaged, both culturally and economically, by the influx of hedonistic and careless Western tourists, who represent 'a form of cultural imperialism, an unending pursuit of fun, sun and sex by the golden hordes of pleasure seekers who are damaging local cultures and polluting the world in their quest' (Turner and Ash 1975: 129).

Relations between these 'local cultures' and the 'golden hordes' have classically been defined in terms of two kinds of impact: acculturation and economic dependency. In terms of economic dependency, it is argued by writers such as Turner and Ash that local service providers are 'supping with the devil' if they sign up to the development agendas of foreign tour operators. Tourist industries often provide only low-waged jobs and encourage various forms of exploitation, such as prostitution, environmental pollution, cultural commodification or the siphoning off of much-needed public services and funds. There are, however, some recent studies which reject the thesis of economic imperialism, arguing that tourism reconfigures relations of dependency that already exist rather than creating them itself (see Ryan 1991). Further, the question remains of what alternative economic activities there are in many tourism-oriented regions. There is some evidence that tourism allows rural economies to survive, albeit with a changed economic base, whereas, in its absence, the loss of small-scale agriculture results in chronic levels of economic decline and out-migration.

Acculturation, on the other hand, refers to cultural rather than economic influences. It is 'the process by which a borrowing of one or some elements of culture takes place as a result of a contact of any duration between two different societies' (Burns 1999: 104). This borrowing is usually seen as asymmetrical, with the culture of the more developed and economically powerful society dominating that of the less developed. An example would be in Goa, India, and many heavily visited parts of Thailand, where a society traditionally intolerant to public bodily display has had to adjust to the beach culture brought by Western tourism. Another example is festivals and processions traditionally held in order to commemorate local events or to celebrate religious occasions, which begin to be held 'on the hour, every hour', in order to coincide with coachloads of tourists. The Semana Santa processions in major Spanish cities, for example, have become key tourist spectacles in their own right.

Acculturation is also said to occur where the tourists' language is gradually assimilated by local people, while tourists make no reciprocal effort to learn the host language (Nunez 1989). Ryan (1991) identifies eight areas in which tourism is likely to introduce socio-cultural change on localities: handicrafts, languages, traditions, gastronomy, art and music, architecture, religion, dress and leisure activities. Some of these transformations are thought of in terms of what tourists bring with them, such as music, language and styles of dress, resulting in a form of 'contamination', whilst others result in the dilution of indigenous cultural traits through the loss or adaptation of traditions, such as religious practices, festivals and local cuisine. However, it is very difficult to make categorical judgments about the effects of these changes, particularly in terms of their desirability or otherwise. For instance, numerous studies have argued that tourism enables disintegrating cultural practices to be revived and maintained, and thus revivifies markers of ethnic identity (see Jamison 1999; and essays in Boissevain 1992). In Nepal, for example, Sherpas have found new support for their culture and skills through the increasing presence of Western trekkers (Adams 1992). Such issues, complicating the host/guest dichotomy, lead Franklin and Crang (2001) to conclude that 'tourism may be less of a one-way street than the all-engulfing westernizing tidal wave it sometimes seems'.

Beyond hosts and guests

Three problems with the idea of host–guest acculturation can be identified. First, acculturation posits a clear distinction between those cultural attributes imported into a society by tourism, and those that were there 'before'.

This suggests the existence of an original, pristine cultural identity, existing in isolation from influences brought in through travel. This plays on a classic trope of early anthropological discourse, famously deconstructed by Clifford (1992). Clearly, the economic inter-dependence which global trade has brought makes it difficult to credit the existence of economic or cultural oases sealed off from outside influences. Many multi-ethnic societies attest to the fact that cultural identity is always in flux, shifting around both internal and external divisions.

Tourism is not, therefore, the sole domain wherein identity becomes (re)defined and contested. It can, however, work to reinforce ethnic boundaries by introducing images of 'the outsider' – both by creating local backlashes against cultural values perceived as threatening, as in Islamic rejections of touristic culture in Egypt (Aziz 1995), and by providing an 'other' around which previously diverse ethnic groups can coalesce. Jamison (1999) shows some of the complexities involved in his case-study of competing ethnic groups in Malindi, a popular tourism resort in Kenya. Here, tourism both engenders ethnic conflicts by instigating relations of economic inter-dependency, leading to competition among different ethnic groups, but also instils recognition of a wider community of interests requiring inter-ethnic cooperation.

Secondly, acculturation suggests that cultural changes can be traced to one source, namely tourism. This is problematic, not least because it is so difficult to distinguish the effects of tourism from those of other influences emanating from the economic activities of the developed world, especially through global capitalist initiatives such as neo-liberal trade (for example, the economic 'structural adjustment' programmes devised by the World Bank and the International Monetary Fund). The wide-ranging influence of globalized media networks cannot, either, be ignored. Does the summer tourist really explain changing local attitudes more than the year-round TV set?

Thirdly, it is too simplistic to see culture as being absorbed or 'borrowed' wholesale. Host–guest assimilation takes place on different levels and to different degrees: some attributes of tourist lifestyles will be welcomed by local people whilst others are rejected, and some host groups might be accepting whilst others might be hostile. The precise effects of tourism on locally situated social relations can be difficult to predict. Lever (1987), for example, found that tourism enabled female workers from a small rural village in Spain, employed seasonally in bars and hotels in the Costa Brava resort of Lloret de Mar, to live for long periods free from the constraints of male-dominated village homes. It also allowed them to command a more independent and respectful role when they returned home, having won the status of breadwinner by sending much needed money back to their families.

Finally, tourists are often simplistically seen as the 'perpetrators' of negative cultural influences upon local 'victims'. Some studies suggest that different local groups will enter into a range of different relationships with tourists, including ignoring them, being hostile towards them, seeking romantic or friendship encounters with them and seeing them purely as a source of commerce. In fact, as Tucker's study of Goreme cited above and below suggests, certain groups of locals may see tourists as the spectacle, rather than the other way round. This perspective has been developed by Cheong and Miller (2000), who argue that the Foucauldian concept of the gaze, utilized by Urry (1990) to describe the structuring power of the touristic imaginary, is less a property of tourists than of brokers engaged in marketing, promotion and hospitality services. Tourists become the targets of a gaze deployed by *agents* – such as government officials, tour guides, travel agents, hotel/restaurant employees, guidebooks, academics and market researchers/promoters. These do not serve a neutral role, but constrain the movements of tourists by channelling them into pre-selected enclaves, directing their gaze towards certain sights rather than others and ensuring their conformity to particular itineraries. Especially on organized package tours, tourists thus find themselves socialized into quite restricted comportment agendas and are far from the all-powerful, sovereign consumers or adventurers that they often appear.

Nevertheless, although the question of how to assess the cultural effects of tourism is a difficult one and the host/guest dichotomy simplistic, it is necessary to recognize certain concrete impacts on the socio-economic and cultural organization of places that have rapidly become highly visited tourist destinations. In locations such as the small island of Boracay in the Phillipines, studied by Smith (1988), where a farming and fishing economy based on family production had historically produced a relatively slow-changing environment and society, the suddenly accelerating influx of visitors in the 1980s brought intense pressures to the island's traditional way of life (see Harrison 1992). In small agricultural economies such as this, a process occurs whereby local entrepreneurs start to provide facilities and offer services for the incomers. This is often followed, as development increases, by the arrival of foreign workers and firms, creating the infrastructure to cater for large numbers of visitors (through hotels and restaurants, leisure facilities, services, roads, airports, and so forth). The cash economy expands, wage-labour systems make an appearance, land values rise astronomically. Such far-reaching changes in the locality's economic base have inevitable implications for social and cultural organization.

These can have depressing consequences. A recent article in a British newspaper[1] revealed the far-reaching changes wrought upon three remote valleys in Himal Pradesh, Northern India, by 20 years of Western 'hippy' tourism. In a scenario echoing the plot of Alex Garland's bestselling book, *The Beach*, the local economy, it seems, has been completely transformed by the arrival of a ready market for the area's prodigious crops of marijuana. Previously used only in religious rituals and to provide hemp products, the 'charas' has now sucked many local people, as well as incomer Westerners, into intensive (and illegal) cultivation and smuggling networks. The result is villages seemingly dominated by a cut-throat industry that has turned yet another erstwhile Shangri-La, famous for its low crime rates and welcoming people, into a violent, paranoid and hostile area, which foreign embassies now advise their nationals to avoid. Thus, tourism appears to have instituted a drugs trade which has subsequently replaced the tourist trade altogether. Such outcomes are undesirable in terms of the region's visitability, yet, for (some, but by no means all) locals, the economic prosperity brought to their villages has allowed them to access previously unimaginable goods and services. The question of how to assess these transformations in terms of their desirability is, in this sense at least, a difficult one.

Being ourselves for you[2]

This brings us to the classic contradiction haunting tourists – the fact that their arrival transforms the indigenous culture they came to see. Such questions are bound up in the key issue in any discussion of touristic cultural display, namely, the question of authenticity. MacCannell (1976, 1999) argues that tourists – who come in the main from highly industrialized and technologized countries – are seeking the authenticity that is lacking at home. He argues that the popularity of tourism can be explained by modernization and the increasing detachment from traditional values of work, family, home and neighbourhood in Western societies. Of course, not all forms of tourism search out pre-modern destinations. Some turn on the fantasy of encountering a technologically advanced future (including visits to science parks and to busy, cosmopolitan cities associated with high-tech, fast-paced lifestyles, such as Los Angeles, New York, Tokyo or Sydney). Yet the appeal of travelling backwards in time does seem to be predominant in many forms of tourism (see Frow 1991). One Australian woman visitor to the cave-house villages of Goreme in Turkey remarked that she 'would hate the Goreme people to all be driving cars in twenty years. Donkeys and horses and carts are much nicer. It's nice for time to stand still in some places' (Tucker 1997: 117). In such ways, as MacCannell observes, tourists put a value on the ideal of 'primitive culture', exclaiming, ' "Look, there are no fences around their fields. That's worth a picture!" "They work only for their own subsistence. That's worth reporting back to our overly commercial society at home!" ' (MacCannell 1992: 29).

For MacCannell (2001), the tourist gaze takes two forms. One is content with the apparatus of conventional touristic representation, in which satisfaction occurs through the spectacle's conformity to pre-given expectations. (MacCannell equates this form with Urry's (1990) use of the term). The other form comprises a 'second gaze', which refuses to be satisfied with constructed sights and gains its pleasure from looking beyond the surface, for unexpected and idiosyncratic details. The tourist industry takes advantage of this search for authenticity by fragmenting the market into niches aimed at key social groups, including tailor-made guided tours to remote regions (the Himalayas, for example) or, more mundanely, by including 'authentic cultural experiences' in package tours. For MacCannell (1976, 1999), this encourages local responses of 'staged authenticity' – the provision of contrived performances in a locality's 'front region' that allow barriers to be maintained screening off the real 'back regions' in which local culture is enacted (see below).

Authenticity is not an objective quality but a subjective judgment, always open to contestation and dissent through conflicting interests. As Getz (1994) shows in an overview of how to 'manage' authenticity in tourist festivals and events, there may be a disjuncture between visitors' perceptions of authenticity (does the spectacle concord with the images in my head?) and the anthropological understanding of authenticity (does it succeed in communicating the cultural meanings of its original social context?) A third measure of authenticity can also conflict with both of these: that of the tourism planner and promoter, who may see authenticity merely as community acquiescence (does it meet with the community's approval?) These different sites of authentication (the academic's, the visitor's, the planner's and the local community's) are not equivalent, neither are they equal. It is the planner who has the political-economic power to construct and promote the spectacle, wherein authenticity may be reduced to the variables of customer satisfaction and community acceptance. Groups within the local community rarely have the opportunity to express an opinion on tourist influxes, never mind affect their scope, focus or volume. This is especially so where, as is often the case, local governments have already accepted the arguments about the economic benefits they bring.

Sealing off the other

To what extent, then, do tourists seeking glimpses of local cultural life find themselves actually sealed off from 'real' local people and the spaces they inhabit? Does cultural display merely offer the tourist a facile and stereotyped substitute for the 'other', thus sparing him or her the effort of meeting real people in the context of their everyday lives? Daniel Boorstin, writing in the US in the 1960s, argued even then that the tourism industry insulates the visitor from interactions with local people:

> The traveller used to go about the world to encounter the natives. A function of travel agencies now is to prevent this encounter. They are always devising efficient new ways of insulating the tourist from the travel world. In the old traveller's accounts the colorful native inn-keeper, full of sage advice and local lore, was a familiar figure. Now he is obsolete. ... One reason why returning tourists nowadays talk so much about and are so irritated by tipping practices is that these are almost their only direct contact with the people.
>
> (Boorstin [1961] 1992: 91–2)

Boorstin yearns for a more exclusive age of travel, before the rise of mass tourism, and blames the latter for the loss of individual, culturally authentic relationships between travellers and locals. His reference to the obsolescence of the 'colorful native inn-keeper' ignores, of course, the desire for encounters with 'genuine' local people that, following MacCannell, we have been discussing. However, we have already noted above the key role of 'culture brokers' in tourists' interactions with the local environment. In managing tourists' contact with local markets and sights, culture-brokers and other hospitality service-providers form the bulk of their encounters with local people. This, it is argued, constructs a kind of cultural bubble inhabited by tourists and tourist-oriented locals, in which everyone is playing the game of making the holiday destination live up to its advertised cultural identity (see, for example, Jafari 1987; Boniface 1998). The very fact of being away from home brings for the foreign visitor the likelihood of behavioural challenges and comportment or language difficulties. These, however, which are the very stuff of the concept of 'foreign-ness', are stripped away by hotel personnel and 'comfort' services, leaving the tourist to consume only the spectacular aspects of the cultural 'other'.

Cultural performers

Simply by virtue of 'being there', local people often seem to be required to perform their own identities for tourists. Yet this performativity is even more starkly apparent where it takes place within organized, commercialized tourist programmes and display-sites. Costumed performers of all kinds now people open-air museums and ethnographic theme parks around the world (see Stanley 1998). In museums which display a long-distant past, most performers are actors, whether professional or otherwise, playing more or less scripted or ad-libbed parts in scenes from a historical epoch. However, at many 'living history' sites and cultural centres, on-site performers are not actors but members of the cultural community on display. For example, ex-miners guide tour groups at Blaenavon's Big Pit mining museum and the Rhondda Heritage Park in South Wales. Similarly, in so-called ethnographic theme parks, many performers are representatives of existing ethnic minorities, recruited in order to provide demonstrations of customs, dress and traditions from the cultural enclave on display (Hendry 2000).

In the US, Ghost Town at Knott's Berry Farm, near Anaheim, California, has a collection of abandoned Western buildings, pulled down and reconstructed to form a Wild West themed town. 'Locals' in period costume are available to chat, and an 'Indian Trails' section has crafts, wigwams and two cultural shows presented by Native Americans who do actually come from particular tribes and are qualified to talk in detail about their customs (see Hendry 2000). MacCannell (1992) sees such living displays as commercial exchanges between 'performing primitives' (who are all in reality ex-primitives) and 'moderns' (the tourists). They are 'a response to a mythic necessity to keep the idea of the primitive alive in the modern world and consciousness', and an outlet for the collective guilt that 'moderns' hold for their societies' destruction of the primitive world. In MacCannell's analysis, the spaces of local culture that tourists explore are thus inevitably staged performances, standing in to mask the destruction of traditional environments left behind by the relentless onslaught of a Western-style global monoculture.

Stanley (1998), on the other hand, takes MacCannell to task for an overly pessimistic analysis which, he argues, consigns 'primitives' to the status of modernity's passive victims. Stanley prefers to use the term '*indigène*', arguing that touristic performance is not necessarily a manufactured creation but can, potentially, function to allow individuals and groups to maintain and affirm their sense of identity. He cites the case of Hawaii's Polynesian Cultural Centre (PCC), whose performers are all students of the Mormon-funded Brigham-Young University-Hawai'i, dedicated to the education of all the Pacific islanders. They are all paid for their performance work and receive an education in the skills and customs of traditional island cultures, including studying its anthropology. The university is also supported by scholarships funded by the PCC. Stanley notes that these performances have come in for trenchant criticism from those who see them as contrived tourist spectacle or sops to the Mormon vision of a 'unifying spirit' among the diverse Pacific cultures it has evangelized. Yet he ultimately rejects the critique of ethnographic performance as 'othering', arguing that, in an age of ubiquitous performativity and the consciousness of theatricality, 'there is no ethnographic self divorced from the other, [for] we become ourselves in our performances for each other.' (Stanley 1998: 182). He proposes that the whole point of living display is that its participants are not seen as archaic but as embodying a critique of, and an alternative to, urban industrial life.

Clearly, the use of living cultural representatives, selected to give the visitor insider insights into the culture on display, raises difficult issues for the self–other relations we have been discussing. There are, of course, many opportunities for exploitation, degrading work and low wages, particularly where living history parks are managed by commercial organizations. These seek to make a profit from selling the markers of ethnicity or cultural difference literally embodied in other human beings. In cultural centres, however, where there is a strong educational function alongside tourist spectacle, local people may participate out of a conscious commitment to local history. At the Polynesian Cultural Center, students do, it seems, learn local crafts and traditions which are disappearing. In my own case-study, the Rhondda Heritage Park, local ex-miners become costumed guides because they want to commit to public memory the past life of mining villages, preventing its erasure along with the bulldozing of the collieries (Dicks 2000b).

The politics of performance

In many ways, where performance is voluntarily undertaken, is paid and provides employment, it seems at least more equal than the alternative – where locals are required simply to 'be themselves' for free in front of a curious, detached tourist gaze. In the latter case, locals are likely to make efforts to re-appropriate some of the surplus value for themselves by engaging in the selling of tourist services. This, however, is often seen as a sign of inauthenticity by tourists, who expect them just to *be* themselves rather than to *sell* themselves. The latter situation is explored in detail in a fascinating study of Goreme, a highly visited 'troglodyte' village in Central

Turkey (Tucker 1997). It is a site visited both by independent travellers and backpackers as well as by organized tours of package holidaymakers. The bizarre volcanic rock formations of the landscape are inhabited by people who have for centuries carved out cave-like dwellings from the rock itself. Unlike neighbouring villages that have been artificially preserved, it offers visitors the experience of contact with actual inhabitants. Rather than being a deserted museum, it is sought after as a repository of 'living culture'.

Tourists in Goreme, as in other destinations, are looking for authenticity, but they are also seeking to purchase services that will afford them pleasure and relaxation. This gives rise to numerous difficulties in tourist/local interactions. First, the economics involved, in which local people are reliant on tourist custom, work to foreground the many gaps (both cultural and economic) between tourists and locals. The ways in which local entrepreneurs try to service, and profit from, tourist needs, such as by sales-people offering them goods and tour-guide services, is interpreted by some tourists as 'hassle'. In turn, tourists who refuse to acknowledge invitations to buy or insist on lengthy bargaining are seen by some locals as greedy and disrespectful. When tourists find themselves invited into local people's houses, seemingly in a spirit of hospitality and friendship, the revelation that the true motive is the selling of a carpet or headscarf strikes the tourist as a con. The local entrepreneur, however, observes Tucker (1997), does not see such commercial activities as incompatible with the values of hospitality and friendship for which their 'living culture' is famed.

Secondly, both locals' and tourists' ideas of local culture come into conflict, particularly in terms of gender politics. Local men find themselves censured for 'losing their grip on the moral codes of life' by becoming preoccupied with relationships and encounters, often of a sexual nature, with tourists. For their part, women tourists find that their attempts to interact with locals are restricted to interactions with men (local women being 'kept under lock and key'), who view them primarily as potential sexual conquests. Whilst some enjoy the attention, others find themselves pursued for the duration of their stay and their freedom of movement curtailed. Thirdly, there are tensions around the issue of cultural preservation. Tourists are both highly critical of other tourists' effects on the 'ideal village' they are seeking ('there is a very fine line between that which is considered worthy of tourist attention, and that which is perceived to be too touristy for "real" experience' (Tucker 1997: 115) and of locals who, they worry, might harbour 'modernizing' urges.

Since the local economy of Goreme is dependent on tourism, there is a powerful strand of opinion arguing for keeping people in their 'chimney houses' in order to preserve the 'living museum', and resisting moves to relocate families outside the village. Many villagers, on the other hand, see their caves as dark and uncomfortable, and express a wish to move out to safer, more practical and more prestigious locations. In addition, they see the tourists' constant picture-taking and their endless quest for unposed and spontaneous glimpses into locals' 'back-stage' lives, as showing a lack of respect towards their culture. What Tucker's case-study points to is a central misrecognition or misunderstanding lying at the heart of tourist/ local interactions. The tourists want to believe that genuine oases of cultural survival can be accessed, explored and preserved, while the oasis inhabitants are actually just as consciously embroiled in modernity's relations of exchange as the tourist. Locals know that they have a commodity to sell – the display of their cultural identity – and are thus quite knowingly involved in performing that identity rather than simply living it.

Beyond authenticity

The discussion so far shows that identifying the 'real' local culture from the 'artificial' tourist culture is an elusive task, suggesting that authenticity is too slippery a concept to be of much use in analysing the cultural effects of tourist spectacle. Two other counters to the charge of inauthenticity can also be mentioned here. First, there is no clear dividing line between the myths and imagery of place that tourists see as locally authentic, and those that local people themselves may hold about their home town or country. It is too simplistic to see the tourist as the only consumer of formulaic images of local culture, as though they were kept in circulation purely for him or her. Various discourses of cultural authenticity are often already sedimented in the place-myths of many countries that have had to struggle to assert a distinct identity in the face of colonial power (see Shields 1991). Graham (2001), for example, discusses authenticity's role as a core cultural value in Ireland during centuries of nationalist struggle against British rule. This stock of images and legends – folkishness, natural wilderness, empty roads, perfectly preserved historic centres – has been politically and culturally useful to Irish identity quite independently of its associations with tourism. Resting on images of an unchanging cultural particularity, they tend to downplay the cosmopolitanism, vibrancy, contemporaneity and diversity of Irish culture today, i.e. those qualities that it shares with other globalized Western societies. It is then hardly a surprise when tourists arrive interested only in sprites and folk songs.

Secondly, tourists are not necessarily seeking cultural authenticity. MacCannell (2001), for example, recognizes that some tourists are content with inauthenticity, recognizing it for what it is. Feifer's (1985) well-known discussion of the 'post tourist' suggests that authenticity is no longer taken seriously by all tourist groups. She points out that since TV and video, there is little surprise element left in going abroad. Further, there is a multitude of choices of where to go and what kind of cultural experience to consume. This results in a widespread and self-conscious awareness that tourism is neither authentic nor serious, but a kind of game with multiple texts, in which most views are contrived and constructed for the gaze. And Graham's (2001) above-cited account of the trope of authenticity in Ireland's tourism iconography identifies an alternative voice in contemporary Irish popular discourse which makes fun of the traditional tropes and commonplaces. Television advertisements in the 1990s began to figure ironic representations of 'Ireland – the Brand'. This kind of promotional discourse addresses and flatters a 'knowing' consumer whose postmodern sensibilities supposedly prevent them from believing in complacent mythologies of national identity.

Cultural exchanges?

Can touristic cultural display find a way out of the entrenched positions of authenticity/inauthenticity we have been examining? Taylor (2001) suggests it can, arguing for a recognition of the distinction between authenticity and sincerity. Contrasting two kinds of Maori cultural tourism on offer in New Zealand, he describes how packaged but supposedly 'authentic' Maori performances laid on in the restaurants of big hotels actually prevent any contact between tourists and Maoris, turning the 'colonial enclave' into 'enclave tourism in which cross-cultural understanding is discouraged in favour of voyeurism through a clear demarcation between the tourists and locals, the hotels and homes' (Taylor 2001: 8). Maoris appear in the same, standardized costume, engaged in the same, standardized activities, frozen in a past era, with no recognition of regional, tribal or individual differences or the actualities of their present-day lives. As an alternative to this, some Maori groups have set up their own 'cultural exchanges' in which tourists are taken to the environments in which Maoris actually live. These *marae* visits emphasize communication and interaction between tourists and locals, which potentially short-circuits the objectification and temporal distancing that the hotel packages – with their insistence on authenticity – involve.

Taylor (2001) suggests that this kind of exchange of 'sincerity' can liberate touristic experiences from the constraints of the authenticity ideal, since it is set up in human interaction and contact rather than being an internal quality to be appropriated by the tourist gaze. This kind of distinction is always slippery, and Taylor does not suggest that tourist–Maori encounters can be neatly divided into two models, perhaps the 'packaged authentic' and the 'bespoke sincere'. Claims to authenticity are made within Maori-operated *marae*, too, where traditional performances remain on the itinerary. This indicates the impossibility of sustaining a clear distinction between the symbolic content of local, community-managed displays of the self and the tour company's packaged displays of the 'other'. The economics may be different, and, importantly, the opportunities for communicative exchange either closed off or facilitated, but the same stock of essential cultural images and narratives are the inevitable fodder for both. Since tourists arrive already loaded up with these cultural expectations, it is difficult for cultural providers not to offer them a mirror.

This suggests that cultural repertoires, when put on display, are inevitably condensed and inter-textual (i.e. made to resonate with wider cultural commonplaces and images), whoever is charged with displaying them. So it is not so much that local cultures have simplistic images foisted on them, but that all public representations involve the selection and use of a narrative framework that is oriented to the audience's expectations. The question, rather, is what the display then manages to achieve in terms of disrupting complacent assumptions and stereotypes, and enabling more challenging and complex messages to be communicated. The economic organization of much tourism (through large tour operators and hotel services) is too distanced from the spaces of local culture, and too preoccupied with the commodified provision of tourist pleasure, to engage with the local community in careful, participatory ways. However, local groups have inevitably become more aware that they, too, can get involved in self-display for an audience. This means that the potential always remains for tourist–local encounters to generate more challenging kinds of self–other display.

Notes

1 Levy A. and Scott-Clarke C., Valley of the Shadows, *The Guardian Weekend*, 20 April 2002.
2 The title of a recent book by Nick Stanley (1998) which discusses the many varieties of 'living' ethnographic display and tourist-oriented performance around the world.

Further reading

Abram, S., Waldren J. and Macleod D.V.L. (eds) (1997) *Tourists and Tourism: Identifying with People and Places*. Oxford: Berg.

MacCannell, D. (1999) *The Tourist: A New Theory of the Leisure Class*, 2nd edn. Berkeley, CA: University of California Press.

Rojek, C. and Urry, J. (eds) (1997) *Touring Cultures: Transformations of Travel and Theory*. London: Routledge.

Stanley, N. (1998) *Being Ourselves for You: The Global Display of Cultures*. London: Middlesex University Press.

Urry, J. (2002) *The Tourist Gaze*, 2nd edn. London: Sage.

CITIES ON DISPLAY

There will be no Beatles. Liverpool is being rebranded away from its 1960s glories and as far from its tragic self-pity image as possible. With multiple agencies involved, the aim is to attract visitors, especially from the South-East . . . But will all this change our perceptions of Liverpool? Well, the closest model is Glasgow, and that changed our reflexes from gangs and Gorbals to art and architecture. Here in the 'pool of life', as Carl Jung called Liverpool, the task is to rid itself of the scallies and shellsuits, and place itself as an agenda-setting, twenty-first century city. Its cultural tourists could claim to be helping rewrite Liverpudlian folklore.[1]

Cultural display is not only geared to tourists from afar. It is also aimed at luring in weekenders and day trippers from affluent areas and local urban populations with money to spend. These are people who, rather than rushing home from the office, will linger in the city to shop, eat, have a drink or see a film, provided there is a sufficient concentration of attractions to keep them there. Urban planning strategies of the past 20 years have focused on the creation of spectacular, design-led, retail and entertainment zones that encourage strolling, promenading and gazing, providing a variety of spending opportunities along the way. Cultural references are displayed at every turn. Shopping arcades and plazas are replete with restaurants, cafés and shops that attempt to invoke the 'feel' of particular times and places – such as South Street Seaport in Manhattan, with its invocation of a maritime past. And urban shopping enclaves strive for a cosmopolitan feel through continental-style, café-bar piazzas and whimsical art-works. Streets, squares, arcades, shopping centres, leisure complexes, restaurants and cafés embellished with symbolic designs and reconstructions organize the city's visual environment into recognizable 'motif milieus' (Gottdiener 2001).

All of these environments claim to be cultural – both in the sense of displaying a wealth of cultural products (through architecture, artworks, performances and exhibitions) and in the anthropological sense (by making overt references to the vibrancy and diversity of local histories and ways of life). By striving to re-make themselves in 'human scale', cities are aiming, above all, to become urban magnets – to pull people in and keep them there. But this is for a target audience conceived primarily as middle class – affluent consumers and tourists, attracted by the suggested presence of artists and other 'cultural innovators'. As a result, the spectacular, celebratory image on display in urban enclaves seems very distant from the miles of ordinary, unadorned housing estates that lie outside. In an age of display, these seem more invisible than ever, reinforcing the impression of their social and cultural exclusion. Culture is proclaimed to be where the new signs are pointing, not in the run-down estates or the older city suburbs. So what constitutes the public cultural identity claimed by today's city planners? This question points us to the foundations upon which the idea of urban culture are built. In what follows, I consider what kind of culture cities are constructing in the process of turning themselves into beacons of display.

Cities are fun; cities are different

Contemporary cities have been seen both negatively and positively. On the one hand, they are celebrated as a dynamic space of cultural difference, characterized by a lively and diverse street life (Raban 1974; Young 1990). In Young's (1990) perspective, for example, urban consumption encourages and feeds the city's sociability, and affords the experience of cultural difference. She writes enthusiastically:

> We spend a Sunday afternoon walking through Chinatown, or checking out this week's eccentric players in the park. We look for restaurants, stores, and clubs with something new for us, a new ethnic food, a different atmosphere, a different crowd of people. We walk through sections of the city that we experience as having *unique characters which are not ours*, where people from diverse places mingle and then go home.
> (Young 1990: 239, my italics).

For Young, cities nurture cultural difference and particularism, and the urban dweller or visitor (like the classic 'flaneur') can find in them a mosaic of 'unique' and different cultural identities. She does not see these as superficial images stockpiled merely visually, as in the tourist gaze, but as meaningful encounters and interminglings between people 'from diverse places'.

In other approaches, today's cities are seen as spaces of surveillance, domains of a segregating power which reserves and polices key consumption zones for those with money to spend, whilst ruthlessly ensuring that homeless and poor people are kept out (Davis 1990; Marcuse 1994; Zukin 1995). Zukin describes how New York's 'business improvement districts' (BIDs) have led to highly segregated and privatized zones. They utilize symbolic imagery and themes to create the appearance of social order, and 'reflect Disney World values of cleanliness, security, and visual coherence' (Zukin 1995: 67). Relying on the production of unity in visual terms, they try to disguise their lack of solidarity in social terms. In place of the older industrial territories comes an increasingly fragmented, competitive and specialized urban environment in which different zones develop according to the logic of disaggregated 'islands of regeneration' and 'flagship' redevelopment areas (Harvey 1989b; Bianchini and Schwengel 1991). Los Angeles becomes the frightening exemplar of an unnavigable 'postmodern urban condition' entirely turned over to the needs of capitalism (Dear and Flusty 1999).

What kind of city is being described in these accounts? It is a city dependent on ebbs and flows of private investment, highly vulnerable to collapses in consumer spending, property prices and the vicissitudes of the finance and service industries. Accordingly, if capitalism is the bedrock of these entrepreneurial cities, it is also their potential nemesis. This makes the new city an edgy, insecure place, its leaders locked into a never-ending bid to prevent capital flight and to lure in new investment. In the process, it becomes a place of both pleasure and divisions, where public sociability and leisure is organized within and confined to certain sanitized zones of consumption and display. It is a city where culture has become something to be planned and designed, to be transmitted from drawing-board to sidewalk.

Central to the emergence of the contemporary entrepreneurial city has been the organization of consumption. This has made cities today look very different than in the immediate, post-war era, when many were centres of industrial production. In a historical overview of the US urban experience, Hannigan (1998) sees cities today regaining the leisure role they held in the first three decades of the twentieth century. That, he argues, was the golden age of city social life – featuring 'amusement parks, theaters, night clubs and cabarets, baseball stadiums, ballrooms, burlesque houses, storefronts, nickleodeons and grand movie palaces' (Hannigan 1998: 15). However, from the 1950s to the 1970s attendance at these city-centre venues trickled away as television, domestic entertainment and suburbanization kept people at home or propelled them to the new out-of-town theme parks, shopping malls, cinemas and sports centres. City centres became synonymous with urban blight, crime and decay.

By the late 1970s, explains Hannigan (1998), a completely new approach was beginning to take hold in urban planning circles. It was realized that office and retail development alone were not enough to keep workers in the city after dark and at weekends. Instead, 'flagship destination projects' (Hannigan 1998: 51) were needed, to create aesthetically appealing, festive and safe leisure zones. They had to compete successfully for the 'new breed of consumer who is hooked on fun' (Hannigan 1998: 89) and to keep him or her on site long enough to generate maximum sales. Accordingly, retailers, restaurateurs, stadium managers *and* traditional cultural institutions all began to realize the role that spectacular cultural display could play in the environments they provided. Making the environment visually varied and stimulating, with plenty of historic and cultural references, was central to the strategy. The Rouse Company in the US, for example, became a market leader in the construction of historic-flavour 'festival marketplaces' in city after city (Boyer 1992). By the 1990s, the buzz-word was the 'convivial' 24-hour city, designed to provide entertainment opportunities round the clock to keep the crowds flowing through (Bianchini 1995; Griffiths 1998).

Culture is central, in at least four respects, to this revitalization of city-life. First, the aesthetic, design-centred principle which guides it is based on the visual referencing of particular times, places and ways of life. This is achieved through the construction of 'scenographic tableaux' (Boyer 1992: 190). For example, Times Square in New York has deliberately recreated the glitter of its golden age of theatres, huge neon-lit shop-fronts and flashing advertising billboards. Cardiff Bay, a massive docklands redevelopment scheme in Wales, discussed further below, incorporates a panoply of maritime references into its street design and architecture. The idea is to create the impression of being immersed in an environment suggestive of other times – granting the consumer a vague feeling of being elsewhere. As a deliberate contrast to suburbia, urban enclaves cultivate the sense of being inside an enchanted space, counterposed to the mundane world. This contrast with the mundane is part of the logic behind the principle of visitability, and, as Urry (1990) has argued, behind the tourist imaginary itself.

Secondly, cultural display becomes a means of urban management. As Zukin's work (1995) shows, the staging of public festivals and performances provides a tool for governments to secure public spaces such as parks and squares and to police the streets. It also protects and fosters capital investment in real estate. New Urbanism in the US, for example, is a design movement dedicated to the creation of (contrary to its name) strictly neo-traditional, affluent, socially exclusive townscapes. Its most famous products are the constructed town of Seaside in Florida and the Disney-owned town of Celebration (see AlSayaad 2001). But cultural display is ubiquitous in all kinds of ordinary urban 'interpretation'. From the provision of visitor signs and seating to the commissioning of artworks for waterfront locations, it is aimed at making aspects of the urban environment stand out and address visitors, thus organizing their movements and encouraging them to locate, enter and remain in the visitable areas.

Thirdly, traditional urban cultural institutions are themselves embracing the principles of cultural display and design – mimicking the city of display itself through their interior layout and architectural identity. Museums, for example, are becoming hybrids – providing film theatres as well as exhibition spaces, shopping areas and dining facilities (Chapter 6). Reconstructed streets in 'living history' museums provide three-dimensional, strollable simulations of the historical town or city, whilst the new generation of high-tech, ultra-modern museums offer light, airy galleries with stylish seating, art installations, shops and cafés. These latter are usually housed in spectacular new buildings designed by high-profile, contemporary architects (such as Bilbao's acclaimed Guggenheim), and thereby contribute directly to the city's 'look', as well as to its international image and status. Attracting funding for these prestigious exhibitionary institutions has thus been central to countless urban redevelopment schemes.

Finally, culture in urban design has come to be equated with identity, and identity with the transmission of a coherent, clear set of messages. These are themed environments, in the sense that their image is carefully managed and controlled to furnish particular connotations. Julier (2000) describes how new building development in the ex-industrial, northern British city of Leeds in the late 1980s was carefully overseen by city planners, ensuring that developers conformed to the 'Leeds Look', i.e. to certain stylistic conventions vis-à-vis building materials and architectural details. Reflecting current trends in cultural display towards wrap-around, multi-sensory simulation rather than purely visual spectacle (see Introduction), Julier (2000: 122) notes how urban design now encompasses a broader, more experience-centred view of culture, which has 'shifted from the purely visual consumption of architectural exteriors...to the more holistic experience of seating, signage, sounds and smells', in pursuit of the somewhat amorphous ideal of 'good European city'. It seems that, in the scramble to keep consumers' attention, urban design is no longer content with being gazed at, but seeks to construct an entire sensory life-world.

Legible cities?

The above discussion shows how the incorporation of cultural display is taken very seriously as a sub-discipline of public planning and policy, where it is viewed as a crucial site for cities' 'communication strategies'. Cultural display enables the promotion of various zeitgeist values, such as economic dynamism, multiculturalism, green-ness, artistic innovation, youthfulness or historical pedigree. Urban planning today, accordingly, is dedicated to addressing consumers through *readable* cultural representations. This is impelled by a widespread dislike, in design circles, of confusion. In order to be stages for the communication of messages, urban space has to embody meaning. And spaces which, through unplanned development, betray haphazard allusions or fail to signify much at all are seen as meaningless. Unable to address the onlooker, they fail to be 'legible'. Instead, the urban environment should be 'an enormous communications device' with clear nodes, paths, landmarks, edges and districts with defined characters – thus enabling people to perceive 'the relatedness of a complex thing' (Lynch 1990, cited in Kelly and Kelly 2003: 30–1). Legibility means the execution of a worked-out communications strategy, carved out in streets and buildings, cemented into walls and pasted onto pavements.

Some writers, however, understand legibility in quite different terms. For them, cities today are characterized by its loss (see Jameson 1991; Sorkin 1992; Short 1996). What has been lost, it is argued, is the transparency through which social and civic functions used to be inscribed into material, urban environments. In the late nineteenth and early twentieth century modernist city, it was clear where power operated and what roles it assumed. It was visible in the awe-inspiring, grandiose public buildings and obvious functional demarcations of the Victorian and Edwardian metropolis. New 'recombinant' cities or 'cities of bits' have abandoned the old pretensions to universality (Sorkin 1992). Now 'anything seems to go with anything – hierarchies are both reinforced and concealed, at once fixed and despatialised' (Sorkin 1992: xiii). In the 'city of bits' a myriad of enclaves shout for the attention of the consumer. They offer cultural images galore, but an environment where centres of power are hard to locate and where a generalized commercialism has spread into every quarter. Achieving legibility, in this perspective, cannot come from the design-based formulas of thematic coherence and consumer-accessibility, but only from the provision of 'maps' for meaningful mass participation in civic, public space (see Jameson 1991).

Many trace the loss of this mapping to the rise of urban simulation. Soja (1992), for example, announces the arrival in the US of 'exopolis' – space outside conventional city centres, which used to be given over to suburbia but which now forms a corporate, decentred, growth-oriented, manu-factured land-complex, housing a network of business and industrial parks, shopping malls, office complexes, residential areas and cultural venues. What is distinctive about exopolis is its simulacra – its buildings and spaces, public and private, which function as theme parks or enormous billboards, using high-tech displays as self-promotion to tell their own stories, and literally to make exhibitions of themselves. This is a place which has 'moved well beyond the simpler worlds of the artificial theme parks that you visit when you want to. The new theme parks now visit you, wherever you may be' (Soja 1992: 121). What they offer are places rich with cultural images, snapshots and identity-tags all busy communicating lifestyles and histories, but where the social, political and economic relations of the city today become obscured and unreadable.

The global, the local and the marketing of place

In the 'entrepreneurial city', there no longer appear to be clear demarca-tions between city government, commerce and civic culture (Hubbard and Hall 1998). These developments need to be understood in the context of local political-economic strategies centred on economic growth rather than redistribution, and aimed at securing the regeneration of towns and cities devastated by the loss of manufacturing industry. The phenomenon of using cultural symbolism to promote cities is not by any means new (Barke and Harrop 1994; Ward 1994). It increased substantially, however, in the early 1980s, when governments in localities that were being rapidly blighted by deindustrialization, and in which vast areas of ex-industrial land were becoming derelict, found themselves unprepared to deal with the situation (Fretter 1993). They adopted place promotion in an attempt to attract much-needed capital. This was in a US-inspired ideological climate in which policies of wealth creation through physical capital were replacing those emphasizing welfare provision, redistribution and social capital (Oatley 1998). Property-led redevelopment, organised by private business concerns rather than governments, has been a key feature of neo-liberalist US efforts at urban regeneration (Zukin 1995).

   In the UK, largely following the US example, the business of place pro-motion became even more market-driven, slick and competitive in the 1990s due to the replacement of centrally allocated and locally adminis-tered regional aid with a system of competitive bidding. Central government planning policy inherited from the 1960s allocated resources on a formula basis to Urban Priority Areas, on the basis of 'special social need' (Oatley 1998: 11). But in the 1980s, this needs-led, spatially-targeted approach was accused by the then Conservative-led government of leading to a 'dependency culture', counterposed to its preferred values of 'enterprise and vision, opportunity and incentive' (Oatley 1998: 11). It was replaced in the early 1990s by a system of competitive bidding in which places were invited directly to compete with each other for money awarded 'on merit' from various government 'Challenge Funds'. This bidding process transforms the role of local government into place-promoters, and institutionalizes the role of the private sector in creating 'partnerships' for the launching and delivery of bids. It has thus instituted, in Oatley's summation, 'a shift from local government to local governance' (Oatley 1998: 17).

The language of this new entrepreneurialism makes much of the idea of partnership, not just with local businesses, but also with local community organizations and groups. However, this community rhetoric is often merely gestural. In a discussion of culture-led urban development in Lancaster in the UK, Bagguley *et al.* (1990) distinguish between consumerist postmodernism on the one hand and local vernacular postmodernism on the other. The former involves generating wealth for businesses through prestigious projects employing star architects, rather than producing an improvement in opportunities and facilities for local people (especially those most disadvantaged through the loss of manufacturing jobs). The latter involves popular participation, channelling resources to local residents, reducing the power of the architect and ensuring that redevelopment is carried out in tune with local vernacular building styles. There have been some recent examples of this in 'community-centred planning' (see Miles 1997), but all too often, urban redevelopment is aimed at the production of prestige, consumer spend and visitability. Neo-liberal thinking holds that community benefits are produced through the trickle-down effect of makeovers, but as the example of Glasgow in the UK suggests (its image madeover but its unemployment still high), there is little concrete evidence that this occurs (Hubbard and Hall 1998; Loftman and Nevin 1998).

Culture in the shop window

It should be clear from the above discussion that many of the new uses of urban cultural display are organized around the careful provision of shopping opportunities. However, it should be noted that the link between cultural display and the selling of commodities is not new. Department stores were the exciting new urban arrival of the late nineteenth century. They made use of the new electric light to produce spectacular shop-window displays. These functioned as simulacra of the interior retail space, which itself housed displays of 'exotica' designed as a spectacular counterpoint to the conventional bourgeois home (Rojek 1993). Department stores thus functioned as display cases for both the cultural 'other' and the 'self'.

This tendency intensified in the late twentieth century, and, with the expansion of retail export and import flows, it has been the 'ethnic commodity' which has come to prominence. The shopping mall and, increasingly, the high street, make window shopping akin to touristic excursions from country to country. We expect most high streets to feature craft and design shops displaying items from Africa, Indonesia and India, and most restaurants to offer menu items from a range of different countries. A sandwich shop that fails to feature Italian mozzarella now seems hopelessly old-fashioned. Spectacular shopping malls deliberately seek to recreate the feel of a cosmopolitan city, with enclosed plazas, galleries, arcades and streets, along with seating 'outdoors' around fountains, statues and displays of public art.

In reality, one should remember, many shopping malls and streets offer few, if any, attractions geared towards overt cultural display, especially in the developing world (although see Appadurai and Breckenbridge 1999 on the 'exhibition complex' in contemporary India). And even in the hyper-real West, it is important to note that much consumption remains tied to mundane, routinized household provision taking place in ordinary supermarkets, rather than spectacular sites of display (Lunt and Livingstone 1992). Yet mega-malls in the US and Canada, such as the West Edmonton Mall and the Mall of America in Minneapolis, show how tourism, entertainment and shopping are becoming increasingly fused. Ritzer and Liska (1997: 103) point out that 'more Canadian package tours now go to the West Edmonton Mall than to Niagara Falls'.

However, single-use malls and department stores are increasingly being overtaken by the 'festival market-place' pioneered by the Rouse Company in the US. This transforms redundant but historically rich waterfront space into a multi-use shopping and entertainment zone (Griffiths 1998). Quincy Market in Boston was the first example, followed by the phenomenally successful Harborplace scheme in Baltimore. The model has since been applied in numerous other cities, such as Sydney's Darling Harbour, Liverpool's Albert Dock and Cardiff Bay (see below). The aim is to create a heritage ambience and construct a carnival atmosphere by staging 'impromptu' artistic street performances amongst arcades and plazas of small, high-class designer and craft shops. The idea is to foster a convivial and carnivalesque atmosphere, where consumers will want to linger – and spend.

Art and the city

Key to the creation of carnivalesque cities has been the promotion of their artistic identity. As a result, art has moved into the city streets. Traditionally contained within designated museum and gallery spaces, art has now joined 'the flight from museum to city' (Lamoureux 1996: 116). Permanent, monumental art has always been displayed outdoors for the public, but, from the 1980s onwards, temporary exhibitions, too, began to dissipate into new areas of the city. For example, in 1987, the German city of Munster held the *Sculptur Projekte*, which positioned some 60 works around the city at outdoor locations, all of which had to be closely connected to the city or its history. This reflects the increasing importance given to *location* in the display of art, such that setting and, increasingly, timing are seen as integral aspects of the work's meaning and its ability to communicate. Lamoureux comments: 'Fifteen or twenty years ago, stereotypical congratulations affirmed that a work "held together"; today, the facile but supreme compliment is "it works well in that space"' (Lamoureux 1996: 114).

Through the proliferation and mainstreaming of a new (post-1960s) art form – the temporary, site-specific installation – artists have been able to reach new audiences, beyond those who can be enticed to enter a gallery or museum building. Zukin (1995) describes, for example, how the abstract, large-scale paintings of Al Held were put on display in a vacant ground-floor storefront of a former bank in Manhattan. This is a decentralizing, self-promoting strategy of display, in which art finds spectators among shoppers and passers-by rather than confining its address to visitors with high cultural capital. Artists can thus try to link themselves into the spatial and temporal loops of the strolling urban tourist/flaneur.

If artists themselves now think of the city as location, rather than being confined to the gallery space, city planners, too, are highly aware of the benefits of bringing art into the city. Certain key Western cities, such as Barcelona, Vancouver, Rotterdam, New York, Glasgow and now Liverpool, have sought to portray themselves as 'cities of culture' which have placed art at the centre of their planning policy over the past decade. The European 'City of Culture' competitions originated by Greece in the 1980s have been a major spur, and now the title is vigorously fought over. The staging of high-profile, accessible art shows has been key to such competitive initiatives. For artists, placing their work in public city spaces allows them to explore new contexts for communicating creative meaning. For planners, art is a means of introducing identity and distinctiveness to urban space. It also allows 'world cities' to display their avant-gardist credentials in milieux – such as ordinary streets and arcades – which can claim to be populist and inclusive.

In particular, public art is seen as a vital prop in urban regeneration projects. In the UK, Gateshead (Newcastle), Birmingham, Cardiff and now Liverpool have all adopted the tried-and-tested millennial arts-led regeneration strategy. In 2002, Liverpool hosted its second Arts Biennial: this took the works of over 300 artists and placed them around the city in both conventional art galleries and more eclectic spaces – from take-aways to churches, from the Cammell Laird shipyard to Lime Street Station. At the time of writing, Liverpool had just won the nomination for Britain's turn to host the European City of Culture in 2008, overcoming competition from Gateshead (Newcastle), Cardiff, Oxford and Birmingham. Liverpool is trying to follow in Glasgow's footsteps. Holding the title in 1990, the latter managed to transform its image from poverty-stricken, drugs-infested hell-hole to city of culture, art and architecture (Short 1996). In the process, efforts were made to banish from public view the city's unemployed and poor (linked with the wrecked industries of yesterday), and promote in their place a dynamic, prosperous, middle-class identity. As the newspaper quote at the beginning of the chapter advises Liverpool, 'the task is to rid itself of the scallies and shellsuits' – that is, to disassociate itself from connotations of the 'underclass'. The idea of Liverpudlian artists in shellsuits has clearly not occurred.

As well as dedicated exhibitions in city spaces, art is used in urban redevelopment schemes as a permanent feature of the material environment. 'Percent for art' policies adopted in the US and Europe set aside 1 per cent of capital development costs for the commissioning of dedicated works of art (Miles 1998). Some of this comprises specially commissioned, eye-catching, signature works from well-known sculptors, such as those of the UK sculptor Anthony Gormley in Belfast, Birmingham, Gateshead and Derry, or Jonathan Borofsky's giant 'Hammering Man' in Seattle. There are also, however, more modest commissions for street furniture, such as lamp-posts, benches and street paving embellished with particular motifs and themes. The most mundane and dreary urban spots can be enlisted into the artistic landscape – roundabouts, building hoardings, school railings, electricity sub-stations, car parks, pavements, even retaining walls. Rather than the monumental public statuary of the early twentieth century, this new public art embraces more whimsical, vernacular themes. The emphasis is on artworks which play with shapes, textures and movement, and which reference local industrial heritage.

Many of these artworks are supposed to communicate messages about the places in which they are situated. For example, pairs of wild geese mounted on street-lights in the Welsh castle town of Caerphilly were intended by the artist and planners to represent both 'new beginnings' and 'old values', as well as to reference, more prosaically, the castle's famous wild geese. (In a survey of local people's responses, unsurprisingly, no-one 'got' these messages – see Penberthy 2001). However, a countervailing trend can be seen in the widespread use of conceptual and modernist art which has little connection to its site and no local references (Miles 1998). In corporate enclaves of consumption aimed at professionals and office workers, such as Broadgate in London, a collection of contemporary sculpture placed in the plaza displays its own credentials as an avant-garde, 'value-free' prestigious asset (Miles 1998). Similarly, Phillips (2000) describes how the development firm Olympia and York invited artists and architects to display artworks for 'The New Urban Landscape' in the trade/consumption enclave of Battery Park City in Manhattan. By 'dangling the bait of abundant and chewy art' the firm succeeded in promoting the World Financial Center as a public space and itself as a public patron (Phillips 2000: 98). She points out that the concept of the 'public' is seen here merely as a spatial location, whereas it should refer to people – in all their diverse and complicated relations to city life.

Cultural quarters

The US has provided a model for many of the culture-led regeneration strategies subsequently applied in Europe. The 'cultural quarters' formula has been particularly widely copied. Pittsburgh, Cleveland and Boston were the original trail-blazers. The idea is to create a zone of entertainment and art, by building or refurbishing museums, art galleries, cultural centres, independent film studios and theatres, and then installing among these a variety of up-market café-bars and restaurants (Griffiths 1998). They address a highly mobile professional and managerial class, high in both economic and cultural capital. Such projects are not always uniformly successful. The ex-steel-making British city of Sheffield provides a good example. Its Cultural Industries Quarter was planned by the City Council as a strategy of capitalizing on the popular music scene that had grown up in the city in the early 1980s.

Sheffield's council-run cultural initiatives of the 1970s and early 1980s belonged to an earlier paradigm of community-oriented cultural policy, in tune with the political principles of the city's then socialist-dominated council. They were part of the council's policy of providing access to culture for ordinary working-class residents. It set up Red Tape studios for local musicians and a council-run independent cinema. However, in the late

1980s, Sheffield joined the gravy train of consumption-led, public-private regeneration (Goodwin 1993). Now seeing its indigenous artistic and musical talents in instrumental terms, as 'cultural industries', the Council pursued a calculated strategy of boosting the profile of the city's connection with popular music. Its new Cultural Industry Quarter was designed to promote a cluster of artistic networks. It managed to draw in enough public and private funding to open in 1999 the UK's first-ever National Centre for Popular Music. This soon closed ignominiously, having failed to attract either sufficient visitors or critical acclaim.

The key problem in such initiatives remains that of harnessing creative energies for instrumental ends, for economic profitability and transmission of the 'right' messages. In Sheffield, planners were trying to capitalize on a locus of musical talent that was resolutely counter-cultural and anti-bureaucratic, situated within shifting, informal social scenes and networks of people that could not easily be identified, accessed or manipulated by planners (Brown *et al.* 2000). There is, inevitably, a tension between planners interested in culture purely for the purposes of economic development, and cultural practitioners themselves, who are primarily concerned with cultural experimentation in its own right – including both economic successes *and* failures. Artists, for example, tend to be cynical about the provision of public amenities on the basis of promotional or corporatist goals, and such amenities can easily lose credibility, be labelled inauthentic and completely miss the ground-level cultural trends and currents where creative networks are germinated.

The most notorious British example of a disastrous attempt to make culture an instrument of regeneration and place-promotion was, of course, London's Millennium Dome. It was specifically constructed, with considerable public investment, in order to trumpet the cultural and scientific talent of the UK at the millennium, whilst at the same time to assist in the massive regeneration efforts in London's redundant docklands. When commentators and critics almost universally derided the Dome as boring, predictable and uninspiring, visitors decided to stay away, and it duly closed after only one year. The Dome was so over-burdened with government promotional hype and with the endless pursuit of commercial backing, that it ended up entirely failing to showcase the real loci of cultural creativity in the UK. In this way, culture can easily end up as a means for developers and governmental agencies to create an aesthetic gloss for corporate, profit-led development, and to provide a legitimation for the destruction of existing environments (Miles 1997).

The problems of urban culturalization

The problem with these instrumental uses of culture is that they often lead to a depthless, placeless form of cultural representation (see Relph 1976). Culture is not a free-floating resource or commodity that can be scooped up by revenue-hungry planners, politicians and developers, and has little meaning if it is viewed merely as a set of available symbols and images, divorced from its roots in real social and historical contexts. Below, I examine three aspects in particular of contemporary urban cultural display that have problematic implications – for the look of the city, and, more importantly, for the experience of city life.

Conveyor-belt cities

The first contentious issue relates to the widely noted blandness and sameness of urban regeneration projects (Griffiths 1998). They often rely on tried and tested, formulaic development plans that produce only standardized results. The dozens of urban redevelopment schemes claiming to flag local cultural distinctiveness – from waterfronts and canal-sides to cultural quarters – all too often end up replicating each other in terms of architectural style, retailing outlets and the now ubiquitous café culture. Their architecture is often characterized by 'a similarity of red brick, false colonnades, bands of orange colour, painted wooden circles or diamonds set in the walls' (Ryan 1991: 140). The surfeit of cultural referencing emerging in centres of consumption seems not to represent particular places so much as a generalized and ill-defined 'elsewhere' (Shields 1989). Each development tries to distinguish itself by adopting a unifying theme – often, unsurprisingly, a maritime theme. As Boyer notes of Manhattan's South Street Seaport, 'there can be no better stage set for the spectacle of capital than a recycled mercantile area' (Boyer 1992: 201).

This standardization is partly the result of local government tendering out building contracts to a few large, high-profile companies and offering high-rent consumption spaces to retail and leisure chains that have already gained a recognizable image and amassed the necessary initial capital from elsewhere. It is also the result of entrenched ideas in planning circles about what constitutes a desirable cultural milieu and a dependable consumption strategy for urban areas. Further, it is the product of a global 'star system' of architects, employed as status symbols by city planners eager to keep up with the competition from other image-conscious cities. In this sense, nothing succeeds like success. Keil (1994), for example, notes a new 'global sprawl' characterizing urban redevelopment that produces endless replicas of the same city architecture and street design. Short (1989) calls it the new international 'blandscape', while Holcomb (1993: 142) identifies an 'international aesthetic' organized around the principle of 'eclectic conformity'. The notion of 'eclectic conformity' is a suggestive one, capturing that sense in which standardization means not homogeneity but an endlessly reproduced series of thematic variations (an analysis reminiscent of the 'culture industry' thesis developed by members of the Frankfurt School – see Marcuse 1968; Adorno and Horkheimer 1979).

Such analyses give weight to critiques of globalization which argue that it results in cultural homogenization across previously diverse environments. Relph (1976) argues that places are becoming increasingly homogeneous at the same time as being embellished with superficial markers of distinction. They are thereby turned into 'pseudo-places' (see also Augé 1995). Similarly, Ritzer (1999) argues that rationalized systems of MacDonaldized production inevitably produce standardized, 'disenchanted' corporate forms in urban consumption outlets. This means that marketers are caught up in a never-ending effort to 're-enchant' them, in order to keep their consumer appeal. The result is that 'MacCities' compete to provide ever more spectacular and alluring simulations – employing an excess of cultural symbols – so as to differentiate themselves artificially from each other. Sorkin (1992) sees this process as the institution of a 'universal particular, a generic universalism inflected only by applique', a place where 'locality is efficiently acknowledged by the inclusion of the croque-monsieur at Mac-Donald's' (Sorkin 1992: xiii). Anomalies and disjunctures – characteristics of traditional city life – are replaced with themes and quotations.

However, others refute the cultural homogenization thesis (e.g. Appadurai 1990; Castells 1994). For Castells (1994), it is a mistake to lump together the planning practices of Europe, founded on longstanding left-leaning political traditions and ideals of popular participation and support for indigenous cultures, with those of the US, oriented to a neo-liberal agenda of consumerism and privatization. McNeill (1999) argues that global styles do not result simply from the logic of economic flows, but from conscious decisions on the part of political parties in government, which can result in several different scenarios. Some local governments use it to engineer the spectacular entrepreneurialism we have been discussing; others, such as those in France where support for the National Front party is high, deliberately employ metaphors of cultural 'invasion' which buttress the appeal of racist policies. Global styles may also represent a conscious strategy of self-differentiation in relation to neighbouring competitors, as in Bilbao's agreeing to become the site of the new American Guggenheim Foundation museum, which allowed the Basque city to differentiate itself from wider Hispanic culture. For McNeill (1999), rather than cultural homogenization, this points to the complexity of global–local inter-relations, which are better understood as the 'indigenization' of globalized processes to enhance particular local claims to identity and status. There-fore, every individual manifestation of cultural display within globalized city economies is the outcome of a complex global language of systematized local particularities (see also Robertson 1992).

Cities of fragments

Local cultural particularities, however, do not only take the form of capital-available images. They are also manifested in the patterns of residence, travel and work which have been sedimented through the industrial history of cities. Redevelopment of ex-slum or ex-industrial areas often involves pushing out, marginalizing or ghettoizing indigenous population groups in areas targeted for redevelopment (Archer 1997). As Bianchini (1993) describes, there is a tension between efforts of local planners to lever-in flagship projects given over to corporate interests and the efforts of local community-based groups to obtain funding for small-scale, community-oriented cultural projects. High profile, high investment cultural pro-grammes dedicated to economic gain run the risk of neglecting decentralized, community-based cultural provision for low-income social groups. The rationale behind flagship redevelopment projects is to generate new consumer spend by attracting visitors and shoppers into the area; it is rarely directed primarily at improving the quality of life of existing resi-dents. Such planning approaches risk reducing the question of culture to aesthetics: to 'issues of embellishment and beautification' rather than the more anthropological definition of how people use and relate to their living environments (Mercer 1999: 398).

The creation of symbol-rich streetscapes, plazas and frontages, all dedi-cated to addressing the consumer and catching his or her attention, makes the contemporary city seem almost human, at least from the street. By addressing us as the universal consumer, it seems to be speaking equally and personally to each one of us. But this is a chimera, for stark inequalities divide the city now as in the past. As Soja (1989: 246) comments, 'when all that is seen is so fragmented and filled with whimsy and pastiche, the hard edges of the capitalist, racist and patriarchal landscape seem to disappear, melt into air'. Behind the references to multiculturalism in architecture, café design and art, the city can hide the homogeneity and exclusivity of its dominant corporate culture.

Fortress culture

Urban make-over projects of the kind developed at Baltimore Harborplace have depended on making urban space secure for investment and resettlement by the wealthy. This has meant introducing cultural images associated with the taste cultures of targeted consumers, and excluding ones tarred by the area's previous cultural identity (particularly where this revolved, for example, around heavy industry or crime). It has also often involved 'pacifying' the streets and carefully controlling who will be attracted to wander along them. Davis (1990) has been particularly critical of such policies in relation to attempts to clear social 'undesirables' from the streets of Los Angeles. 'Hostile' street furniture, such as wavy benches or narrow bus-shelter perches, prevent homeless people dossing down. Loitering is encouraged for 'respectable' consumers who behave in accord with the spaces provided; it is not encouraged for others.

On the wealthy hillside around Los Angeles the private, heavily policed shopping enclave is taken to its logical extreme at Universal CityWalk. This is a fortified citadel of shops and amusements built by Universal Studios on their own private hilltop, as a means of containing and managing the flow of visitors from the company's vast car parks to its famous Studios. Entering this safe replacement for the city below requires conformity to a list of bill-posted rules: the citadel tolerates no 'boisterous behaviour', no 'rummaging in trash cans', no 'sitting on the ground for longer than five minutes' and no wearing clothes 'likely to cause a disturbance' (Beckett 1994: 146). Indeed, any form of 'expressive behaviour' is prohibited without the prior written permission of the management. Similar, although less overt, rules govern behaviour in Disney World (see next chapter). It operates entirely outside the public sphere, for the Disney Company now has full administrative and fiscal control over its domain – having become, in effect, the area's own local government (Fjellman 1992).

Closed-circuit TV and private security guards are a more visible response to commercial demands for secure, crime-free local trade and protection for property values in gentrified residential zones. For example, in the case of Glasgow, cited above as an early holder of the title European City of Culture, a flagship regeneration initiative created new cultural institutions, high-class shopping malls and gentrified enclaves. However, as elsewhere, this redevelopment has been accompanied by a 'fortress impulse', which has installed a network of surveillance cameras and private policing systems throughout the city (Fyfe and Bannister 1998). There appears to be a 'cleansing' of urban space, so that only orderly cultural and social activity is allowed to thrive. Such security initiatives can, indeed, make certain city-users, such as women and older people, feel more empowered to take to the city's streets at night, people who might previously have felt safer staying at home. Nevertheless, the attempt to banish certain visible groups, such as homeless people and groups of teenagers, who might commit little actual crime but do disturb the impression of public order, narrows and segregates the social and cultural life of the city.

Ironically, cultural redevelopment projects often displace culture on the ground in that the street-level unruliness of urban cultures is exchanged for safe, official displays. The loss of multiplicity in city cultural space threatens to 'purify' urban life by destroying sites of social interaction and the variety of cultural forms they generate, so that consumers are shielded from any contact with otherness (see Sennett 1996). Difference may be on show in the city's cultural displays, but is therein granted only textual, artefactual or architectural visibility. Redevelopment strategies may seek to represent, and even celebrate, resistant and disorderly culture in public displays, but are less willing, it seems, to accommodate the people who create it within the physical space of the city.

A tale of two make-overs

In the last section of this chapter, I consider two case studies from Wales in the UK. In the one case, an ex-docklands area bordering the flourishing city of Cardiff was converted into a vast office, residential and consumption zone financed with almost £500 million of public money. Cardiff Bay, currently putting the finishing touches to its massive makeover, is now striding confidently on into a dizzying and seemingly prosperous future of round-the-clock shopping, entertainment and cultural display. In the second case, an ex-colliery and railway complex in the city's impoverished Valley hinterlands was targeted for leisure redevelopment, but failed to win the public money and consent necessary for the projected overhaul. A mining museum was built, but the area continues to suffer considerable and seemingly endemic social and economic problems. These two examples of culture's co-option into ex-industrial make-overs give some insight into the considerably different outcomes, vast inequalities and spatial unevenness that characterize such projects.

The dock of the Bay

Cardiff Bay is a newly invented urban entity. It covers an area of 2700 acres, which includes Cardiff's extensive docklands, built to service the

South Wales coal export trade in the 1840s and subsequently declining into disuse in the 1950s and 1960s. It also includes the residential and commercial area of working-class Butetown, which in its heyday was home to 'one of Britain's largest immigrant and minority communities ... to more than fifty nationalities from virtually all over the world' (Jordan and Weedon 2000: 168). The top half of the area was known as Tiger Bay, a name with many historical associations (see below), while the lower area was known as the Docks. Today, while Butetown continues to exist, the names Tiger Bay and the Docks have been erased from the map. Instead, Butetown now sits in the middle of Cardiff Bay – a vast docklands regeneration scheme, which is transforming the area into a centre of consumption providing leisure attractions and retail services for visitors and tourists, as well as new rentable office accommodation and swathes of waterfront residential apartments. Over £444 million of public sector grant money was received by Cardiff Bay Development Corporation, who used it for massive infrastructure projects (such as the creation of a grand, ceremonial boulevard to connect the Bay with the city centre), financial inducements to lure in private companies and, of course, on the controversial Cardiff Barrage (which turned the Bay mud flats – ecologically significant, but not consistent with the waterfront vista desired – into a freshwater lake). As Thomas (2000) makes clear, this vast redevelopment project would never have taken place without very substantial public funding, and yet the returns generated in terms of long-term jobs and economic benefits to the local area have been difficult to identify. Claims that 13,000 jobs have been created do not seem to be substantiated, and many of those that have been provided are in short-term construction work (Thomas and Imrie 1999).

Attempts to manipulate local cultural identity have been central to the development ethos underpinning the Cardiff Bay story. Catapulted into decline in the 1920s after the collapse of Cardiff's sale coal trade, the docklands were for the next 50 years almost entirely neglected by local government, business and the labour movement (Thomas 2000). During this period, the area acquired a reputation for being both socially backward and threatening – a place of high crime, prostitution and delinquency. Jordan and Weedon (2000) point out that these images have been used to represent the area both negatively – as 'dirty, violent, diseased and immoral' – as well as romantically, depicting it as 'exotic and a Mecca of racial harmony' (2000: 171). Both kinds of representation have worked to sediment an image of Butetown residents as different and other, marked off from the rest of Cardiff, Wales and Britain.

Integrating Cardiff Bay into the capital city vision of the 'new Cardiff' entailed changing this image of otherness. This meant distancing the project from the area's old associations, and thus from the existing local culture of the area. It meant embracing fresh, new images and a discourse of modernism and progress – that of transforming Cardiff into a world-class capital that would be fit to lead Wales into the new era of political devolution. It meant remoulding the old dockland physical layout, seen as 'conducive to ghettoisation and criminality' (Jordan and Weedon 2000: 175), into a space where new cultural values and lifestyles, consistent with images of a modern, consumerist capital city, could be displayed. The Corporation's promotional discourse hence focused on the provision of consumption venues, housing and offices, blanking out any mention of industry.

The Cardiff Bay Development Corporation was not set up to meet the needs of local Butetown residents, nor to tackle docklands poverty or unemployment. Instead it was charged with the remit of creating 'an exciting, internationally significant waterfront development' (Thomas 2000: 30). Although it did include a community team, comprising several officers charged with ensuring the distribution of benefits to local residents, the Corporation spent a very small proportion of its vast budget on amenities specifically geared towards the local community (Thomas and Imrie 1999). However, this does not mean that the project has neglected the *images* represented by community. On the contrary, these are promoted vigorously in the area's planning discourse. For example, an independent consultancy devoted to arts-led regeneration, the Cardiff Bay Arts Trust (now known as CBAT), has since 1990 commissioned a number of artistic installations around the Bay area, many of which are consciously aimed at invoking local culture and involving local school children. In fact, community participation is one of CBAT's stock phrases.

Yet, in a very real sense, the existing docklands community of Butetown has been pushed to the periphery, both socially and spatially. This is reflected, for example, in the site's road infrastructure. The new boulevard connecting the Bay and the city centre runs parallel with an older access road, which could have provided the main entrance to the site. This existing road, however, was known as Cardiff's red light area, and lay at the heart of the older docklands community. 'More prosaically', comment Thomas and Imrie (1999: 113), 'it is fronted on one side by the poor-quality Butetown housing estate, which does not present the kind of public face CBDC aspires to'. The old road remains as access to the estate, while visitors to the Bay arrive via the new Lloyd George Avenue. The two roads are separated from each other by the rail-line (to Cardiff's original city centre), large-scale urban planting and a barbed wire intruder fence. As Cardiff poet and writer, Peter Finch, asks: 'Does the fence protect the residents there from death by diesel two-car? Or does it just keep them out?'[2] The social divisions between Butetown, with its high unemployment and housing problems, and the new high-tech consumerism of the Bay are sedimented in this literal dividing line, effectively screening the estate off from the boulevard.

The culture showcased in the Bay is a resolutely mixed high/low blend. It includes Mermaid Quay, a festival retailing complex with shopping malls, plazas, arcades and performance space, a 12 screen cinema and leisure complex, and the new Wales Millennium Centre. This houses the Welsh National Opera, theatre and dance groups as well as venues for more populist cultural events. The Millennium Centre has been subject to particularly fierce struggles over defining the cultural patrimony of Cardiff and the Bay. Its original experimental architectural design by Zaha Hadid and exclusively high-culture use (as home of the Opera) were subsequently rejected by a nervous local council in favour of a 'safer' design and more populist, mixed-use identity. The cultural mix of the Bay is thus carefully orchestrated. An existing museum, the Welsh Industrial and Maritime Museum, with an old-fashioned emphasis on material artefacts in the form of 'puffing machines', was exiled from the area. Instead, the Bay favours the high-tech image of Techniquest, an interactive science discovery centre. This is all part of a plan to construct 'an arc of entertainment' to attract 2 million visitors per year (Thomas and Imrie 1999: 112).

The installation of street art projects has been a key feature of the cultural landscaping of Cardiff Bay. John Masefied's maritime poem, *Cargoes*, is reproduced in several wall panels around the Bay and its images provide the inspiration for a string of artworks positioned around the quaysides. This is in spite of the poet having no connections to the Cardiff area. Other artworks exploit the area's nautical references to the full. Benches and seating feature inlaid imprints of sea creature fossils, huge terracotta whales, wooden keel-shapes and decking. Sculptures include anchors, rope knots, curlews and chain links in bronze and steel and a 'circle of sea timbers' fashioned out of reclaimed oak. The most impressive sculpture, Brian Fell's memorial to local merchant seamen who lost their lives in wartime, is made from riveted steel in the shape of a ship's hull, the underside of which is fashioned into the mask of a human face fallen to the ground. Whilst this piece and several others do succeed in providing meaningful – even moving – cultural referents for the area, the endlessly repeated maritime iconography in the Bay's architecture and street art simply reproduces an easy waterfront theme that could characterize any ex-docklands area.

Of course, public art cannot easily represent complex historical stories reflecting particular local conditions. These are both explained and displayed in the Butetown Historical and Cultural Centre. Here, there is a fascinating archive of oral histories, material evidence and testimonies from ex-dockers and sailors and other Butetown residents. Established independently of the Corporation, and operated on a voluntary basis as a local charity, the Centre is dedicated to recording and preserving the history of the local area through the active participation of local residents. One cannot escape the impression that the Centre is a peripheral stage at the edge of the Bay's corporate 'vision', yet its community activities do provide important forms of legitimation and authentification for the redevelopment project as a whole. Far more than any of the Corporation's expensive theming and public art ventures, the Centre provides channels between the new space and the old, between the corporate vision and the local community. It is a side-effect of the redevelopment project – motivated by the rapid disappearance of docklands industry, but not sharing in the bonanza of financial resources lavished on the Bay. Yet it is here that cultural display takes its most meaningful and richly layered forms, providing quite a contrast to the curiously placeless identity of the Bay.

How real is my valley?

Just 10 miles away from Cardiff Bay, to the north of the city, are the mouths of the Rhondda, Cynon and Merthyr ex-coal-mining Valleys. Separated by the urban sprawl of Cardiff in their midst, which owes its existence to both of them, Valleys and Bay are nevertheless intimately bound up with each other through their linked histories. What united them was the sea coal trade of the late nineteenth and early twentieth centuries. Coal was produced by miners in the Valleys, from where it was transported down by rail and canal to the docks (built by Lord Bute, the major landowner in the coalfields), and then exported to every corner of the British Empire by dockland workers, on ships manned by dockland sailors. Many Valleys women who had come to Cardiff to find work ended up marrying seamen of diverse ethnic and national backgrounds and settling in the Bay. Thus there was a blending of Welsh identity, itself a hybrid made up of different regionalities both from Wales and from England, with the cultures of India, China, Egypt, the Yemen, Somalia, Sierra Leone, Liberia, Nigeria, the Cameroons, Gambia and South Africa as well as the islands of the Caribean. Tiger Bay ended up as a multi-ethnic community resisting classification into the conventional black/white binary (Jordan and Weedon 2000).

Now, however, the Bay and the Valleys seem worlds apart. The massive redevelopment of the docklands contrasts painfully with the situation in the

Valleys, a disparity which has been described as 'the great cultural divide' between 'deprived Welsh valley communities' and 'the brave new world of Cardiff Bay' (*Western Mail*, 17 March 1995). As we have seen, however, the disparity is more complicated than this simple Valleys/Bay contrast suggests. Cardiff Bay itself is fractured both socio-economically and culturally through the entrenchment of the divide between the corporate, consumerist spaces of the Bay and the impoverished, community spaces of Butetown. The upper Valleys, on the other hand, remain largely unified in terms of their unremitting economic decline, notwithstanding decades of local government attempts to regenerate the area after the loss of the collieries and coal-related industry.

It was the 1980s that marked the virtual eclipse of the Valleys' coal industry. Their collieries shed 70 per cent of their workforces in the decade up to 1988. 18,000 coal-mining jobs were lost between 1980 and 1988 alone as 23 collieries in the region closed down (Fretter 1993). As we have seen, the 1980s and 1990s were also the decades of privatist, market-oriented strategies for urban regeneration, where public grants were offered on a competitive basis in the hope of encouraging public–private partnerships (Prentice 1993). In 1988 the Welsh Office instigated its Programme for the Valleys, which made funding available for a 'new image' for the coalfields, in which promoting the area's cultural assets and heritage became a central element. Prior to this, there had been virtually no tourism or heritage development in the Valleys, as local economic policy had been dominated by attempts to create an alternative manufacturing base to replace the collieries. The new entrepreneurial model saw the Valleys' future as lying in 'modern' forms of employment, i.e. in small and medium business enterprises organized around leisure and consumption (Humphreys 1995: 140).

Heritage tourism depends, of course, on the display of historic cultures. In the case of urban redevelopment in ex-industrial areas, however, emphasizing the past can work against the promotion of a future-oriented entrepreneurial identity. This is an identity that needs to be conducive, not politically resistant, to venture capitalism and consumerism. As Robins (1991) points out in his discussion of Newcastle's ambivalence towards its historical cultural icon, Andy Capp[3], during its own efforts to harness heritage for economic regeneration, images born of an industrial past may sit uneasily alongside ideologies of modernization, flexibility and enterprise. If the Wales Tourist Board was to be successful in capitalizing on the Valleys' past, it had to approach the area as an enterprise-heritage hybrid, capable of generating images both of traditional industrial heritage as well as dynamic, post-industrial renewal.

Thus were plans for an ambitious, three-site development instituted for the Rhondda, incorporating not only a disused Victorian colliery but also three other parcels of adjoining land to be conjoined into an integrated heritage-leisure hybrid (for a full account of this story, see Dicks 2000b). Historical interpretation of the coalmining culture was to be confined to the colliery buildings, whilst a countryside recreational function was envisaged, complete with forest centre, pony-trekking, woodland walks into the adjoining forest, an activities holiday centre and an adventure playground, for the other main area of the site. This adventure park would even include a cable car and a dry ski-slope. Later plans added in more retail outlets, including a garden centre to be housed in a bizarrely conceived 'glass mountain'. The proposal for the multi-site development reflected an awareness of the financial benefits of a strategy offering a variety of visitor attractions, requiring movement between sites to encourage long-stay and high-spend visitor activity. Visitor attendance predicted was 400,000. It was to be a truly flagship development, providing a 'gateway to the Rhondda' by opening up the rest of the Valley to visitor penetration as well as uniting the Valleys with Cardiff Bay through a rail link to a proposed 'mineral railway centre'.

Unlike Cardiff Bay, however, the Rhondda had no development corporation to oversee and manage the proposals. Instead, funding had to be sought by a consortium of interested local councils and development agencies. Perhaps inevitably, these parties failed to cooperate or to achieve consensus, and, in addition, the funding required – some £15.49 million – failed to materialize. Repeated efforts to secure funding throughout the 1980s resulted in a piecemeal development, which ended up comprising only the heritage museum, centred on the colliery buildings. Whilst development in Cardiff Bay was fully backed by both central and local government, there was much more prevarication, and less local government commitment, in the case of the Valleys project. Private sponsorship failed to materialize in a much more capital-risky area.

At the Rhondda Heritage Park as it is today, local history is given a vivid and fairly detailed treatment. This is in spite of (or perhaps because of) its confinement to a one-site interpretation facility. Although some have accused it of aping a theme park, I think this unjustified. It does tell the story of the coalfield communities in a direct and uncompromising manner, without romanticizing the past – such that most visitors come away with a clear sense of the harsh and unjust way that the miners were treated (Dicks 2000a). The simulation itself does at least grant the Rhondda Valleys a memorial to their coalmining history, bestowing on it a highly capitalized asset that has certainly had far more resources directed at it than the

Butetown Historical and Cultural Centre. In fact, the differences between the two heritage centres point to some of the major underlying tensions in the uses of cultural display for community and regeneration uses. In the Rhondda, local history was harnessed for regeneration; in Cardiff Bay, it was relegated to a marginal site. Yet few visitors come up to the Rhondda Heritage Park, compared with the hundreds and thousands who flock the quays and plazas of the Bay.

In the Rhondda, local people have not, on the whole, been invited to participate in the construction or development of their heritage museum (Dicks 2000b). In Butetown's historical centre, the indigenous community's participation is actively solicited. Yet this independent historical centre remains detached – even sidelined – from the affluent Bay itself. In the Butetown centre, participatory heritage display is managed on a shoestring in isolation from the leisure-consumption zone of the Bay; in the Rhondda, a powerful representation of local history is performed seemingly in isolation from the surrounding residents. In the Bay, economic regeneration has come in spite of the area's own cultural-historical resources; in the Rhondda, it has failed to come in spite of being sought within those resources themselves. In a sense, local history in Butetown was merely sidelined by redevelopment, whereas in the Rhondda it was actively exploited and appropriated. Butetown residents were seen as onlookers in the Bay's corporate mission; Rhondda residents, by contrast, were expected to provide the cultural resources for regeneration (it was, after all, 'their' history), but without any meaningful sense of popular participation.

In the Bay, the corporate vision succeeded, hitched as it was to a powerful, politically and economically secured vision of Cardiff as modern capital of Wales. In the poverty-stricken Rhondda, it failed, unable to rely on such buttresses and separated off from the highly capitalized nucleus of Cardiff and the M4 corridor. In both instances, however, the indigenous resident populations of *now*, in their every day, ongoing and complex contemporaneity, have continued to be marginalized. This suggests that high-profile, instrumental cultural display, oriented to economic ends, will not easily find a place for local people's participation, especially for those who have lost most as a result of industrial restructuring. Popular participation is, perhaps, best organized from within more ground-level, non-instrumental initiatives which are aimed at local memorialism, not at catching the distracted attention of visitors or consumers. Unfortunately, such projects rarely attract the capital investment or secure the visitor reach and interpretative resources achieved by the consumerist flagship developments. The latter serve to routinize the expectation of a spectacular stage-set for culture, and promote the idea that culture resides only where it is on display – in the historic past or in spectacular leisure-zones. One is unlikely to find it, they seem to suggest, in the ordinary streets, houses and communities of today's working-class.

Notes

1   From Bennett, O. (2002) The quality of Mersey, *Guardian*, 15 September.
2   From Peter Finch's Real Cardiff web-pages: http://dspace.dial.pipex.com/peter.finch/cardiff.htm
3   Andy Capp is a cartoon figure, representing a working-class, cloth-capped, beer-drinking 'Geordie' (from Newcastle) who holds traditional values regarding both trades unions and issues such as women's rights.

Further reading

Hall T. and Hubbard P. (eds) (1998) *The Entrepreneurial City: Geographies of Politics, Regime and Representation*. Chichester: John Wiley and Sons.
Hannigan, J. (1998) *Fantasy City: Pleasure and Profit in the Postmodern Metropolis*. London: Routledge.
Julier, G. (2000) *The Culture of Design*. London: Sage Publications.
Miles, M. (1997) *Art, Space and the City*. London: Routledge.
Zukin, S. (1991) *Landscapes of Power: From Detroit to Disney World*. Berkeley and Los Angeles: University of California Press.

4 | THEMING CULTURE, THEMING NATURE

The idea is that visitors can take in all the pleasures of California – the Golden Gate Bridge and the redwood forests, Hollywood and the wine country – without actually having to go to the places themselves ... But what is weirdest about the whole idea is that you can wander down the real Venice Beach some 45 minutes away for absolutely nothing: real sand, real ocean and real lifeguards in real bathing suits. Rather than walk down an abbreviated Hollywood Boulevard in California Adventure, you can walk down the real one less than an hour away without paying anything. And if you listen carefully in the LA mornings these days you can hear a real mockingbird rather than having to follow a sign to a recording of a California quail.

(From Campbell, D. (2001) Duncan Campbell@Anaheim, *Guardian*, 12 February)

At Disney's new California Adventure theme park at Anaheim, one is guaranteed to find the concentrated essence of California-ness. In visiting the actual Golden Gate Bridge, Hollywood, redwood forests and famous wine country, one would have to bypass large areas in between (such as freeways, farm tracts, industrial districts, schools and other anonymous, everyday places), which might not seem very California-like at all. Even though some of the places it features exist in reality, and for free, only a few miles away, one can visit them at the Park within a *totally* Californian scenic world. California Adventure embodies the promise that, via technology, nature's own reality-effect can be improved upon – made more condensed and vivid. Theming seeks to recreate a simulacrum of reality, which is convincing in its use of perspective, texture, colour, form, and so forth. But it does not pretend to *be* reality. It is aimed, rather, at eliminating the 'dead space', i.e. the non-symbolic, ordinary, unreadable spaces which real environments always contain (Kirshenblatt-Gimblett 1998).

Theming is a technological effect which aims to make environments thematically coherent, through deploying a particular, recognizable set of symbols. Theme parks are the epitome of the totally themed environment, but they do not have the monopoly on theming. Indeed, theming has moved out of the theme-park to the city street. Many kinds of themed environment now exist, and they appear to be proliferating: restaurants, cruise liners, hotels and hotel rooms, pubs and cafés, streets, shopping malls – even airports are now themed (Gottdiener 2001). And now nature is following suit (see below). In this chapter, I am concerned with theming in all its visitable forms – with places and environments which offer a constructed but meaningful cultural coherence.

Theme parks provide the experience of immersion in a three-dimensional, wrap-around little world, 'breaking down the wall of the second dimension, creating not a movie, which is illusion, but total theater' (Eco 1986: 45). They do not set out to recreate reality, therefore, but to construct a believable, yet fictional, dream-world – an imaginative and alliterative world where Morocco is composed of Tangier Traders, the Brass Bazaar and Casablanca Carpets. They offer intensifications of place, in the form of bounded worlds, centres, adventure and discovery parks, villages and cities, stuffed with cultural experiences. Busch Gardens, Williamsburg, US, offers visitors the chance to explore four 'typical' English, French, German and Italian villages, while the Chessington World of Adventures in Britain includes the 'Mystic East', where Japanese, Thai and Chinese cultural symbols are combined into one attraction (Rojek 1993). Flambards Village Theme Park in the UK offers both a 'Victorian Village' and 'Britain in the Blitz'. Terms such as 'glimpse', 'experience' and 'journey' pepper the promotional rhetoric of these parks offering to transport you to an 'elsewhere' and an 'elsewhen', within conditions that are safe and professionally managed.

Rather than fooling spectators, these little worlds are designed to induce wonder at the mimetic, spectacular and transportational capacities of technology. Beardsworth and Bryman (1999) note the operation in theme parks of the 'Barnum Principle' – the circus entrepreneur who realized that spectators do not mind suspending disbelief, as long as they are rewarded for doing so. They effectively sign up to a kind of contract with the entertainer, which lasts as long as they are presented with a high-quality, successful simulation. If they can see the wires, disappointment occurs – not from the puncturing of an illusion, but from the inadequacy of the staging devices they have been offered.

From expositions to theme parks

This appreciation of staging-effects is not new. In Chapter 1, I mentioned Mitchell's (1988) work on colonial-era Egypt. He notes that Egyptian visitors to the Paris Exposition Universelle of 1889 were spellbound, and disconcerted, by the attention to detail displayed by the Egyptian exhibit – a full-size, reconstructed Cairo street complete with peeling paint, dust, dirt and donkeys. He suggests that spectators to the fair were being inculcated into a way of apprehending the world as an exhibition. This exhibitionary mode of understanding provided the well-spring for the great colonial-era international expositions of the nineteenth and early twentieth centuries. As well as rides and amusements, expositions constructed special zones dedicated to simulating different cultures and nations. 'Ethnic villages' contained living villagers from various corners of the West's Empires, dressed in 'ethnic' costume and displaying local crafts, dances and rituals. In these expositions, the origins of modern-day theme parks can be found.

The 1893 Chicago World Fair, staged to commemorate the 400th anniversary of Columbus's landing and to celebrate American technological progress and political union over that time-span, was described by a Smithsonian Institution curator as 'one vast anthropological revelation' (quoted in Rydell 1999: 285). The 'ethnological' living villages, copied from the earlier Paris Exposition of 1889, had Algerians, Samoans, Brazilians, Egyptians, Javanese and other national groups performing various dances, arts and rituals, in an area of the festival called the 'Midway Plaisance'. This area was an amalgam of spectacle, noise, entertainment and 'living tableaux'. It provided a clear contrast, notes Rydell (1999), to the quiet and serious atmosphere of learning cultivated at 'White City' and in the official 'Anthropology' and 'Government' buildings. Here, the scientific achievements, architecture and technologies of white 'civilization' were displayed. The separation communicated a clear message that whilst white culture was scholarly and orderly, non-white culture was quaint, undisciplined, childlike and not to be taken seriously (Rydell 1999). The chaotic Cairo street at the earlier Paris Exposition had served the same purpose – to exhibit its own, pre-modern lack of order and discipline (Mitchell 1988).

The accounts of early World Fairs show their clear reliance on a discourse of cultural particularism – what I referred to in Chapter 1 as the idea of the world as a cultural mosaic. Through displaying the culture of individual nations, they set up a close homology between places and cultures (see Gupta and Ferguson 1992; Kahn 1995). This logic has continued to structure today's expo, even though the references to imperial conquests have been replaced by a focus on nations' technological achievements and commodities. During the twentieth century, the modern, purely commercial, orderly expo became a showcase for invited countries to promote their own, distinctive image, particularly through technology. Post-World War Two expos began to display this cultural identity in entire themed environments. By the 1950s, the idea had germinated of making permanent enclosures of this kind of exhibition: expo had given birth to Disney (Bryman 1999). It encapsulated a trend that soon spread to other leisure spaces – namely, the carefully planned production of coherent backdrops and totalizing environments, in contrast to the diverse and haphazard collections of attractions at early fairs, carnivals and amusement parks.

Wilson (1992) suggests that expos have always sought to bring technology and culture together, but have traditionally consigned these to separate pavilions. It is only recently, in an era of scepticism about its benignity, that technology has sought actually to wrap itself up in culture. Replacing an earlier, post-war emphasis on the 'white heat' of technology, expos in the 1980s increasingly tried to connect technology with reassuringly human cultural traditions – especially those which could be considered intrinsically 'natural'. At Expo 1986 in Vancouver, Canada, for example, the General Motors pavilion hosted the 'Spirit Lodge' show (directed and produced by Disney-trained personnel), which featured a Native Canadian elder reflecting on the human anxieties thrown up by technological progress (Wilson 1992: 174–5). Conjuring up his culture's traditional icons in the smoke of the fire, he concluded that modern technology, in enabling 'change' and 'the freedom to move', reflects ancient human themes and the fact that 'though our machines have changed, our dreams remain the same' (Wilson 1992: 175). This was a deliberate attempt to reference, out-face and ideologically incorporate the then-raging controversies in Canada over the land-claims and politics of Native Canadians. Thus, in a neat but unsubtle double message, General Motors celebrated the survival of authentic cultures whilst also trying to position the automobile as their natural heir.

From the 1980s on, then, showing the human face of technology and science became increasingly crucial in public, state-sponsored displays such as expo. New Age values of 'the old ways', nature, ecology and spirituality were found to be particularly useful for countering the empty, alienating, machine-controlled vistas of corporate technology familiar via sci-fi and Bladerunner-esque films. By suggesting that technology simply reflects mankind's striving to live in harmony with nature, culture becomes the bridge by which corporate profit in the guise of economic growth is reconnected into the human/nature loop. Accordingly, although today's expos may seem less overtly concerned with cultural display than in the days of the living ethnological villages, culture has actually become more integral to them. For instance, technology is never linked to the idea of corporate gain, but always located within a universalizing discourse of progress that celebrates the 'innovations and advances of mankind' (from Expo 1992 Official Guide, cited in Harvey 1996: 101).

In the 1990s, certain expo exhibitors began to express these themes through cultural displays which became more self-consciously artistic. In the 1992 Seville expo in Spain, Fujitsu erected a high-tech spherical cinema, in which a three-dimensional, full-colour, wrap-around film – 'Echoes of the Sun' – immersed the audience in a shower of flying molecules and a 3-D 'virtual vineyard' of natural creatures, to demonstrate the conversion of sunlight into living, organic energy (Hendry 2000: 69). It invited the audience to

> discover the art in technology. And the technology in life ... Fujitsu welcomes you to a world where the only frontiers are in your mind, and where art, technology and life become one.
> (Expo 1992 Official Guide, cited in Harvey 1996: 122)

Harvey (1996) sees the Fujitsu cinemascope as a technology of simulation, as opposed to the older Expo technology of representation. Exemplified by the 1986 General Motors show described above, the latter represents technology as a means of enabling human culture to thrive and progress. In the Seville Expo in 1992, this representational relation between culture and technology was still widely in evidence in many of the exhibits. However, Harvey notes the emergence of a new, simulational logic in the Fujitsu exhibit and others (such as Spain's computer-generated figures dancing flamenco on a real lake). These were created by high-tech Western states and companies concerned to show technology *as* art – no longer simply enabling or enhancing it, but embodying it. Harvey suggests that such simulational devices are more effective at communicating the inseparability of human culture, nature and technology than older, representational devices relying on explicit messages telling us so. Thus, the technologies of simulation *themselves* 'generate beauty', 'bring people together' and 'enable communication' so as to 'produce the essence of life itself as outcome not origin'. (Harvey 1996: 125). Rather than bringing technological progress and human liberation as distinct values into a relationship with each other, as in The Spirit Lodge, the most cutting-edge displays at Seville 1992 showed technology *as* human, and vice versa.

Harvey goes on to point out that 'there was no hyper-reality in the African Plaza' (1996: 127), which showcased instead indigenous products from African countries. Painfully exposing the irrelevance of computer simulation to Southern economies, this suggests that the technology of simulation becomes another means for the wealthiest countries and corporations to distinguish themselves from others via an 'informatics of domination' (see Haraway 1991). Thus, Expo still enables global hierarchies to be demonstrated as in the colonial era, but rather than showing the power of nations through object-centred collections from their colonies, it shows their position within deterritorialized networks of power wherein culture and nature themselves becomes commodified. Countries who fail to show their embeddedness in these global informatics networks are forced to appear as old fashioned, by seeming tied to particularist, material, nation-bound realities. This connects to Eco's earlier (1986) observation that rather than opportunities to vaunt new technology and goods, expos are really opportunities for countries and corporations to display their powers of display.

Theme parks today

Theme parks today have taken this amalgamation of technology and culture to new heights, making it not a spectacle but a bodily experience. In the phenomenon of the themed ride, machines are literally clothed in symbols and set within symbolic environments – ones that are always recognizable from popular culture. However, today's theme parks offer much more than rides. Instead, they have scenic tableaux and built reconstructions representing well-known cultural iconography or places, as well as swathes of shops and themed restaurants, performances and shows. Some of these are recreations from famous legends, stories and films, whilst some are organized around tableaux representing ethnic or national identities, historical periods or ways of life. Indeed, the first Disney park at Anaheim in California (Disneyland), opened in 1955, initially shunned the typical fairground rides and attractions, only adding them later due to popular demand (Bryman 1995). Disney's corporate mission draws a careful distinction between Disney theme parks and conventional amusement parks:

> Rather than presenting a random collection of roller coasters, merry-go-rounds and Ferris wheels in a carnival atmosphere, these parks are divided into distinct areas called 'lands' in which a selected theme ... is presented through architecture, landscaping, costuming, music, live entertainment, attractions, merchandise and food and beverage.

Within a particular land, intrusions and distractions from the theme
are minimised so that the visitor becomes immersed in its atmosphere.
(From the Euro Disneyland share prospectus,
quoted in Bryman 1995: 64).

The emphasis, therefore, is on 'immersion' – the creation of wrap-around,
totalizing environments, with no 'intrusions' (there are close affinities here
with virtual reality – see Chapter 7). The removal of 'distractions' and
intrusions suggests that the idea of authenticity is not entirely at odds with
the theme park experience. It is produced through the 'feel' and 'look' of
the place, however, rather than through verisimilitude or aura. Authenticity, in this theme-park sense, is attained through attention to detail,
careful design and utilization of the latest technology. Since theme park
designers are catering in the main for the non-expert, outside visitor rather
than the informed insider, their task is simply to hold up a three-dimensional, animated mirror to the ready-formed expectations of their clientele.
In some, mainly fun-oriented theme parks, there is a cheerful negligence
about historical and geographical accuracy. For example, 'Big Ben' at
Banbury Cross, the 'English town' at Busch Gardens, US, resembles an
outsize Swiss grandfather clock, with only superficial echoes of the London
original. Yet, in others, there is considerable attention paid to the credibility
of cultural detail, something on which Disney parks, in particular, pride
themselves.

Walt Disney World in Florida, opened in 1971, takes the emphasis on
themed lands further. This is actually a multi-theme park, a set of interlinked lands which includes the Magic Kingdom, the Epcot Center, Disney-
MGM Studios, River Country, Discovery Island, Typhoon Lagoon and
Pleasure Island, all situated on 27,400 acres of reclaimed swamp and scrub
forest in central Florida. It is a constellation of attractions representing
different points on the entertainment–educational axis. The original
Disneyland is mainly tied to entertainment and fantasy themes. Disney
World, by contrast, initiated a much more ambitious and adult-oriented
genre of quasi-educational cultural representation, with the opening in
1982 of the Epcot Center – comprising Future World and World Showcase.
Fantasy and thrills are still provided in abundance, as at Magic Kingdom,
but at Epcot we are presented with information in themed, three-dimensional form. At Future World we are offered science and technology and at
the World Showcase it is travel and culture. Thus, Disney World offers an
experience aimed not only, or even predominantly, aimed at children, but at
adults, too. For every one child that goes there, four adults visit (Bryman
1999).

At the Epcot's World Showcase we are presented with what Fjellman (1992) calls a 'synecdoche heaven' – mini-lands representing (some of) the world's nations, through scaled-down replicas of their most famous buildings:

> Let us walk to the bridge just beyond the China Showcase ... and look around us. To the immediate right we see the Chinese ceremonial gate from which we have just come; beyond it are the roofs of Norway and the Mexican Pyramid. Off in the distance to the right lie the totem poles of Canada and the gabled rooftops of the United Kingdom. To the left rises Germany's castle, and next to it the Campanile from the Piazza San Marco in Venice. Directly across the lagoon, side by side, are the Georgian facade of the American Adventure, the Nara Pagoda of Japan, Morocco's towering minaret, and France's Eiffel Tower.
>
> (Fjellman 1992: 240)

At World Showcase, cultural references from a country's different epochs and regions are all sucked into one amalgamated national identity. Each national site is a bricolage of national icons, and the Showcase itself a bricolage of the 'World'. Here, all the totemic national signs are conveniently gathered together into a compact and organized environment with no dead space or wasted time. Significantly, the industrialized countries have restaurants and shops, offering opportunities to consume, whereas the more 'exotic' countries, such as Morocco and China, have an ethnographic framing with labels describing ethnic groups and customs (Stanley 1998). The 'other' becomes the picturesque, and the ethnic label is reserved for those cultures deemed most 'exotic' and 'traditional'. As MacCannell (1992: 121–2) has asked, rhetorically: 'in their interaction with others, how can groups in power manage to convey the impression that they are less ethnic than those over whom they exercise that power; in other words, how can they foster the impression that their own traits and qualities are merely correct, while the corresponding qualities of others are "ethnic"?' The answer, it seems, is through the Epcot Center.

At Epcot's Future World, by contrast, history is nothing to do with traditional cultural oases where things were done differently, but an onward march of machines, governed by a unifying rhetoric of freedom, progress and understanding that links together the past, the present and the breathtaking new future. An underlying new-age, one-world vision suggests that 'humankind' will achieve harmony, unity and freedom only through trusting those (i.e. the corporations) who can enable and develop these technological breakthroughs (Fjellman 1992). Much of Disney World is, indeed, barely concealed corporate promotion. At Future World, the language of 'partnership' and 'awareness' provides the rhetorical casing for quite overt corporate promotion (the Kraft sponsored show entitled 'The Land', for instance, teaches us the benefits of computerized irrigation and the merits of agribusiness). It also constructs an attempted alliance – a rhetorical 'we' – between the visitors and the corporations (Fjellman 1992).

Theme parks try to cloak consumerism in a form of disguise. As Eco points out: 'The Main Street USA facades are presented to us as toy houses and invite us to enter them, but their interior is always a disguised super-market, where you buy obsessively, believing that you are still playing' (Eco 1986: 43). Jane Kuenz (The Project on Disney 1995: 58) comments that her Disney experience was like overhearing an interminable conversation in which all she could make out was the 'sound of commodities talking to each other'. Theme parks are indeed very efficient and concentrated selling spaces, achieving secure and high levels of sales per square metre. And many no longer take the form of stand-alone, pay-bounded attractions. Instead, mini-themed areas are sited within spend-driven environments to complement their leisure-oriented image and act as beacons for developers who want to invest in profitable adjuncts, such as hotels, campsites, res-taurants, car parks and, of course, other leisure attractions.

In this way, the theme park logic comes to colonize whole areas. It re-constructs them as concentrated and potentially lucrative holiday and resort destinations – Las Vegas, Orlando and Orange County being the prime US examples (Davis 1996). Shopping malls, international hotels and theme parks are becoming more difficult to distinguish (Bryman 1999). The ori-ginal Disneyland opened with a joint Disney/ABC television network strategy for mutual cross-promotion. Since then, all the major theme park chains in the US have been taken over by media conglomerates, such as Time Warner, Viacom and, of course, Disney itself (Davis 1996). Disney theme parks set up deals with high-profile corporations whereby, in return for capital investment in the Parks' infrastructure, they showcase the company's products – a good early example was Disneyland's collaboration with Carnation Milk (Davis 1996).

Davis (1996) describes how cash generated from the parks can then be used to finance other arms of the conglomerate, such as film production and the operation of cable networks, while, most importantly, characters and stories can be cross-promoted within each outlet, whether film company or theme park. Along with Time Warner (who acquired the Six Flags theme parks), Disney operates hundreds of stores selling media memorabilia. Each product adds interest, novelty, visibility and, thus, value to the others. Film motifs provide that crucial 'what's new' element to the permanent structure of the theme park, preventing it from ossifying and becoming out of date.

Time Warner's film, *Batman: the Movie*, was showcased at Six Flags through the carefully timed unveiling of new Batman rides and laser shows. Davis (1996) sees theme parks as a new form of mass medium, bringing together into one site the previously separated commercial activities of entertainment, advertising, marketing and public relations. They are 'a kind of physicalised advertising, a performative and kinetic space that makes the electronic or filmic product and its promotion literally material' (Davis 1996: 411).

Within this selling complex, visitors are not merely the passive recipients of a package; rather, their active participation is required. Everyone joins in the game of participating in the fakery as though it were completely normal – even if this is rationalized as being 'just for the sake of the children' (The Project on Disney 1995). Visitors to Disney World submit to playing bit-parts in a living Disney cartoon, in which they and their children are frequently button-holed by the ever-present and determinedly playful outsize characters. Gaining enjoyment and pleasure from Disney's 1950s Prime Time Café, for example, involves willingly adopting the themed behaviour of Mom and apple pie, and obediently playing the required part when the waiter speaks in character. Some visitors (notably, it seems, the British) may feel embarrassed and awkward, yet most appear willing to conform to the demands of the simulacra in which they find themselves caught up.

The Disney experience offers a palette of extraordinary cultural environments all delivered within the same utterly ordinary, controlled and managed regime. Inside, you can wander freely around and explore, safe in the knowledge that no one is going to harass you, and that encounters with others will be predictable and risk-free. Disney thus has elements of a kind of utopia. There are colourful and noisy amusements, spectacles and exhibitions everywhere you turn – all arranged for you to sample at your whim. Food and drink can be consumed at any time – everything is available in the land of plenty. And this abundance is experienced alongside crowds of others, all enjoying the same pleasures without any apparent competition or social divisions. In this way, theme parks, like other sites of mass culture, are sites of intensive consumerist activity which nevertheless stage capitalism's antithesis: a society where (it seems) no one has to work and where everyone is equal and everything communal (The Project on Disney 1995). Yet, this is a utopia that has to be paid for, where each purchase (the ice-creams, the food, the merchandise, the entrance fees) seems a necessary step in the accumulation of pleasure and enjoyment, and where the achievement of happiness and togetherness becomes dependent on the exchange of money. The pressures to fulfil family members' desires through purchases is immense, readily producing repeated disappointments, rivalries and disagreements. Such tensions can easily turn utopia into dystopia.

Ethnographic theme parks

Although many theme parks still concentrate on child-oriented thrill-rides and enchanting fantasy-journeys, there is a marked tendency around the world towards the construction of theme parks which belong to the more culturally ambitious, adult-oriented 'living tableaux' model (Stanley 1998). This means that there are very blurred lines between many theme parks, market-fairs, festival complexes, heritage centres, cultural centres and, indeed, museums. As Stanley observes:

> What perhaps is new and audacious [about theme parks] is the sub-
> version of the authority of the conventional museum that these
> exhibitions offer. The national tableaux and pageants at Disney World
> attempt to cross the traditions of World's Fairs with those of Skansen.
>
> (Stanley 1998: 32).

Theme parks are not just a Western phenomenon. Of the top 50 largest parks in the world in 1993, with annual attendances of over 2 million, no fewer then 15 were located in Asia (Davis 1996). Japan, as we shall see below, has long had a booming theme park industry. Hong Kong, Singapore and Taiwan are all key players, while new areas of growth are occurring in China, South Korea, Thailand, Malaysia and the Phillippines. Such investments are funded both by Asian media conglomerates anxious to diversify, as well as by Western interests. Tokyo Disneyland attracted over 16 million visitors in 1993, and has become a phenomenal success. Large-scale, commercial Disney-type parks sit alongside smaller, local, less consumer-oriented ones. Stanley (1998) distinguishes, for this reason, between 'ethnographic theme parks', set up by entrepreneurs and oriented primarily to outside tourism, and 'cultural centres', the product of 'indigenous curation' and oriented both to tourism and to education, in the name of local cultural-environmental sustainability.

However, such a dividing line is not easy to sustain, for many theme parks appeal both to the local and to the foreign tourist gaze. In the Pacific region, for example, neighbouring white 'settler' nations have typically adopted an 'exotic' island destination as a favourite holiday destination: Fiji for Australians, Hawaii for North Americans, the Cook Islands for New Zealanders (Stanley 1998). These islands have responded by building their own sites of cultural display. At Fiji's Pacific Harbour Cultural Centre and Marketplace, visitors are transported around a set of displays by canoe, whilst at the Polynesian Cultural Centre (PCC) in Hawaii, different villages are brought together to represent Tahiti, Hawaii, Samoa, Tonga, Fiji and the Maori people. They are the settings for various displays of Polynesian arts, crafts and customs, as well as lectures and demonstrations (Hendry 2000). The PCC was constructed in 1963 through Mormon Church sponsorship, with the aim of funding Polynesian students to attend the Islands' university.

The displays and shows at the PCC are aimed at showing local islanders the traditional customs of all the Islands, whilst simultaneously offering them a sense of a unified identity – something called Polynesia. It also, however, very successfully manages to attract the tourist gaze of Westerners holidaying on the Pacific Islands. It appears to address both locals and visitors, by turning the customs and cultural practices of the area into a visitable attraction. It functions rather like a Western heritage museum, in providing a sanctuary for cultural customs that are perceived as lost, threatened or misunderstood. There is, therefore, an ethos of 'salvage ethnography', cultural preservation and education, through the elaboration of an identity for 'here' which is held to be in danger of being lost. This *is* different to the Disney model, but perhaps less in terms of the audience it addresses and more in terms of the emphasis on local place-identity. Instead of one place containing unrelated 'elsewheres', as in Epcot's World Showcase, one place sets out to represent and bring together related 'heres'.

This ability of the cultural centre/theme park to proclaim the identity of 'here' also makes it a potentially valuable tool for state-sponsored political policies, such as the cultural incorporation of ethnic minorities. Indonesia's Taman Mini, for example, provides a means of displaying the state's territorial claims. The site is dedicated to the doctrine of 'unity in diversity' and is designed to speak to Indonesians as much as to foreign tourists (Stanley 1998). It has a heavy-handed educational message for Indonesian visitors, through naming, displaying and describing the officially designated ethnic groups and proclaiming their essential unity. In China's Shenzhen, similarly, 'Splendid China' provides a trip round the country's famous topography and culture, whilst the Folk Culture Villages display the non-Han cultures living mostly in the farthest reaches of China's political territory. The latter houses reconstructed villages, complete with living representatives of each ethnic minority. These people act as re-interpreters of their own cultures, patiently answering questions and explaining the displays on view. They also allow China to advertise publicly its own proclaimed tolerance and sensitivity towards its ethnic minorities.

This example shows that theme parks are not simply vast, disguised selling and tourism machines. They offer a potent and very public expression of key aspects of national identity: costume, religion, traditions, music, but most importantly the relation between the political centre and the 'provinces'. Through miniaturization, viewing towers and aerial rides (via cable cars, elevated mono-rails and the like) they allow vast and sprawling national terrains, such as the Indonesian archipelago or China, to be viewable and containable within one unified vista.

Like Disney, many of the larger theme parks in south-east Asia are not content just to represent 'here', but also try to bring 'there' over 'here'. Alongside its 'Folk Culture Villages' and 'Splendid China', Shenzhen has a park called 'Window of the World'. Rather like Epcot, it displays reconstructions of various famous national landmarks contained within 'lands' – the UK, for example, has Stonehenge next to Buckingham Palace. Like Disney, it 'brings the rest of the World to China, but, it should be stressed, strictly on Chinese terms.' (Stanley 1998: 73). Japan, too, has a very particular and interesting collection of cultural theme parks dedicated to the representation of foreign cultures. The *gaikoku mura* (foreign country villages) studied by Hendry (2000), represent a sizeable proportion of the country's 28 theme parks. Unlike comparable theme parks in the West, many feature only one country: separate parks showcasing Denmark, Germany, Spain, Britain, Holland, Russia and Canada are amongst those that Hendry studied. Various indigenous musicians and artists from the original country are employed to perform in the parks, and there are extremely well-executed replicas of famous buildings, usually designed and constructed by indigenous architects and craftsmen. According to Hendry – who has also studied comparable parks in other countries – they manifest 'an extraordinary degree of attention to detail and to an internal idea of authenticity' and 'try to create a space that will induce visitors to feel that they have actually entered the foreign country featured' (Hendry 2000: 20).

Although many of these *gaikoku mura* represent Western cultures, there are also parks specializing in Asian countries, including one that has an 'Oriental Trip' featuring excursions into the landscapes of Nepal, Bhutan, Thailand, China and Korea. Many have popular literary themes, such as the Brothers Grimm in the German park, Ann of Green Gables in the Canadian site and Don Quixote in the Spanish one. In her book, *The Orient Strikes Back*, Hendry (2000) ponders the question of whether these highly elaborated examples of foreign cultural display represent a form of 'reverse orientalism'. They certainly suggest that Japan has enthusiastically appropriated the gaze on 'the other', which was previously the monopoly of the West.

In the Great Exhibitions in Europe and the US from the mid-nineteenth century to the early twentieth, Japanese art and architecture were initially exhibited through the lens of orientalism, as examples of the 'exquisite' and 'exotic' workmanship of the 'oriental mind' (Hendry 2000). Increasingly, however, as Japan modernized and became a unified, industrial, imperial nation, its technological, military and manufacturing skills went on display – first, as evidence of the 'civilized' spirit it shared with the West and its success in 'aping' the West's achievements, but, later, as evidence of its power and military might – whereupon it immediately began to be greeted with fear and suspicion. In this way, Japan has been displayed in the West via an orientalizing gaze which has successively exoticized and demonized it. Now, however, Japan has not only the technological wherewithal to outdo the West's exhibitionary techniques, it also has an affluent, tourism-hungry and consumer-oriented populace which, like the West, seeks the same kind of travel-free, wrap-around simulations of the world-as-cultural-mosaic that theme parks in the West provide. This time, however, the West finds itself on display. Hendry (2000) notes the initially unnerving feeling these parks produced for a Western anthropologist not accustomed to having the 'tables turned'.

However, many have seen Japan's obsession with Western culture as evidence of a continuing American-led cultural and economic imperialism. The presence of Disneyland in Tokyo seems to confirm this. However, Hendry (2000) notes that there have been few voices within Japan echoing those that greeted the opening of Euro-Disney in Paris. Disney's arrival in France was the occasion of an outpouring of almost universal scorn from most European newspapers, arguing that it was a 'cultural Chernobyl' in which American values (such as commercialism, materialism, regimentation, political conformism) were trying to insinuate themselves into 'European culture', through a process of cultural entryism (Bryman 1995). By contrast, American-style attractions in Japan, argues Hendry (2000), are not seen in the same way and, according to her, most local commentators on Tokyo Disneyland reject arguments that see it as an example of Western cultural hegemony.

Indeed, the importation of American theme parks into other countries could also be interpreted as the reverse of Americanization. For example, it has been argued that Tokyo Disneyland represents a Japanese appropriation of American cultural symbols, and in this sense is indicative of Japanese rather than American cultural imperialism (Van Maanen 1992; Brannen 1993). It seems plausible to see the spread of theme parks and cultural display as indicative of a proliferating world techno-capitalist consumerism, which invites affluent population sectors to consume culture in visitable form. This serves to illustrate the extent to which, far from being a Western phenomenon, there is now a swathe of countries, concentrated in wealthier regions of the world, which are fully signed up to the project of creating their own high-tech version of the global cultural mosaic.

Discovering the art in nature

Cultural particularism is not the only force behind the proliferation of theme parks. 'Discovery' has provided the motif for a new generation of parks dedicated to the display of science, nature, art and the environment. Indeed, the theme of the environment is now a central, perhaps the central, organizing feature in many discovery parks. The referencing of environmentalist discourse, it can be argued, humanizes science and technology in the way that was noted above in relation to recent expos. It allows technology to partake of a new-age, quasi-environmentalist vision which celebrates the idea that humans have now, allegedly, come to recognize their shared interests with nature. It also references a fused science–art discourse, in which human creativity and 'the wonders of nature' are shown to work in harmony with each other. This is closely tied to a popular-educational principle. Indeed, many of these new discovery parks conjoin the domains of art, science and nature through a populist, educational ethos that draws on the action-oriented framework of interactive pedagogy.

The UK's Millennium Commission, a public fund set up to finance 'Year 2000' visitor projects throughout the UK, has been responsible for a number of these discovery centres. For example, The Dynamic Earth is Edinburgh's newest attraction, which presents the story of the earth from Big Bang, through its climatic evolution to humankind's arrival. Another new UK Discovery Centre, @Bristol, offers Wildwalk, 'a living rainforest in the heart of the city', which takes visitors on an 'immersive' walk-through tour into six domains displaying different environmental stories. For example, People and the Planet provides insights into 'the ways in which we can ensure the sustainable future of our living planet'. The environmentalist message focuses on resource depletion and 'vanishing wildernesses'. There is also an Imax cinema showing *S.O.S Planet 3-D*, which invites visitors to 'experience the plight of our fragile planet and its changing environments, in a totally new way, on the giant four-story IMAX® screen in cutting-edge 3-D'. It covers 'three of the most pressing environmental issues of our time: global warming, ocean depletion, and deforestation' (from @Bristol web-pages).

The newly opened and highly acclaimed Magna Science Adventure Centre in South Yorkshire, UK, built on an ex-steel plant, is another example, this time highlighting the inter-dependence of art and technology. It combines technological discovery, organized around the base elements in steel-making of air, earth, fire and water, with an environmentalist message. It brings these together through commissioned artworks 'that cross the boundaries between science and art, as part of Magna's aim to fuse art, history, science and technology' (from Magna web-pages). The four pavilions use spectacular technological effects to stage the symbiosis of technology, industry and nature. It also humanizes technology by adding in human faces and voices. Its multi-media exhibition, the 'Face of Steel', presents steel-workers past and present telling their own life-stories.

Some of these science discovery parks eschew complex cultural interpretation and concentrate on technical wizardry, special effects and interactive gadgetry. Techniquest, a very popular interactive science park in the UK, is an example. Yet even here we find overt references to the inter-dependence of culture, technology and nature through its educationalist ethos of 'bringing science alive'. Indeed, Techniquest now has a publicly funded role in providing national curriculum 'learning experiences' for visiting school-children. Live performances in the science theatre create dramatic, attention-grabbing scenarios for the demonstration of scientific principles. The *Mo Mo Forest*, for example, a special display for schools, 'focuses on the care of the environment, using shadow scenery, animal puppets and lots of audience participation' (from Techniquest website). And many of Techniquest's interactive exhibits demonstrate the fusion of technology and human creativity, by showing the workings of creative optical and photographic effects. Indeed, the site's whole *raison-d'être* is to convince 'ordinary folk' that they can 'do' science and technology. By offering the latter in toy-like form, which visitors themselves activate, they invite their users to experiment, be creative and to feel in control.

The environment on display

Addressing the environment and self-consciously appropriating the language of conservation seems to be the latest way of pulling in visitors. Japan is planning its 2005 World Exposition on the theme of 'The Environment'. Even zoos and acquaria, which now prefer such nomenclature as wildlife parks and Sea Worlds, are careful to reference the values of conservation through focusing on 'habitat' and 'community'. For example, at SeaWorld Adventure Park in Orlando, Florida, various sea creatures including dolphins, stingrays, turtles, sea lions, otters, sharks, penguins and manatees have become themes, each providing a separate attraction. The Anheuser-Busch theme park chain, who owns the site, claims:

With every visit to SeaWorld or Busch Gardens, you are supporting wildlife conservation around the world. In fact, in a typical day at our parks, a portion of your admission might help rescue an orphaned whale, protect threatened habitats, recycle a ton of plastic or even help save an entire species from extinction.

(SeaWorld official visitor guide and map)

On the same brochure, SeaWorld cheerfully acknowledges its commercial partners, including Fujifilm, Motorola, Pepsi, Little Tikes, Pampers and Southwest Airline, seemingly quite oblivious to these companies' own contribution to environmental degradation. In such venues, the discourse of conservation becomes little more than an ideological cloak. However, its very mundane ubiquity suggests that environmentalism, long marginalized as the stuff of minority pressure-groups, has become since the 1990s a taken-for-granted and mainstream concern – something which large corporations are unafraid, even eager, to highlight. This shows the extent to which, by the 1990s, nature had been substantially reinvented *as* the environment – they had become seen as one and the same thing (Macnaghten and Urry 1997). We could see this reinvention as itself the product of a fused culture/nature discourse (culture + nature = the environment).

Referencing environmentalism is easy because it is a very wide term, and capable of being interpreted in the vague and general language of 'care', 'protection' and 'sustainability'. Eco-tourism is a manifestation of this. In the words of Klaus Toepfer, Executive Director of the UN's environment programme, eco-tourism attempts to 'develop tourism in ways that minimize the industry's negative impacts and actively promote the conservation of Earth's unique biodiversity'. It is supposed to help finance 'the protection of ecologically sensitive areas and the socioeconomic development of populations living in or close to them'.[1] Regardless of the fact – acknowledged elsewhere in the form of tree-planting carbon-replenishing schemes (such as Future Forest) – that every air flight burns thousands of gallons of jet-fuel and emits polluting carbon dioxide, eco-tourism nonetheless suggests that visiting itself can help save the planet. Increasingly, holiday brochures eschew the label 'tourist' and instead solicit 'adventurers', fieldwork assistants, exploraholics, volunteers and travellers, to go on expeditions, projects, treks and adventures and do their bit for environmental conservation.[2] Eco-tourism remains a minority interest for now. But it taps into the same concern for the sacrosanct qualities of 'natural' places that underpins many of the sites of nature-display we now see proliferating in 'destination countryside'. Below, I turn to a discussion of these visitor sites and consider how they reproduce a vision of what we might call 'the world as environmental mosaic'.

Destination countryside

Just as urban areas have been branded, interpreted and made accessible for the visitor, the countryside, too, has entered 'the economy of signs' (see Zukin 1991, 1995). Nature has long been produced as a tourist destination. The parks and menageries of Victorian Britain, for example, show how, by the nineteenth century, nature had already become a leisure destination and an object of the bourgeois gaze. Already then, 'one no longer lived in nature, one visited it as a tourist from the real world of the metropolis and the money economy' (Rojek 1993). However, the last twenty years or so have marked a new phase in the 'culturalization' of nature, in which these managed sites of nature are recast as sites of cultural consumption and visitability (Wilson 1992). Urry (1990, 2002) links this to the rise of the service class (see Chapter 1), whose tastes are centred on a host of 'natural' products, processes and environments. These all play the role of embodying an alternative to the perceived onslaught of technocratic modernism. The myth of the countryside and nature, as places outside of and resistant to these forces, impels a fascination with visiting them – presumably to check they are still there.

MacCannell's (1992) analysis of tourism as a search for authenticity as modernity's 'other' shows how the US's great national parks serve a similar purpose. Here, nature is still staged as an escape and an antithesis to the urban metropolis, but is thereby revealed as dependent upon it. This is because, as designated zones of non-urban development, they simply re-affirm the city's power to assist in the staging of nature and the management of its visitability. MacCannell sees the US's nature parks as evidence of capitalism's final destruction of the pre-industrial world. They are 'the good deed of industrial civilization' for they 'are symptomatic of the guilt which accompanies the impulse to destroy nature'. Thus, the parks are 'marked-off, interpreted, museumized nature', 'a reminder of what nature would be like if nature still existed'. They function well for capitalist expansionism, since 'by restricting "authentic" or "historic" nature to parks, we assert our right to destroy everything that is not protected by the Park Act' (MacCannell 1992: 115).

MacCannell's discussion of Yosemite valley, a beautiful natural land-scape which has been crowded out with visitor amenities (to the extent that it now houses a mini-city managed by the Curry Company), shows that 'nature' can still be sold as such even where it is surrounded by shops and gas stations. Nature thus comes packaged in different guises. In some destinations, it is decked out in layers of cultural interpretation, in others, such as wildernesses, it is deliberately left to stand alone. However, even in the last case, we still find the gradual but visible encroachment of theming and amenities, oriented to the production of visitability. Of the many types of nature-oriented visitor destination, I will mention just four here, which indicate this trend.

First, we can note the popularity of visitor sites which enclose nature within interiors – such as environmental and botanical gardens, often housed in vast glass domes and greenhouses, which allow tropical plants to be grown and a totally constructed visitor environment to be created. A good example is the phenomenally successful Eden Project in Cornwall, UK, where two vast glass domes enable the visitor to wander at will amongst a unique collection of tropical plants, trees and flowers. Then, secondly, there are enclosed outdoor parks and gardens, which have usually been created specifically for leisure purposes – either for the public or for an elite household, as in the grounds of country houses. Thirdly, there are local countryside parks and nature reserves – large areas of naturally occurring but managed habitats with clear boundaries around them. These have become more popular just as the traditional, local municipal park appears to be on the wane. Finally, there are whole swathes of non-bounded, but well-marked and well-known national landscapes and parks, often forming part of the state's countryside patrimony – including mountain-scapes, lakelands, dales, vales and valleys. These, too, are increasingly provided with visitor-oriented accessories.

Of these, there is some evidence to suggest that the municipal park in its traditional guise is undergoing a gradual decline in relation to the others, perhaps due to its failure to embody the currently favoured conservationist, environmental ethic (see Urry 2002). The manicured, rule-bound, mono-cultural and formal look of municipal parks seems to pit them against an environmentalist spirit. Country house gardens have been able to repackage themselves as conservationist projects by the recent emphasis on reclaiming heritage garden designs and reconstructing the auratic spaces of the pro-ductive, self-provisioning country house (for example, the immense popularity of the UK's Lost Gardens of Heligan). In such gardens, visitors are invited not only to gaze upon wealth and splendour, but to learn about the historic provisioning of households and the principles of domestic horticulture. They thus embody a heritage appeal. This provides a con-trastive experience to the new eco-domes, bio-spheres and glass houses, where a future-oriented vision of natural eco-system survival is invoked. In both site genres, however, an informal learning environment is created, which invites one to identify a kind of utopian alternative to the urbanized and degraded life-world of today.

Interpreting nature

These new enclavic spaces now pepper the countryside, marking it out into a plethora of small micro-environments, all offering different kinds of visitor appeal. This reflects a marked diversification away from the large national parks and reserves of the earlier twentieth century (Wilson 1992). In all of these sites, nature is *interpreted* for the visitor. This reflects a new ethos of consumer-oriented accessibility and visitability. In order to attract people other than nature enthusiasts (bird watchers, ramblers, climbers, etc.) nature is given a more human face. This is achieved through adding in human cultural artefacts and amenities, often in the form of interpretative signage, way-marked 'interpretative trails', viewing platforms and benches, graphic displays, visitor centres, cafés, and so forth.

Interpretation at nature sites serves two functions. First, it announces the site as a *sight* – a place which qualifies as a day out, and which promises to meet the demands of the leisure and tourist gaze. Entrances, maps, brochures, paths, visitor centres and signage all serve this purpose. Without such markers the site remains undifferentiated from its surrounds, unidentified as a destination. Secondly, interpretation allots cultural meaning to the site, by suggesting how it is to be read and interpreted. By adding cultural iconography and narratives to natural landscapes, interpretation turns it into a site where certain meanings – particularly those belonging to environmentalist discourse – are pre-selected for us. Visitors enter a landscape of signs and are invited to interact with it in manageable ways. Thus, we are confronted with the cultural display of nature.

This is evidenced in the increasing appearance within nature parks of artistic works such as sculptures, mosaics and art installations. Thus the worlds of art and nature are brought together, each making the other more visible. The UK's Yorkshire Sculpture Park is a good example, where way-marked trails take the visitor on a journey through both landscape and sculptures. Even in non-bounded stretches of countryside (forests, lakes, dales, moorland, cliff and coastal landscapes, etc.) artistic and design-led signage and trails are increasingly in evidence, as are art installations. In the grounds of the whimsical Edwardian, mock-medieval Castell Coch, in South Wales, the woodland pathways are dotted with benches – not mass produced park benches, but artisan-crafted benches using natural materials and sculpted into unusual shapes. Every now and then the visitor encounters along the footpath a life-size sculpture of a fox, a badger, an owl or a hare.

This is all quite a move away from the romantic ideal of nature as unspoilt wilderness that was inherited from the eighteenth century. It also provides quite a contrast to the experience of the countryside with which Raphael Samuel, the socialist historian of the British Isles and, late in his life, defender of 'the heritage industry', grew up in the 1930s and 1940s. He recalls his fellow working-class ramblers' 'adoration of the rugged', their 'romantic primitivism' and their subscription to the values of the 'open-air movement':

> Our idea of natural beauty – or what was called in the 1930s and 1940s 'scenery' – was also very much of our time. The fetishization of the unspoiled might plausibly be related to the agitation, on both Right and Left of the political spectrum ... against what was seen as the menace of ribbon development. The accent was on large and open vistas ... 'Nature in the grand'. The favoured views ... were panoramic. The optic was that of the outsider, one for whom villages were mere dots on the horizon. 'Beauty spots' were, by definition, uninhabited and ideally places where there was not a soul to be seen.
>
> (Samuel 1998: 143)

There was nothing picturesque, sentimental, historically interesting or, indeed, overtly cultural about such a landscape: rural villages were considered simply poor and scruffy and never objects of the gaze. There was no attachment to the rural architecture or lifestyles of the past. The countryside was, above all, expected to be empty, bracing and unadorned with signs of human habitation or intervention. By contrast, today's countryside is fetishized in human terms, either as a relic of the past and of values that take us back to older, more desirable ways of life, or as a resource for ecologically inspired future visions. Of course, Samuel's countryside was charged, too, with representing certain cultural values, yet these (values such as primitivism, wilderness, loneliness) specifically eschewed signs of human activities, 'interference' and culture. Today's countryside, by contrast, is reinvented as a form of 'partnership' between nature and humans via the discourse of conservation. In order to survive, nature is now required to present itself as a human-friendly place.

Visitor-friendly nature

Natural wetland sites are a good example of nature's dependence on human-friendly cultural values. Long regarded as unattractive, smelly, ambiguous (neither wholly land nor water) and therefore unvisitable, many wetlands have been allowed to disappear (or, in some cases, such as that of Cardiff Bay discussed in the last chapter, actively destroyed in the name of urban, visitor-oriented redevelopment – see Cowell and Thomas 2002).

Recently, however, the tide has literally been turned by strategies designed to make them visitor-friendly. In the US and Canada, for example, Ducks Unlimited is a private, not-for-profit conservation organization that 'conserves, restores, and manages wetlands' both for the waterfowl themselves but also for the 'benefit of those of us who cherish outdoor experiences, whether those experiences include carrying a shotgun or a pair of binoculars' (from their website). Their website highlights the way in which conservation is tied up with the production of visitability and 'outdoor experiences' – including hunting.

Making wetlands visitable involves endowing them with layers of cultural interpretation. In the UK, for example, the Wildfowl and Wetlands Trust manages a number of visitor sites in the UK, and its partner organizations have wetland visitor sites in Hong Kong, Singapore, US (Maryland), Australia (Newcastle) and Trinidad. The Trust makes these wetlands visitable, first, at the simple level of amenities, such as the construction of access routes and pathways along with consumer facilities such as toilets and cafés. These enable visitors to be both guided (towards the best viewing spots, for example) and managed (so as to prevent environmental damage from undisciplined access). Secondly, instead of leaving visitors to discover the landscape on their own, directly and perhaps haphazardly, it is made into a symbolic 'text' that welcomes them in and guides them along various interpretative paths. Signage, interpretative trails and itineraries, graphic panels, sculptures, artworks, visitor buildings and exhibitions all clothe the landscape in cultural meaning that suggests to the visitor how it should be 'read'. At the London Wetland Centre there is even an art gallery where different artists' work is on show, and events include exhibitions of wood carvings and paintings.

As in urban public art schemes (Chapter 3), these artistic interpretation designs are usually organized around a coherent visual theme. At the National Wetland Centre in South Wales, a 'landscape sculptor' was employed to design creative installations that would add interest and meaning to the visitor itinerary. His chosen motif takes the form of a heron's wing, the 'watcher of the marshes'. The visitor enters the site by means of a visitor centre with an impressive façade of wooden interlocking herons' wings. Viewing benches have been sculpted in the form of a heron's feather, and replica nests perch on tall, wooden, tree-like structures along the pathways. The materials utilized all signify the values of nature – reeds, twigs, willow, local stone. At the centre is an installation of giant stone swans' eggs, each complete with a viewing window into its interior. Here, the embryo at each stage of development can be viewed, mirroring the depictions of human embryo development with which we are already familiar. Finally, there is the usual children's play area constructed to match the site theme – in this case, with tunnels imitating the habitat of water voles. Countryside interpretation thus fuses together the values of art and nature in order to communicate to the visitor the message of their essential unity. This is something which is, again, recognizable from ecological discourse, emphasizing the inter-dependence of humans and nature.

However, there is some scepticism about the educational value of the ecological messages propagated at such sites. In a study of a well-known eco-tourism site, Fogg Dam Conservation Area in the Northern Territory, Australia, it is argued that its visitors, self-defined as eco-tourists, are accessing a consumer-oriented spectacle under the guise of educational eco-tourism (Ryan *et al.* 2000). Visitors, it seems, respond to the site in sensory rather than cognitive ways. First, they see it as an emotional 'experience', allowing them to feel the 'naturalness, openness, space, peace, quiet, and natural sounds' that are essential elements of 'the outback' (Ryan *et al.* 2000: 160). Secondly, it becomes an opportunity to consume spectacles marked out by the site's interpretative apparatus. Encouraged by wall displays showing the impressive birds that populate the area and carefully placed viewing paths and platforms, visitors concentrate on scooping up views of the most spectacular inhabitants of the site, rather than gaining any insight into the relationship between the birds and their habitat. The gloss of education that eco-tourism enjoys may often, this study suggests, be quite unsubstantiated.

Retailing nature?

It is important to note that such transformations do not only reflect a vague cultural shift towards the embrace of environmental values, but are also determined within a given political economy. Ideas of nature conservation, increasingly mainstream in the past decade, have been absorbed, too, by planners in the private and public sector, and set to work to meet economic goals. Much of the current professional discourse of local authority countryside planning departments emphasizes conservation. Environmental planners advise and, in turn take advice from, experts in wildlife and nature trusts and charities. Many of these nature parks undertake important conservation work; indeed, many see conservation as their core activity, with the visitor amenities conceived only as income generators for this work. The Wildfowl and Wetlands Trust in the UK carries out extensive habitat restoration, captive breeding programmes, conservation research and land and water management (see their website).

However, none of this important conservation work could take place without the income and sponsorship opportunities provided by the visitor facilities. Strategies of conserving the countryside are bound up with making it accessible and an interesting day out, transforming it in ways that help it to attract the gaze. Appealing to the ideal of the 'unity of culture and nature' within environmentalist discourse has been a means of bringing cultural display into nature parks, and thus enhancing these places' visitability. This is part of a wider, pragmatic response to the marketisation of planning for land-use. As pressures on public funding have increased, countryside planners dedicated to preserving green space have also recognized that it has to be made accessible for users. Public funding to support the preservation of natural landscapes has been made dependent on their ability to be claimed as a useful and popular public resource. If no-one uses a park, a wetland, a forest or a public right of way, it soon loses this claim and public funding will be hard to find.

Thus, green spaces have had to enter the economy of signs in order to survive under market conditions. Or, to put it another way, changing market conditions have made them into an economic asset that can signify a new era. Short (1996) discusses the example of Syracuse's Onondaga Lake in New York State. This was heavily polluted during the city's heyday as a thriving centre of chemicals and manufacturing industry. Short identifies three political-economic periods which serve to mark out the lake's changing role within the city's identity. During one hundred years of industrial growth, the lake was allowed to act as a repository for sewerage and chemical waste, since city leaders and residents alike prioritized the needs of industrial production, which was not be subjected to 'stifling' controls. In a middle, transitional period, after the Second World War, environmental groups campaigned for a clean-up of the water, but their voices were not able to gain ground until the 1970s, when industry was beginning to close down or move out. Only then were civic leaders and businesses together convinced that leisure-led regeneration was the key to Syracuse's economic survival.

Once leisure and consumption were placed firmly on the agenda, then, miraculously, the environmental arguments for cleaning up the lake found powerful backing. This indicates the alliance that post-industrial political-economic realities potentially institute between environmental discourse and economic regeneration. In an industrial era, environmentalism goes against dominant political and economic interests, and thus struggles to be heard. In a post-industrial, leisure-led economy, polluted environments become a handicap to visitability and a drain on resources. This can surely help to explain the rise of environmentalist movements since the 1970s – the period when rampant industrialism in the West began its long process of decline.

None of this should imply that before we had countryside interpretation, we somehow had unmediated, direct experience of nature. As Wilson (1992) points out in his book, *The Culture of Nature*, this experience is always mediated through the practices and discourses of photography, industry, advertising and aesthetics, as well as by social institutions such as governments, tourist agencies and schools. There is no such thing as an unmediated experience of nature, since we are part of a culture that has already loaded nature up with particular cultural values, such as freedom, simplicity, contemplation or adventure. The difference with the new interpreted sites, however, is that explicit signifiers are provided to activate these meanings for us, rather than leaving us to summon up particular connotations on our own. In this sense, the idea of 'discovery' and 'exploration', centrally flagged at nature parks, is to an extent factored out by the practices of theming and interpretation they employ. These seek to 'discover' the place for us in advance and equip it with meaning on our behalf. Rather than discovering it, we are accessing it through encountering a pre-coded environment. This does not mean that visitors to nature theme parks are passive, brainwashed or devoid of their own interpretations. However, it does show the extent to which visiting the countryside is becoming increasingly dependent upon the deliberate insertion and display of cultural signs. Increasingly, it seems, the countryside appears in the guise of theme park.

Notes

1   Quoted in (2002) How to be an eco-tourist, *Guardian*, 9 March.
2   See Birkett, D. (2002) Are you a tourist or a traveller, *Guardian*, 24 August.

Further reading

Gottdiener, M. (2001) *The Theming of America: Dreams, Visions and Commercial Spaces*, 2nd edn. Boulder, CO: Westview Press.
Harvey, P. (1996) *Hybrids of Modernity: Anthropology, the Nation State and the Universal Exposition*. London: Routledge.
Hendry, J. (2000) *The Orient Strikes Back: A Global View of Cultural Display*. Oxford: Berg.
Macnaghten, P. and Urry, J. (1997) *Contested Natures*. London: Sage
M. Sorkin (ed.) (1992) *Variations on a Theme Park: The New American City and the End of Public Space*. New York: Hill and Wang.

The Project on Disney (1995) *Inside the Mouse: Work and Play at Disney World*. Durham: Duke University Press.

Wilson, A. (1992) *The Culture of Nature: North American Landscape from Disney to the Exxon Valdez*. Cambridge, MA: Blackwell.

HERITAGE SOCIETY

5

Heritage is a mode of cultural production in the present that has recourse to the past. Heritage thus defined depends on display to give dying economies and dead sites a second life as exhibitions of themselves. A place such as Salem, Massachusetts, may be even more profitable as an exhibition of a mercantile center than it was as a mercantile center.

(Kirshenblatt-Gimblett 1998: 7)

Heritage is symptomatic of a much-discussed 'turn to the past' in contemporary society. This is a cultural trend manifested as visitable history of all kinds and not just in the guise of museums (which are discussed in detail in the next chapter). In what follows, I focus on the intertwining within heritage of two – potentially competing – forces: its visitor-oriented market relations, on the one hand, and its claims to stage and pay tribute to 'authentic' culture, on the other. Heritage production involves both salvaging the past, and staging it as a visitable experience. It makes the two interdependent. This reflects a wider tension in the local ownership of heritage – on the one hand as a resource for professional interpreters and planners, on the other as a resource for people's attempts to represent their own history and identities on a public stage. These two sets of interests are likely to be interrelated in different ways in different heritage projects, with some giving greater space and some less to people's active participation in their own self-display via heritage.

The turn to the past

Heritage is not a new phenomenon. As Lowenthal (1985, 1998) points out, historical landscapes, cityscapes and buildings have long been consecrated as attractions and sights on a tourist trail. The second half of the nineteenth century, in particular, produced a boom in museum-building and historical record-keeping in the West. It was then that the goal of recording and disseminating history to the mass public started to become a matter for governments, political elites and powerful interest groups such as trusts and learned societies (see Bennett 1995). Nevertheless, the recent turn to the past represents a distinctive second-wave of heritage-mania. This second wave has largely rejected the didactic forms of the earlier public museums, which appealed in practice only to a small, well-educated section of the public, and adopted instead more accessible techniques of display which seek as wide an audience as possible.

It was in the 1980s that heritage audiences began to soar. Most countries in the Euro-American axis witnessed a boom: heritage visits in Europe, for example, rose 100 per cent between 1970 and 1991 (Richards 1996). Visits to heritage attractions in the UK rose from 52 million in 1977 to 68 million in 1991 (Light 1995). And most commentators agree that the years since the 1980s have continued to witness a remarkable explosion of popular interest in heritage and the past (Urry 1990, 2002; Samuel 1994; Lowenthal 1998). Samuel, for example, describes contemporary society as 'an expanding historical culture' dominated by the power of 'Clio's hand', where history has become a 'mass activity' with more followers than ever before (Samuel 1994: 25). Lowenthal (1998) writes, similarly:

> All at once heritage is everywhere – in the news, in the movies, in the marketplace – in everything from galaxies to genes. It is the chief focus of patriotism and a prime lure of tourism. One can barely move without bumping into a heritage site. Every legacy is cherished. From ethnic roots to history theme parks, Hollywood to the Holocaust, the whole world is busy lauding – and lamenting – some past, be it fact or fiction.
> (Lowenthal 1998: xiii)

In the 1980s, the heritage boom was still a novelty, and the subject of fierce debates by cultural commentators (see below). Now, heritage has become so ubiquitous that it is simply an expected aspect of any visitor environment.

One of the obvious reasons for this expansion is the fact that heritage has become a lucrative resource for marketers, who see it as a key lifestyle indicator. Accordingly, corporations and other commercial sponsors have enthusiastically cultivated a 'retro' market-niche, and public planners, similarly, have exploited the potential of heritage for luring in consumer spend to development zones. Nevertheless, for all they wish they could, marketers do not have the power single-handedly to implant desires into people's minds. They cannot conjure up the popularity of cultural forms out of thin air: these also have to strike a chord with the particular concerns of the day (or, better, with what Williams 1961: 63–5 called an epoch's 'structure of feeling'). As the above quote from Lowenthal suggests, the recent heritage boom probably owes at least some of its impetus to the surge in a popular 'identity politics'.

In an age of identity, people come to think of their sense of self as something they can actively shape and construct, rather than something which is fixed for them by stable or inherited familial or working roles (Bauman 1996). Gaining a sense of one's past becomes integral to this project of claiming an identity for the self – hence the boom in popular practices of genealogy, archaeology and collecting. Such practices remain minority activities, however, and it has rather been in the form of public, visible, built culture that heritage suddenly seems to be everywhere – indeed, wherever there are exhibitions, buildings, performances and townscapes designed to pull in visitors. And this is not grand History in the form of state figures and official events. It is rather history in the guise of people's lives and lifestyles: the ordinary but 'colourful' life of the self. As I shall suggest below, what heritage visitor sites provide is a public platform for the past-self, and it is this public acknowledgement and display of self-identity which seems to be fundamental to the particular heritage boom we have been witnessing in recent years.

Heritage for everyone

To many, the heritage explosion of the 1980s seemed a reactionary force. In the UK, popular television programmes (such as the BBC's adaptation of Evelyn Waugh's novel, *Brideshead Revisited*) yearned for a long-past aristocratic England, and visits to 'elite' heritage sites soared. Alongside religious buildings such as cathedrals and churches, 'open' to the public as a matter of course, a large number of previously private historic properties and gardens were opened up to the public for the first time. In the 1980s, such developments were widely seen as constituting a backward-looking, elitist and conservative 'heritage industry' (Wright 1985; Hewison 1987). Many buildings were suddenly added to the government's list of those with 'architectural or historical merit': a staggering 32, 603 obtained listed status in 1987 alone (Hanna 1998). And since the 1980s, visits to these traditional heritage attractions have continued to be immensely popular. Since 1975, visits to English historic properties have increased by at least 35 per cent (Hanna 1998). In the UK, the body charged with, among other duties, conserving and displaying stately homes (the National Trust) had nearly two and a half million members in the mid-1990s, and visits to its properties now number some 12 million a year (Urry 2002).

However, from the 1980s on, these traditional display-sites of elite heritage were quickly joined by sites specializing in 'ordinary' history, or history-from-below. The 'living history' movement has been spectacularly successful, appearing in various locations: in the new breed of open-air industrial museums, within the older, more 'serious' museums and also in the new generation of hybrid culture/technology/art centres that frequently include living history displays and performances. In the process, elite venues, too, have had to adjust to the new popularity of vernacular history. As we shall see below, even grand, state properties now offer the visitor access to ordinary lives, through opening up to the gaze the backstairs life of these homes. In addition, castles and country houses have invested in new interactive interpretative techniques to 'bring them alive' for the experience-hungry visitor. These more vernacular arrivals on the heritage scene have tended to divide the critics, as we shall see later on.

Living history

The phenomenon of 'living history' both refers to 'interactive' heritage museums which use reconstructions and simulations, as well as describing a general tendency towards forms of display that 'bring history alive'. This is a tendency that underpins much of the currently proliferating heritage visitor attractions. It is predicated on the idea of making history more authentic, more real and more immediate; to get beyond, in MacCannell's (1976, 1999) terms, the contrived and distanced historical stages that tourism conventionally offers. The growing popularity of historical re-enactments is a particularly striking example. Viking tourism, for instance, has provided the impetus for a wide range of re-enactments and performances throughout Europe (see Halewood and Hannam 2001). 'First-person' re-enactments about 'us', as opposed to 'third-person' commentary about 'them', involves costumed actors speaking as if they were characters from a past era, ignorant of present-day custom. It has become almost standard at many heritage sites today.

Castles and manor houses increasingly stage first-person re-enactments as a means of enhancing their visitor appeal. Visitors to the Tudor manor house of Llancaich Fawr, for example, in South Wales, are 'calling' on the Pritchards, a well-to-do, seventeenth century family. They find, however, that the family is always 'out' when they arrive. So, instead, visitors are greeted by the costumed servants, who invite them to explore the house while they wait. Along the way they can talk with the servants they encounter in different rooms, who are engaged in daily tasks such as sewing, cooking and cleaning. They thus find out about the backstairs life of the house: the preparation of food, the buying of produce, the keeping of accounts and all the various skills and crafts which serviced the household's needs.

Crang (1996) documents his experience of participating in two re-enactment groups: a society holding recreations of the battles of the British Civil War at various castles around the country, and a group who had volunteered to take part in a reconstruction of an English manor Tudor household. Participant-actors were ordinary people with an enthusiasm for history. They expended much effort on 'getting into' the world of the Civil War/Tudors through assembling the required 'kit' and researching authentic story-lines and yarns. What was produced, argues Crang, was not simply an invented version of the past but a fusion of the 'authenticity fetish' and a carnivalesque principle of ironic, self-aware role-play. Actors and visitors alike were creating together an interpretative frame, geared to the production of high drama, theatricality and an appreciation of successful staging-effects.

The other major forum for living history is the heritage centre or museum, which may itself offer re-enactments and performances. Two types of heritage museum are often distinguished (see Lumley 1988). The first are the modern-day successors of the open-air folk museum first pioneered at Skansen in Sweden. The emphasis here is on careful research of buildings, industries and crafts to ensure period authenticity (for example, the Museum of Welsh Life in Wales and Beamish Open-Air Museum in the north-east of the UK). The second is the simulated 'experience centre', such as the Yorvik Viking Centre in York. Here, visitors climb on board a moving train that takes them through various scenes of Viking life, showing them the sights, sounds and smells of Viking-era York. Similar is the Kerry County Museum in Ireland, where visitors join a 'time-car' ride that takes them to the walls of the medieval town of Tralee. Gaining entry from the sentinel, they enter the smelly, crowded town streets, avoid a bucket of slops being thrown from an upstairs window, and then travel onwards into the ancient castle and abbey. In such sites, the emphasis is on creating sensory drama through technology, multi-media display and high-tech rides and simulations.

Increasingly, however, the line between the two types is being blurred. The first type, such as old collieries, reconstructed villages or canal workings, in which care has been taken to ensure authentic restoration, now also include the second type, through the adding-in of 'experiences', re-enactments and rides which do not pretend to 'be' the past but rather to evoke it. As well as its time-car ride, Kerry County Museum also has a properly curated, more traditional museal display, showing conserved artefacts from the area's history. Even multi-media Yorvik can justly claim to have an authentic geographical and material basis (it is sited on a Viking-era archaeological excavation), and is managed by the York Archaeological Trust, which has public education about archaeology as its prime mission.

In South Wales, two living history mining museums illustrate the twin appeals to authenticity that industrial places offer in their 'second lives as exhibitions' (Kirshenblatt-Gimshblett 1998). They both show the history of two preserved coal-mines via walk-through underground tours led by real ex-miners. In the one (Big Pit in Gwent), visitors move through a real, preserved, abandoned mine-shaft; in the other (the Rhondda Heritage Park) they enter a simulated reconstruction of 'underground', built above the now-capped shafts of the existing underground roadways far below them. A local planner involved in developing the second museum explained to me how he saw their differences:

> Big Pit is a working mine as it was more or less left on the day that the men downed tools and went up out of it. But because of that, and because it's underground, it is very difficult to put back into Big Pit the noises and the feel of what it is like to be underground. You can be underground but it is quiet, there is no one around, the atmosphere is not the same as it is in a working colliery. But it is real. There is a real structure. At Rhondda Heritage Park underground, what we've tried to do there is to make that come alive. It is absolutely accurate in terms if its construction ... because it was constructed by ex-miners. It's not false, although it isn't actually underground. It isn't false. It is a construction ... but it's alive. It's noisy. It has atmosphere... Big Pit is real. It is a real underground mine. Proper. It should be kept exactly as it is. Rhondda Heritage Park is trying to bring that sort of thing to life.
> (From personal interview with tourism officer, Mid Glamorgan County Council 1996)

Whilst Big Pit is 'real' and 'proper' with 'real structure', it is 'quiet' and lacks 'atmosphere'. The Rhondda Heritage Park, by contrast, is 'trying to bring that sort of thing to life'. It is 'alive', 'not false', 'an accurate construction', 'noisy', 'lively' – it is 'constructed by ex-miners' and 'has atmosphere'. Two different orders of reality underlie the distinction between the two attractions: Big Pit's is a material reality, whereas the Park's is experiential. Each complements the other, for each is deficient in the other's virtue: Big Pit lacks the sensory experience, the Park lacks the real structures.

The Park, however, can overcome the constraints imposed by reality (such as the strict safety regulations governing real mining roadways underground), and thus surpass reality, by offering us its very 'essence' – its feel, smell, noises and look but not its material limitations and dangers. Like theme parks, it can 'give us more reality than nature can' (Eco 1986: 44). Yet, in heritage, the 'extras' we are given do not simply represent exoticism or fiction as at the theme park, but stand in for temporal loss. We really cannot have the dead back, for they have gone, but we can at least resurrect the places where they spent their lives. As Kirshenblatt-Gimblett asks: 'Having reconstituted the pot, why not the potter? Why not his [*sic*] studio, home and marketplace? And why limit the reconstruction ... to drawings and words?' (1998: 193). At the Lowell National Historical Park in Massachusetts, for example, a 1920s weave room has noisy, fully-working power looms with interactive exhibits and video programmes about the Industrial Revolution, workers' lives and the history of Lowell. In the Boott Mill boarding-house, visitors can explore the history of 'mill girls', mill workers, immigrants and boarding-house life with the aid of a costumed interpreter (see Lowell National Historical Park web-pages).

In these sites of 'resurrectionism' (Samuel 1994), the voices of the dead that we seem to hear are invariably those of ordinary, everyday people. This vernacular voice is one of the reasons for the popularity of industrial historical display – for it is not usually the bosses who lead us around and talk to us, but the workers. In the reconstructed street, we do not meet the mayor or the mine-owner but the shop-keeper and the housewife. In the manor house, we meet the servants. Indeed, vernacular heritage has become pre-dominant in the production of heritage visitability (Lowenthal 1998; Jordanova 2000). The appeal is that of meeting people and walking through environments that would have comprised, one imagines, the past world of one's own, ordinary self – the self made into 'other'.

The self 'then'

This first-person focus in vernacular heritage suggests that it is not only prompted by wider cultural dedifferentiation (the shift from high to 'ordinary' culture – see Chapter 1). It is also impelled, I would argue, by the diffusion of an identity-centred relationship with the past. As Lowenthal (1998) notes, most people have little awareness of or enthusiasm for history in the sense of national and international events, places, people and processes. What they do have is a sense of how their own lives are changing in relation to those of their peers, parents and grandparents, and how their own selves are affected by these processes. Thus, the idea of history as *dis*interested enquiry runs counter to the prevailing cultural ethos of identity-focused heritage. In other words, the display of the vernacular past is popular because it grants a public stage for self-awareness. I have argued that it provides a means of appreciating the intersection between individual biographies and wider social and cultural changes (Dicks 2000b).

In bringing biography and culture together, heritage displays offer a space for the intertwining of public, exhibitionary space and private, biographical space. Crang (1994) thus sees heritage as a constantly shifting performance, in which 'to each exhibit, people bring a host of metonymic others – personal resonances that are set off, memories and connections triggered by the display' (Crang 1994: 345). In this perspective, heritage is not so much sight-seeing (the public display of the other) as cultural biography (the public recognition of the self and its stories). As Johnstone (1998) suggests, heritage displays can function in this way as 'substitute heirlooms'. They preserve the material culture of past generations that has gradually disappeared from families' own homes, thereby offering visitors the pleasure of seeing their 'own' personal realm displayed and verified in the public collection – 'my granny had one of those!'

Heritage, I would argue, is about journeys. These are not only the itineraries that visitors follow as they move through exhibitions, but also the metaphorical or literal journeys which constitute their own personal life-stories. Moving home as a child or adult, for example, provides one source of heritage-laden biography. The geographical location of early memories – a changed but enduring 'here', for example, or a half-remembered and evocative 'there' – provides a narrative for understanding one's past as a journey. Vernacular heritage activates these different narratives of the journeying self. Where family members have become cut off from previous generations through geographical displacement, the experience of living in diaspora creates a powerful heritage urge (Lowenthal 1998).

The relationship between social class and place-belonging is important here, since different experiences of geographical fixity or displacement reflect different kinds of class habitus (see Fyfe and Ross 1996). Relocations may reflect voluntary middle-class mobility, or they may be the result of forced industrial and colonial migrations, producing generations of families who have had to leave areas to find work. This in turn creates a potential swathe of 'returnees' much later on, revisiting 'home' as part of a recovery of roots and family history. The ex-industrial childhood place, abandoned when Dad lost his job, now has a living history museum to tell *his* story, and by extension one's own. In this way, vernacular heritage taps into the idea that people's autobiographical narratives are never purely personal, but are closely intertwined with wider historical (social and cultural) forces.

My own research[1] at the Rhondda Heritage Park, a living history mining museum in Wales, underscores the relationship between personal biography and public culture in the popular dynamics of heritage. When Bryn Rees, a Welsh miner, tells the story – in his own regional dialect – of the changes he witnessed in the Rhondda Valleys of 100 years ago, he turns history into biography and biography into history. In this way, the personal stories that are told, by real, living characters in heritage museums are also public, in the sense that, by virtue of being on public display, they become part of a public, legitimated narrative – for example, the story of industrialisation, migration or technological change. Such stories are deliberately presented so as to invite visitors' identification with them, and visitors seem to like the idea that their own personal life-journeys (or those of their ancestors) 'make sense' within those wider narratives of public, collective history. Heritage thus grants the private self a public narrative: in place of the solitary perusal of a personal snapshot collection, it offers the visitor public recognition by organizing these snapshots into epic narratives and dramatic scenes and putting them on display.

The biography/culture intersection occupied by heritage suggests a particular category of tourist gaze – one which seeks the means of encountering or fantasizing the self *as other*. The quality of otherness is necessarily part of the heritage gaze, if only through its temporality – we are gazing on the past rather than the present. However, there are multiple gradations of otherness involved here, from a gaze which mirrors the self (as in local mining families visiting their local mining museum) to one which reflects 'the other' (as in Westerners visiting an ethnographic museum of African culture). I suggest the following continuum (Figure 5.1) as a means of representing the different self/other relations potentially set up by heritage:

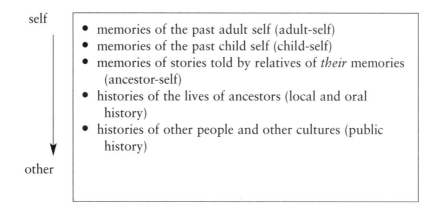

self

- memories of the past adult self (adult-self)
- memories of the past child self (child-self)
- memories of stories told by relatives of *their* memories (ancestor-self)
- histories of the lives of ancestors (local and oral history)
- histories of other people and other cultures (public history)

other

Figure 5.1 Self/other visitor relations set up in heritage display

Tracing the arrow down, there is an increasing distance between the heritage on display and its relation to the visitor-self. At the bottom end, there is only limited personal connection to the heritage on display.

This movement of the arrow arguably has implications for the ways in which visitors understand the authenticity of heritage displays. In my own research at the Rhondda Heritage Park, I found that virtually all of the visitors I approached had some close or distant family connection, either to the place or to coal-mining in general. Further, it appeared that those with the closest and most recent relationship to the history on display were the most demanding and critical in terms of judging its authenticity, whereas those with only a second-hand knowledge were content to be guided by the display's own categories and accounts. The former already had an elaborated narrative in their minds about the history on display, whilst the latter had much vaguer mental pictures. Thus, movement in the direction of the arrow entails a weakening of the visitor's demand for experiential detail in the display, i.e. for the idiosyncratic and everyday particularities of lived memory. Tellingly, I found that those who still lived in the area itself – with the greatest potential investment in the exhibit's experiential authenticity – would only go to the Park to take visiting relatives there, as if they saw it as catering for a gaze more distanced than their own.

One might almost apply Williams's (1961) notion of a 'selective tradition' to the biography/culture dynamic in heritage. As complex experiences become sedimented over time into memories and these in turn are re-mixed and whittled down through selective recall and repetition, what is left, perhaps, is the stuff which provides the common-places of local histories: the apocryphal stories and well-rehearsed iconographics of particular places. As the diagram suggests, where memories are very current, stemming from the adult-self (with the visitor still living there, or having only recently moved away), authenticity is likely to demand considerable detail and layers of complexity. By contrast, where memories stem from childhoods spent in another place, different demands are placed on the display. It may be considered sufficiently authentic if it stimulates personal recognition and accords with one's own childhood memories. Where memories are second-hand, as in the case of the ancestor-self, the display will be considered authentic if it resonates with passed-down stories, such as through the use of well-known anecdotes, reminiscences and iconic details. Conversely, there may be little self-identification with the heritage on display, as, perhaps, in the case of the outside, disinterested visitor looking to accrue anthropological knowledge or simply to find out about history for its own sake. Here, the biographical relationship is minimized and the cultural aspect predominant. In that case, the authenticity of the exhibition is likely to be judged more in terms of its accordance with received, canonical ideas about the subject on display.

My own research suggests that it is the 'childhood-self' and the 'ancestor-self' that find the greatest satisfaction in living history museums and heritage centres. These sites provide vivid stories and anecdotes, often framing them in terms of the personal reminiscences of past characters – such as Bryn Rees. This sets up easy resonances with the already formed imaginations of the childhood/ancestor-self visitor, who also frames the history in terms of personal reminiscences. Conversely, both the adult-self and the 'non-self' orientation are likely to demand a higher level of detail and elaboration than the average heritage display can provide: the former wants it to reflect direct, situated, personal, necessarily complex knowledge, the latter to reflect more formal knowledge. Neither is well-conveyed by personalized narratives, simulacra and images. The arguable predominance of this 'childhood/ancestor-self' orientation to the past certainly resonates with the identity-focused framing of living history discussed above.

Halting a runaway world

Living history also fits in well with the idea that heritage stages the desire to halt a 'runaway world'. It seems to offer an imaginary space of resistance to 'turbo-capitalism', the destruction of traditional environments and the vanishing of communities. By recreating past environments in material form, it seems to make time stand still; we can walk down an ostensibly medieval street and find all its people, noise, sights and smells still there. Outside, redevelopment marches relentlessly on; inside, we can stroll, literally at our leisure, through spaces of non-development. The voraciously destructive drives behind the seemingly solid edifice of capitalism have been memorably narrated by Marshall Berman in his 1982 book *All That Is Solid Melts into Air*. Here he describes the coming of the 1960s 'expressway world' in which the Bronx of his childhood was literally carved up and smashed to pieces by the tank-like onslaught of arch-modern development. Architects, planners and designers throughout the twentieth century, but increasingly after the Second World War, developed the straight lines, clean vistas, overarching freeways and functional buildings of modernity as an explicit rejection of what they took to be the atrophied traditional living patterns and stubborn group identities of old-fashioned neighbourhoods (Mugerauer 2001: 92). Heritage can be seen, in its turn, as a material form of rejection of this rejection.

Yet, herein too lies the fuel for heritage's fiercest critics. Resistance to these transformations has often been seen as a manifestation of that same stubbornness – a failure to move on, an atrophied clinging to the old ways and a 'yearning for yesterday' (Davis 1979). Heritage, likewise, has been seen as the same nostalgic turning away from the present (e.g. Wright 1985; Hewison 1987, 1989). For Hewison (1989), for example, heritage 'will lead to a state of inertia, where we are distracted from the present by ever-improving images of the past, and paralysed by the thought of a future which can only, by comparison with these simulacra, be worse than the way we never were' (Hewison 1989: 22). Below, I examine some of these charges of nostalgia-peddling in a little more detail. In the process, I suggest alternative readings of this resistance which, in my view, are more fruitful in understanding the roots of the heritage-boom.

Nostalgia suggests a kind of retreat from complexity, into the half-remembered vistas of familiarity and simplicity associated with the past. For some critics, this is all we now have left of history, for our saturation with historical signs and simulacra is such that we can no longer identify the real relations between past and present (MacCannell 1976; Bommes and Wright 1982; Baudrillard 1983; Jameson 1991). This view holds that heritage encourages a view of the past as an enclave of lost harmony and social cohesion. Bennett (1995), for example, notes the preponderance of heritage museums in Australia which focus on the 'lives of pioneers, settlers, explorers, gold-mining communities and rural industries prevalent in the nineteenth century, at the expense of twentieth-century urban history' (Bennett 1995: 161). For Fredric Jameson (1984, 1991), heritage is part of a 'nostalgic mode' which proliferates in response to a widespread feeling that the relationship between present and past can no longer be clearly grasped. The turn to the past is, in this way, a *retreat* from the 'crisis of historicity' that characterizes the condition of postmodernity.

Jameson describes North America as obsessed with representations of the past (see also Wallace 1996), but a number of writers have seen Britain as the epitome of the nostalgic mode. It is seen as peculiarly troubled by visions of a lost golden age, and, correspondingly, particularly over-crowded with heritage attractions that look back on it. Hewison (1987) worries that opportunities for tackling the country's current problems are being wished away by the heritage explosion, for it ensures that the populace, busy smiling on the past, has its back turned to the politics of the present. The heritage urge, in this perspective, emerges from a sense of disillusionment and lack of interest in the present, an argument encapsulated in his book's subtitle, 'Britain in a climate of decline'. For Wright (1985), too, the contemporary fascination with the past is moulded by conservative forces, trying to create a vision of old cultural securities pandering to simplistic nationalism and patriotism. In other writings, heritage is seen as a refuge from the maelstrom of postmodernity and its production of continual change. Harvey (1989a), for example, sees heritage as a desire to escape into mythical times of community and solidarity, representing 'the search for secure moorings in a shifting world' (Harvey 1989a: 302). Here, heritage is a retreat from the insecurities engendered by a mobile, globalized, runaway world. These 'retreatist' critiques thus take the heritage brochure's exhortations to escape from the present ('Leave the twenty-first century behind!' 'Take a trip down memory lane!') as symptomatic of its underlying logic.

However, I would argue that it is not necessarily the fantasy of retreat that heritage offers. Some heritage displays do indeed offer cosy and comforting visions of a mythical childhood-that-never-was. But many offer a more ambivalent representation of the past, where both gains and losses in comparison with today are on display. Wright does appear to acknowledge such diversity in his later book, *Journey through Ruins* (1992). Likewise, Bennett (1995) recognizes that vernacular living-history museums do not always portray history through the lens of the dominant culture. Some, such as the Hyde Park Barracks in New South Wales and the People's Palace in Glasgow, succeed in showing the conflicts, divisions and controversies – including those of class, race and gender – within which history unfolds. This is largely because, he argues, they conceive of 'the people' not as a picturesque and homogeneous 'folk', but as 'the norm of humanity to which the museum implicitly addresses itself' (Bennett 1995: 126).

In this way, living-history may succeed in staging a representation of people's 'ordinary lives' which allows them to ponder the experience of change without lapsing into nostalgia. Visitors to the Rhondda Heritage Park, for example, tended to utilize a double framing in decoding the displays: seeing the past on display as both worse and better than now. It was worse in terms of its harsh conditions, better in terms of its solidarity and sense of community (Dicks 2000a). None of those I interviewed expressed a wish to return there. Rather than being a journey backwards, taking spectators away from the realities of the present into a more secure world, heritage can be seen as staging a particular self–other relationship with the past. Visitors enjoy the experience of comparing their own lives to those on display, for it allows them to gain an unusual perspective on their own past and present lives. It is a peculiarly modern, simulating power, which lets them see their own lives as 'other'.

I am suggesting here that heritage is not a retreat from the present but is stimulated *by* the present. It is late modernity itself which allows the past to be represented in forms which seem so real (particularly in wrap-around, interactive, living history simulations). The desire to access the past can be seen as a manifestation of contemporary modes of representation which provide us with multi-sensory, multi-vocal, cacophonous places in which to experience it. Thompson (1995) makes this point when he argues that today's yearning for tradition should not be interpreted as out of synch with modernity, but stimulated *by* modernity. Modernity allows tradition to be disembedded from the constraints of situated and localized interaction, and to be 're-moored' in new and diverse contexts within the multiple forms of mediated spectacle (Thompson 1995: 183–91). Thus, traditions can be consumed and lived without the constraints of authority and obligation inherent in their original contexts. Similarly, we could argue that heritage worlds offer the past as a 3-D experience of the everyday without the dead weight of actually living it.

In his historical study of visitors' accounts of going to Skansen, the early outdoor folk museum in Sweden, Sandberg (1995), too, rejects nostalgia as an explanation for its popularity:

> If the appeal of the institution were simply due to an irresistible nostalgia ... the inadequacy of mimetic representation would ultimately frustrate the spectator-patriots seeking in the representation of folk life the presence of traditional culture...Spectators were more often intrigued by the *in-betweenness* of the folk museums, by the ways in which they both managed the losses of modernity – the weakened connections between body and culture – and celebrated the powers it endowed on spectators – powers of mobility, invisibility, panopticism.
>
> (Sandberg 1995: 333, my emphasis)

Hence, the appeal of Skansen's display of the past need not imply that its visitors were yearning to return there. Instead, the pleasure came from the museum's staging of the experience of transition and dislocation ('in-betweenness') that modernity delivered for newly urbanized ex-peasant families. It provided a space for the visitor to gaze upon that past from the mobile position of a modern-day spectator, i.e. to embody the fantasy of seeing the past as if it were still there, still touchable, suspended in time. This seems to offer an insight into the industrial heritage museum of recent years. Like the Scandinavian folk museum at the moment of industrialization, it, too, preserves and displays an ordinary and working-class world, but at the later historical juncture of de-industrialization and entry into a new global runaway-world. These conditions seem to replicate the intense experience of change that urban industrialization wrought upon the Scandinavian countryside at the turn of the century.

In the newer industrial heritage museums that represent communities of miners, steelworkers, slate quarrymen, canal workers and so on, the visitor walks through a living, multi-sensory world containing ordinary, familiar ways of life, but ones which are no longer the imposed or the obligatory ways of life. They are ones that visitors have left behind, but which are still part of their own or their immediate ancestors' memories. They stage the vanishing of the familiar, but only through the familiar having already become strange. In this sense, they offer an experience of 'in-betweenness' rather than nostalgia. Thus, the popularity of vernacular living history can be seen as a quintessentially modern means of staging and coming to terms with the incessant flow of time. Through being offered the dream of arresting this flow so that we can walk around our own pasts at our leisure, we can imagine ourselves still there: 'what would it be like to go back in time?'

Heritage critiques

Heritage vs. history

For some critics, this self-focused aspect of heritage marks it out as a subjective, and thus intellectually impoverished, practice. In such accounts, heritage is often unproblematically opposed to history – the latter being considered intrinsically objective and truthful. For Hewison (1987), it is simply 'bogus history'. Similarly, we find the following proposition:

> Heritage is not the same as history. Heritage is history processed through mythology, ideology, nationalism, local pride, romantic ideas or just plain marketing, into a commodity.
>
> (Schouten 1995)

Many others who would not insist as straightforwardly as this on the objectivity of history nevertheless accept the distinction. Heritage is often seen as having a particular tie to the present (from which history is free), since it involves specifying some relation to a *legatee* – a person or a collective to whom the heritage 'belongs'. All heritage, therefore, is someone's heritage, whereas history belongs to the disinterested realm of public knowledge.

Tunbridge and Ashworth (1996), for example, argue that, while 'both history and heritage make selective use of the past for current purposes', in heritage 'current and future uses are paramount' (1996: 6). In Lowenthal's view, similarly, while history 'explores and explains pasts grown ever more opaque over time', heritage 'clarifies pasts so as to infuse them with present purposes' (1998: xv). Although history is also inevitably biased, its role is to persuade its audience of its essential truthfulness, whilst heritage 'candidly invents and frankly forgets' (Lowenthal 1998: 121). This argument ignores the many authenticating claims that heritage centres make, suggesting they would all cheerfully align themselves with theme parks. It also suggests that historians are professionals who produce scholarly books, and that history is what is found therein. However, if one sees history as embedded in ordinary people's memorial activities as well as in academic texts, as Samuel (1994) does, such a distinction becomes difficult to sustain.

I suspect that what really underlies the attempt to keep history and heritage separate is the latter's association with visitors and tourists. One does not speak of visiting history, for, as soon as the past is produced in visitable form, it becomes heritage (or, at least, open to the accusation of being heritage). Similarly, one does not tend to think of heritage as assuming book-form (although books may be part of one's heritage). This returns us to the present-day orientation of the term 'heritage'. It is certainly true that, in order to attract visitors and activate the self-as-other relations I have been describing, such attractions do offer a view of the past which resonates with contemporary perspectives. I would argue, however, that most history books do this, too, although for a different audience. Their audience being much smaller, especially in academic circles, the contemporary concerns that history books address may be ones in which only a select group of experts is either proficient or interested.

If we think of heritage as *history made visitable* we can avoid falling into the unproductive debates over truth vs. distortion. What this means is that heritage is produced within the cultural economy of visitability (see Chapter 1), in which the object is to attract as many visitors as practicable to the intended site, and to communicate with them in meaningful terms. This has implications for the definitions of history which are on display. These represent history in terms of people's personal stories and lives, but this does not imply the necessity of distortion or invention. Indeed, many heritage centres are based on careful research into the lives of local people, lives which would otherwise go unrecorded. What we can say, however, is that the principle of visitability works to produce particular kinds of historical representation, which need to be 'readable' by, and interesting to, a wide range of visitors who are there primarily for identity-oriented reasons. For this reason, heritage is, I would argue, never simply about safe-keeping the past 'for its own sake', as it is always produced for an audience whose perspectives and desires (as these are understood by heritage producers) inevitably shape its displays.

Heritage vs. preservation

The question of safe-keeping has provided a further cause for complaint against heritage. For many critics (e.g. Hewison 1987; Jordanova 1989; Walsh 1992; Herbert 1995), preservation reflects the purist ideal of maintaining the past in its original state, for its own sake, and it is this ideal that has become distorted under current commercial pressures. Thus, contemporary heritage becomes an antonym to preservation: 'heritage conservation is creation and not preservation of what already exists' (Ashworth 1992: 97). However, the argument that heritage in a previous era was guided solely by preservationist ideals, reflecting a commitment to saving the past purely for its own sake, is not very convincing. The preservation of townscapes and landscapes for the gaze really took off in the nineteenth century as part of the 'exhibitionary complex' that Bennett (1995) discusses. This was a period when many traditions and ceremonies were positively mass-produced in order to foster patriotic feeling (Hobsbawm 1999). Preservation was not undertaken, in this period, for purely objective, neutral interests, unconcerned with attracting the gaze of spectators or sponsors. More often than not, it was bound up with the projects of various elites to bolster relations of power, status and/or nationalist feeling (see Hobsbawm and Ranger 1983; Gruffudd 1995).

The US case offers a good example of the entanglement of preservation in elite interests. Wallace (1996) describes how, in the late nineteenth and early twentieth centuries, preservation of historic properties was a means by which the genteel descendants of Southern planters and New England merchants could resist and transcend the 'levelling' logic of market value by appealing to the legitimacy of inheritance. Thus, preservation and restoration efforts were dominated by private individuals, wealthy philanthropists and historical societies (such as the Daughters of the American Revolution). Later, it became associated with the demonstration of wealth and power alone, reaching an apotheosis in the preservationist activities of the inter-war multi-millionaire industrialists, Rockefeller and Henry Ford. Later on still, preservation came under the ambit of a more scientist and professionalized perspective through the establishment of public organizations dedicated to the stewardship of the past. The US National Trust (created – belatedly compared to the UK – in 1949) sought to professionalize preservation by tying it to ideas of historical significance, rather than to the whim of individuals.

However, the US National Trust made little progress in the face of the 1950s juggernaut of urban development, and it was not until private developers were themselves persuaded to embrace preservationism (through the evidence emerging in the 1960s of history's tourism potential), that it was able to harness sufficient support for its cause. And even then, heritage projects were the result of compromise between the interests of historical preservation and those of the private developers. Thus, in the US, pre-servation has long been linked, in practice if not in professional discourse, to activities of, first, the self-promotion of elites and, later, the production of commercial visitability. What this suggests is that preservationism gained currency at the same time as preserving the past – and *displaying* this achievement – became politically and socially useful for key groups. If preservationism has grown up in tandem with display, this is because it is necessarily linked into particular social interests, agendas and struggles in which display is a key tool.

Heritage – unlike most history books – is a potentially profitable, audi-ence-attracting business. Moreover, it is cut through by different, often competing, interests. The ways in which these interests shape the content of the displays themselves as well as visitors' interpretations of them cannot, however, simply be assumed in advance. Indeed, the relationship between 'encoding' and 'decoding' in cultural texts is not necessarily one of straightforward determination – as influential media theory has shown (see Hall 1980, on encoding/decoding as a theoretical model and Dicks 2000a on the applicability of Hall's model to heritage texts). Whilst it is important to attend to the economic and social contexts within which heritage pro-jects are set up as visitor-drawing display-sites, we cannot read off the heritage 'message' from such considerations alone. Unfortunately, I do not have space here to examine in detail the question of visitor interpretations of heritage, but the afore-going discussion of the self/other relations it seems to set up does suggest that there is more variation in heritage identifications than is commonly assumed.

A second life as display: heritage as political-economic asset

What kind of political and economic present uses does heritage embody? For a start, it allows places – like its visitors – to lay claim to a strong sense of identity. Globalization does not, as we have seen in other chapters, obliterate place-identity; rather, it increases awareness of it, whilst simul-taneously transforming it. In conditions of 'entrepreneurial' local governance (Harvey 1989b; see Chapter 3), it also means that localities are increasingly thrown into competition with each other to attract new investment. Local economic planning is thus geared towards the marketing of those local resources which will attract high consumer and tourist spend.

Heritage, of course, is high on the list of such local cultural 'assets' (Corner and Harvey 1991; Zukin 1991, 1995). First, in an era of increasingly bland and standardized urban development strategies (Chapter 3), it is one of the few local resources that can be showcased as a 'unique' marker of local identity. Secondly, heritage promises to 'add value' in terms of community acceptance and participation through granting the badge of local authenticity to redevelopment projects and, potentially, encouraging local interest groups to participate in them.

These economic usages inevitably produce a preoccupation with visitor numbers. This in turn reflects a political-economic trend away from automatic state-funding for heritage projects, forcing the traditional purveyors and custodians of heritage (such as museums, archaeological sites, stately homes and country houses, castles, monuments and historic towns) to seek alternative sources of income for upkeep and maintenance. Although heritage projects are often far from being free market enterprises, in that many are funded – initially at least – through public sector grants and subsidies, the rhetoric, priorities and strategies of the market increasingly provide their rationale and managerial direction (McGuigan 1999). Thus, public funding to support heritage in the form of state, local government and lottery grants has not been withdrawn, but marketized. In other words, it has been subjected to a process of competitive bidding in which local projects have to make the case for funding (see Chapter 3). This nearly always involves showing how, through the generation of sufficient visitor revenues, the project will become at the least self-supporting, or, preferably, profit-generating. Public funding is also directed at extracting 'leverage', i.e. using public money to lure in private investment (Bianchini and Schwengel 1991). Heritage projects, in this way, have to show the 'value-added' benefits that they will bring, both economically and culturally, to the area in question.

Heritage, in these ways, can be utilized as an economic asset. However, in another sense, heritage is also a burden to local entrepreneurial governance. It is noteworthy that much place promotion discourse involves casting the local population as key players in an enterprise culture (Corner and Harvey 1991). They are a flexible and adaptive workforce, a self-reliant and forward-looking community, the glossy brochures invariably claim. What they are not is isolationist, parochial, tied to tradition or dependent on central assistance. Neither are they militant or resistant to change. They do indeed possess a great and distinctive cultural heritage, which is of their own making, makes them who they are and, by the way, is very well worth seeing, but this does not in any way detract them from the modern pursuit of enterprise. Such claims may involve neglecting to mention those aspects of local heritage antithetical to the values of enterprise. It is clear, indeed, that if a local people's 'greatness' is to be tapped for tourism, certain aspects of that inheritance might appear a burden. This ambivalence has been noted by Robins (1991: 39–40) in relation to the UK's flat-capped cultural icon of the north-east, Andy Capp, during a period when Newcastle, too, was trying to adjust to economic devastation. As a potent symbol of the city's old, industrial identity, enterprise discourse wanted to proclaim 'Andy Capp is dead – Newcastle is alive'. Yet, in simultaneously marketing Newcastle's industrial heritage of heavy engineering, shipbuilding and coal mining, Andy inevitably came straight back into the picture.

Accordingly, the kind of messages that heritage planners are keen to promote may indeed involve a manipulation or a sanitization of local historical events, figures and stories. Again, everything depends on how local heritage projects are played out. In many cases, planners have little input into the historical content of heritage projects, which is left to the new army of heritage consultants. Contemporary tourist attractions often rely on highly polished, technically sophisticated presentations, ones capable of attracting and holding the interest of visitors conceived of as outside day-trippers, who always have at their disposal many other choices of leisure destination. Professional heritage interpretation companies are in the business of ensuring that displays will catch this easily distracted gaze. In order to live up to an increasingly technologized heritage-industry standard, they construct multi-media displays, audio-visual films, photographic slide-shows and light shows, recorded voice-overs, life-size models and elaborate dioramas, period interiors and streetscapes. The essential characteristic of these interpretation teams is that they are professional culture-industry workers (architects, graphic designers, video producers, photographers, historical consultants, researchers, software developers) who can move from place to place, 'doing' the heritage of any one area. They are not, by definition, limited to one particular locality.

However, these mobile teams of professional interpreters still have to foray out into the real social spaces of localities in order to 'harvest' the material for display. Indeed, this encapsulates the paradox of vernacular living-history. It is a public tourist product, but, as we saw above, one which promises to give the tourist access to his or her imagined past self. It promises to bring real, ordinary people's history *alive*. Thus, encoding (the making of the displays) cannot proceed through interpreters' professional, exhibitionary knowledge alone. Instead, in order to fulfil the mission to display 'authentic' past lives, they have to seek out particular, vernacular knowledge (such as miners' experiences underground, or simply 'the people's memories'). Since heritage has a strong visual element, they also need to find images in the form of photographs, and – probably – video footage of the area. Further, since heritage proceeds by personalization, they must gather reminiscences and anecdotes, perhaps find local characters that can embody the history and bring it alive. This means that living history is, potentially, deeply entangled in the local communities whose stories form its subject-matter. It is also, for this reason, potentially open to local people's active participation. To see heritage purely as a means of marketing the vernacular past is to miss this other half of the heritage project – its local belonging and its use as self-representation. I shall look at this aspect of heritage in this final section.

Heritage as voice of the people?

If agencies of economic governance and commerce can utilize heritage so effectively it is because heritage acts as a badge of authenticity. The 'sign value' of heritage in symbolic economies is not simply dreamt up at the drawing board of marketers and planners. Rather, as we have seen, it is part of a popular feeling for the past and for place-identity, manifested in people's reluctance to see the signs of 'their' history obliterated in a speeded-up world of constant change. Over and above its economic utility for planners and entrepreneurs, heritage thus has meaning for various groups of people – including not only those who do the visiting, but also those who might aspire to become the visited, too. In other words, the more people see other, ordinary lives on display, the more they are likely to see their own lives as worthy of display, too (especially, as we shall see in Chapter 7, in the Internet age).

Accordingly, heritage potentially encourages groups of all kinds to think of their cultural 'roots' as statements about their selves and, hence, their identity, which deserve to be made public. As I shall now discuss, today this is as true for disempowered communities as it is for elites. Like other aspects of displayed culture, heritage is available for touristic commodification, but the tourist commodity-form does not exhaust its meaning. Rather, it allows key local actors to stake a claim to certain values and traditions on behalf of the wider collectivities they claim to represent. Such claims to local representation, however, easily become embroiled in the unequal and divided social relations of the local sphere.

Heritage and local communities

The relationship between heritage and disempowered local communities is a complex one. It is one which is inevitably bound up with divergent class-interests (Bagguley *et al.* 1990). As Wallace (1996) describes, heritage has often gone hand in hand with the *displacement* of local people from their localities. Gentrification, by the 1990s a well-established gravy train in most metropolitan cities in both the US and the UK, invariably operates by evicting poorer residents from historical enclaves. Once an area has been 'discovered' by the middle classes as a historically significant location, developers begin to buy up houses, evict existing tenants and then resell at inflated prices to wealthier buyers; this is followed by shop rents rising and many small, family-run enterprises closing. Strict controls are then imposed on any new development. As a result, virtually all US cities today contain preserved historic districts that have been stripped back to a frozen moment in time, thus wiping out all traces of the communities they had contained over the intervening years (Wallace 1996: 192).

A long-neglected 'zone of discard' in Ottawa, Canada (Lower Town), was 'heritagized' in the 1980s, disinheriting and dispossessing many of its Franco-Irish working-class residents, along with numbers of homeless people (Tunbridge and Ashworth 1996). A similar process has been happening to rural villages in the UK for several decades (Urry 2002). Real estate may thus be treated as material for preservation in a way that people and their traditions are not. Through their purchasing power, middle-class groups thereby wield considerable influence in getting heritage projects off the ground: once in place, they do all they can to prevent any degradation of their historical 'investment'. If they, in turn, are pushed out due to ever-rising prices, there will always be new terrains to take on elsewhere.

Middle-class property owners, however, do not have the monopoly on heritage concerns, in spite of the elision often made between the two. In the 1970s, in particular, various forces converged, some of which were touched on above, to give 'community' history or 'history from below' a new visibility (Samuel 1994). This became the inspiration for various working-class and ethnic groups to save their neighbourhoods from redevelopment. In the US, for example, in 1971 the Chicano *barrio* community of Tucson, Arizona, won a historic battle to prevent a freeway being driven through El Tiradito (the Wishing Shrine) in the centre of their neighbourhood (Wallace 1996: 193–4). The 1970s in the US was the decade of civil rights-inspired community activism which saw history not only in terms of real estate, but also in terms of threatened traditions, festivals and ways of life. The picture is a complex one, though: many US black groups did not subscribe to preserving areas associated in their minds with white supremacy and the bad old days (Wallace 1996: 193–4).

The embroilment of heritage in relationships between powerful and disempowered groups – such as in issues of national belonging, collective identity, political recognition and competition over land and natural resources – means that conflict is a key characteristic of heritage display the world over. In post-colonial settler societies, for instance, heritage claims have a particularly tense history due to the imposition of colonial heritage onto native populations. These kinds of conflict can produce resistance to heritage display. For example, Aboriginal groups in Australia have successfully (so far) staved off plans to convert a brewery on Perth's Swan River into a heritage centre, pointing out that it is the site where their legendary water-serpent, the Waugal, came down to create the river (see Tunbridge and Ashworth 1996: 185).

In complex 'settler' societies, such as that of Canada, indigenous minority heritage claims have clashed with those from more powerful minorities, such as the Francophone Quebecois (Tunbridge and Ashworth 1996). Treatment of the country's Native, Inuit, Chinese, Japanese, African and other minority heritages has to take account of the Quebec issue since it represents a potential challenge to the state union. In an attempt to resolve these issues, the Canadian state has adopted a multi-cultural heritage policy, which grants heritage space to many different ethnic groups. One can see that refusing to recognize a distinctive Quebecois identity would be the surest way of fuelling independence claims; by extension, then, other minorities have to be seen to be recognized too.

Yet, as Tunbridge and Ashworth further discuss, multi-culturalist heritage is a tricky policy for nation-states to operate (1996: 190–1). It can never be seen to be 'complete' (more and more, smaller and smaller groups can come forward with claims to representation), nor to reflect any real possibility of balance (since apportioning exhibitional space to reflect groups' national representativeness brings hierarchical ordering back into the frame). If the state insists on proclaiming all cultural elements to be of equal value in constituting the country's national identity, this is likely to be seen by majority groups as ideological fixing. Alternatively, the state may opt to promote a set of 'core' heritage values, to which every citizen feels an allegiance, over and above their particular ethnic or identity claims (such as is the case with so-called 'American values'). Defining such a core is inherently difficult, however, and may be possible only if it is left so vague and general as to make the term 'national identity' culturally meaningless. Such a policy tries to be safe and non-controversial but runs the risk of simply being irrelevant.

Arguably, it is at the local level that heritage projects can best claim to represent subaltern and marginalized histories. Macdonald (1997), for example, documents the setting up of Aros, a heritage centre on the Isle of Sky in Scotland. She sees this as an attempt to show how the island's story always involved complex relations with outsiders and other places. In Macdonald's view, Aros does not try to portray a pristine cultural oasis but rather demystifies the relation between culture and place. It does this by showing how local history becomes different things in being appropriated by different groups at different times. She sees heritage as 'a transnational symbolic resource for self-definition' which can be inflected at the local level in ways which highlight the forgotten histories of marginalized people (Macdonald 1997: 175). It can be an arena for the display of the self (or selves) as much as for the display of the 'other'.

The desire for 'self-definition' is unlikely to be uniformly expressed. Some people may want a memorial; others do not want to be reminded of the past. But even where this desire can be identified, it can be appropriated by professional interpreters and siphoned away from local people's direct involvement. This was the case, unfortunately, with the Rhondda Heritage Park. It was not, however, according to Marwick (1995), the case with the People's Story Museum in Edinburgh, whose sponsors (the District Council's Recreation Department) deliberately set out to 'tell the story of the life and work of Edinburgh people [and to] involve Edinburgh people in the presentation of their own history' (Marwick 1995: 140). A local oral history project, 'Memories and things', formed the prologue to an intensive period of collaborative encoding, with local elderly people advising on the museum's displays, the layout of text, the writing of soundtracks and the preparation of artefacts. To some extent, there was a transfer of power here from the curator to the public. However, few museums achieve or seek these levels of local collaboration, let alone anticipate the day of the 'autonomous, truly popular and professional-free museum' (Jenkinson 1989: 147). The next chapter will discuss some of these issues in greater depth.

Heritage as magical solution?

Place-based, vernacular heritage appears to offer a magical fusion of two *seemingly* corresponding contemporary phenomena: the shift in heritage towards living history, and the ground-level desire within local groups to put their identity on display and stake a claim for ordinary local history in the construction of official, public heritage. Heritage centres and projects are often able to attract public funding precisely because they are able to make this twin appeal: on the one hand an economic appeal couched in terms of place-marketing ('this will be an exciting and profitable tourist attraction for the region'); on the other hand, a social and cultural appeal to local historical identity ('this heritage attraction will provide a space for local people to commemorate their own history for future generations'). Heritage seems to bring the two together into a planner's dream.

Thus heritage appears to offer a shared agenda: local people want links with their past and visitors want living history and popular memories, so the solution is to ask interpreters to construct their displays around the memories and experiences of local people. In this way, heritage seems neatly to offer the means of regenerating depressed areas, both economically, through outside tourism, and culturally, through inside memorialism. That things can go wrong in this seemingly happy coincidence of objectives should come as no surprise, given the top-down, spend-oriented practices of professional planning and interpretation. Too often, people's pasts are harnessed as a commodified spectacle for tourists. However, if those whose history is considered marketable were also invited to participate in its display, even to direct it, rather than being asked just to hand over the stories, things could turn out rather differently. Whether planners will take such a risk – rather than sticking with the tried and trusted formula of hiring-in professional outside interpreters – is another matter.

Note

1   I carried out interviews with various groups (including local government offi-
    cers, heritage consultants, ex-miner-guides, visitors and local residents)
    involved in the development of the heritage museum in order to understand the
    relationship between the 'encoding' and 'decoding' of heritage texts (see Dicks
    2000b).

Further reading

Bennett, T. (1995) *The Birth of the Museum: History, Theory, Politics*. London: Routledge.

Dicks, B. (2000) *Heritage, Place and Community*. Cardiff: University of Wales Press.

Samuel, R. (1994) *Theatres of Memory*. London: Verso.

Tunbridge, J.E. and Ashworth, G.J. (1996) *Dissonant Heritage: The Management of the Past as a Resource in Conflict*. Chichester: John Wiley and Sons.

Wallace, M. (1996) *Mickey Mouse History and Other Essays on American Memory*. Philadephia: Temple University Press.

6 | OUT OF THE GLASS CASE

In the 1940s, 1950s and 1960s, America's history museums drowsed happily on the margins of a go-ahead culture, tending their genteel artifacts, perpetuating regnant myths in which African-Americans, women, immigrants, and workers figured as supporting actors or not at all. But then came rude poundings at the door . . .

(Wallace 1996: 116)

In contrast to the various heritage sites, theme parks and urban/rural interpretative zones we have examined so far, museums represent a more specialized and, until recently at least, a more tightly defined category of cultural display. A widely accepted definition of a museum describes it as 'an institution which collects, documents, preserves, exhibits and interprets material evidence and associated information for the public benefit' (Selwood *et al.* 1995: 30). However, this definition is becoming problematic as new institutions appear that blur the boundary between science museum, history museum, cultural centre, art gallery and theme park. The latest museum genre is the highly stylized, architecturally striking, technologically-sophisticated, consumption-oriented museum displaying the interdependence of culture, art, nature, science and/or technology (recent examples in the UK include Magna near Rotherham, Think Tank in Birmingham, @Bristol and Urbis, Manchester). These museums do not have stored collections, in the traditional sense of the term, and instead are fully dedicated to the business of display. Even a more traditional, collection-focused museum like London's Science Museum is trying to transform its image from grim, stuffy institution to design-led, interactive and child-friendly space. It, too, is transgressing boundaries by including video sculpture installations and specially commissioned artworks. And art museums themselves are trying out new locations and approaches as they become more geared towards design-led, spectacular exhibitions and attention-grabbing installations.

Museums are, in such ways, trying to solve their inherent accessibility problem – the fact that they portray specialist knowledge to non-specialist visitors. Making museums more visitable involves making this knowledge more accessible and more 'communicative'. Such trends are part of the wider shift discussed in this book towards creating and enhancing culture's visitability. Exhibitionary strategies, it is felt, must allow the displayed knowledge to catch the visitor's interest, to involve them and be easily understood (Sorensen 1989). They must also meet the demands of the contemporary principle of 'cultural rights', both by providing display-space for previously excluded cultures, and by adopting more progressive modes of display that disrupt 'the authoritative cultural voice of the museum' (Bennett 1988: 103). These demands seem to pull the museum in different directions, making it a particularly troubled institution in an age of ubiquitous cultural display. In what follows, I discuss museums as sites specifically constructed around this 'problem' of visitability. For, as Bal asks, 'what is a museum for if not for visitors?' (1996: 208).

Museums and culture

In this section, I discuss museums and exhibitions which put the culture of 'people' on display. These are not confined to museums which call themselves ethnographic. In any museal display which makes an object out of people's lives and culture, the shadow of the ethnographic can be detected (Karp and Kratz 2000). We can see the operation of a kind of 'orientalism', a fascination with the 'otherness' of other cultures, times and places, in exhibitions of all kinds that deal in *absent* people, who are either no longer with us, or over 'there' – in displays about, for example, nations, cities, localities, communities, sub-cultures, industries, lifestyles, the people, the folk, the ancient, the ethnic, the tribal, the primitive. In all of these, 'people' of one kind or another are marked out as being of interest, and their artefacts or art, which are made to stand for them in their absence, are laid out as objects of the gaze. Further, it seems that even technological, scientific museums and discovery centres increasingly feature 'stories of people', as though human voices were needed to bring the machines, gadgets and special effects closer to spectators' own lives. For example, the new UK *Magna* museum, mentioned above, constructed in a redundant Rotherham steel works, offers spectacular, technologically blinding displays of earth, fire, air and water, but it also features the voices of ex-steel workers telling of their past working lives.

Museums are thus fully embroiled in the 'disappearing world' syndrome

(Coombes 1991). Their gaze has classically been directed at 'foreign' places and their 'fragile' or 'vanishing' cultures, but it is also increasingly focused on various kinds of lost domestic 'other' – such as industrial workers, peasants, farm-workers, landed gentry and their servants and, above all, the ordinary past inhabitants of countless places-with-identities. Museums display both the other without (those who are foreign) and the other within (our ancestors). As MacCannell (1999: 82) puts it: 'Every society necessarily has another society inside itself and beside itself: its past epochs and eras and its less developed and more developed neighbours'. Museums are there to show us both, and I look at each in the course of this chapter.

The museum seems to encapsulate modernity's tendency to enclose – or in Mitchell's (1988) term, to *enframe* – other non-modern times and places, and to celebrate the visitor's location outside of these static enclosures: 'they' are in there; 'we' are out here. It thus works to separate out the visitor and the visited, something which has been integral to Western modernity's colonial and touristic incursions into other cultures. In this way, we can see the museum as a key locus where the West's relations of self/other, now/then, here/there and modern/traditional have been formed (see Kirshenblatt-Gimblett 1998). It stages the 'them/us' relation in overt, material ways, through directing the gaze around viewable space: who is doing the looking and who is being looked at? What is being shown to be of interest? This means that museums are powerful agencies for defining culture to the public, and for the public to define itself through the viewing relations they embody. In this, asserts Macdonald (1996: 2), museums are 'key cultural loci of our times'.

Culture as colonial trophy

In the sixteenth and seventeenth centuries, it had already become a marker of status for European aristocrats and princes to place unusual finds within *cabinets of curiosities* for invited guests to peruse. However, these objects were not ordered into hierarchies nor assembled into any historic schema: they were there in order to encapsulate the incredible diversity and inter-relations of the (permanent) wonders of nature. As Bennett (1995) shows, the new public museum of the nineteenth century incorporated a different underlying logic: that of arranging artefacts according to a historical, developmental sequence which culminated in the present. Becoming established at the same time as the new disciplines of history, art history, archaeology, geology, biology, anthropology and ethnology, public museums embodied a new, universalizing, post-Darwinian principle – that all peoples and civilizations developed through time in a series of consecutive stages. As Bennett points out, museums annexed these universal histories to national rhetorics, positing the national collections as the culmination of the universal story of civilization's development (Bennett 1995: 75–76).

The modern public museum, therefore, was not simply about housing collections of objects. Rather, it was a showcase for key modern ideas about the hierarchical ordering and logical progression of knowledge, identity and culture. Indeed, it was the imperialist mindset of the nineteenth century that gave rise to the great museum-building programmes of the era (a legacy from which, like anthropology, museums are still finding it difficult to escape). Museums served the purposes of colonialism by marking out the transition from simple and traditional to complex and modern societies, propagating the message that 'traditional' societies were colonized for their own good in order to 'modernize' them. In the colonial-era museum, objects were displayed as signifiers of something else – they became illustrations of the particular stage of development that any one culture was held to embody. Objects of all kinds – from treasures to everyday artefacts – were scooped up from 'primitive' or 'savage' cultures, and often quite literally looted, by collectors from Europe (including missionaries, explorers, traders, army regiments and colonizers) who took them back 'home' for display.

In the UK's Pitt Rivers Museum, for example, which was inspired by London's Great Exhibition of 1851, everyday artefacts were arranged in order to demonstrate the essential persistence of forms over time, which were portrayed as evolving from simplicity through to complexity. Diverse objects from diverse places were placed next to each other in order to show comparisons and similarities across regional groupings. These were treated as the material evidence of cultures, which in turn evidenced the stages of human development (Coombes 1994). A rough object equalled a savage culture; a technologically sophisticated one an advanced civilization. As Coombes shows in her study of the late Victorian and early Edwardian museums, whenever beautifully made objects were found in so-called primitive cultures, they were invariably treated as anomalies. This was the case, for instance, with the impressive Benin bronzes from Britain's Niger Coast Protectorate, which seemed to contradict the thesis of the 'social savagery' of the originating culture. However, they were simply treated as exceptions, and the dominant evolutionary model continued unchallenged.

Museums were closely tied to the Victorian project of popularizing the idea of an emerging 'world order' of sovereign nation-states. In the European national collection museums, the political identities of nations were elaborated and propagated, whilst in ethnographic museums, these identities were further strengthened by displays of other nations and territorially-defined peoples. Museums in this way served to underline the proclaimed naturalness of national divisions. When colonial regimes toppled, museums in post-independence countries, too, were able to take advantage of this global language of display (Prosler 1996). It enabled post-independence governments to make explicit the relation between their own 'primitives' and the fledgling, modernizing nation-state. In the National Museum in Columbo, for example, Sri Lanka's famed spirit-masks are displayed in a way that highlights their association with the primitive, mythic and peasant-based phase of national development, thus denying their temporal relevance to the modern nation-state (Prosler 1996).

As the twentieth century progressed, the evolutionary ordering of races and cultures was progressively abandoned. Modern professional anthropologists (from Boas to Evans-Pritchard through to Mead) came to embrace cultural relativism, arguing that, rather than being pre-modern or located at an earlier phase of evolution, the non-Western societies they studied were simply different *on their own terms*. Their cultures could not be compared with Western cultures because they had evolved on quite different paths altogether. Franz Boas' museum work in the early years of the twentieth century helped to change the traditional approach by exhibiting artefacts within simulated cultural settings, or contexts (Ames 1992). He rejected the natural-history, 'object-as-specimen' approach to culture, and helped to inaugurate a new kind of anthropology which proposed understanding and exhibiting cultures, in Boas' words, 'from the native point of view' (Ames 1992: 52). This helped to inaugurate a gradual turning away from taxonomies of objects to displays which situated objects within their cultural and place-based contexts. In the Pitt Rivers Museum, the focus was not on any individual culture, but on its comparative position in the complete map, or pyramid, of cultures world-wide. In the relativist approach, by contrast, there came to be much more emphasis placed on the specificity and difference of individual cultures themselves.

Museums, as a result, became increasingly occupied with the relativist anthropological project of describing the homology between cultures and places (on this project, see Gupta and Ferguson 1992). They set themselves up as windows through which one could glimpse 'there' and 'then'. Further, 'there' was produced as coterminous with 'then' so that, especially in ethnographic exhibitions, the displayed people (from the Wahgi to Welsh 'folk') seemed to be frozen in time, condemned to play the same parts forever in a picture that 'holds still like a *tableau vivant*' (Fabian 1983: 67). Indeed, museums' elaboration and popularization of the equation between cultures, peoples and places helped to cement the 'cultural mosaic' view of the world (discussed in Chapter 1, and see Kahn 1995). In this imaginary, culture is understood as something that 'belongs' to a place and a people, something which marks them out as special and distinct and which can be discovered, described, documented and displayed. It is a world-view which underpins the touristic imaginary, predicated as it is on the idea of places-with-identities.

Herein, however, lies a source of tension for museums. For, although the cultural mosaic view remains culturally dominant in popular touristic discourse, it has been subjected to thorough-going critiques within the world of anthropology over the past 20 years or so. The classic anthropological concern with cultural essences enshrined in bounded tribes and peoples such as 'the Nuer' or the 'Trobrianders' has been exposed as a representational trope serving the anthropologist's own professional agenda of laying claim to a people (see, for example, Clifford 1986). It has been accused of 'deep-freezing' cultural difference and propagating a view of the world eternally divided into unchanging cultural islands. The homology between *places* and cultures has also been challenged (Gupta and Ferguson 1992). Yet, for many visitors, the belief that places and cultures are specifiably distinct from each other remains central to their idea of 'how the world is' (or should be). It is only, notes Massey (1995), when we leave the airport and finally reach the café with the smell of Gauloises and good coffee and croissants that we sigh with satisfaction and say to ourselves 'at last – this is the "real" France'.

Museums find themselves awkwardly placed between these competing audiences. On the one hand, they are connected into the recent debates in anthropological discourse (since many anthropologists work in museums, and bring new theoretical outlooks with them). On the other hand, they are visitor institutions which have to appeal to the public, and this is becoming increasingly the case as government policies push them further and further into the market in pursuit of revenue-sources. This means that they are, increasingly, attractions, and therefore under pressure to offer representations which concord broadly with the view of social reality that visitors (and sponsors) hold (Ames 1992). Visitors do, it seems, expect to see clear cultural identities on display. They do not, on the whole, expect to find reflexivity, hybridity and fragmentation. And museums do possess in their collections a wealth of exhibitionary material for the display of clear cultural identities. So, when museums are pushed into representing marginalized or minority cultures, they tend to do so from a perspective which reproduces this idea of the 'global cultural mosaic', often failing to problematize the power imbalances and structural inequalities that lie behind it. This remains the case even in some of the experimental exhibitions which have attempted to embrace a more fluid concept of cultural identity.

Into the cultural mosaic

It is only in the last 20 to 30 years that museums have begun to recognize their role in perpetuating colonialist and orientalist perspectives about ethnicity and cultural difference. Museums were, on the whole, content to reproduce the preoccupations of culturally dominant national mythologies, as Wallace describes in the quote with which this chapter begins. It was not until the 1970s and 1980s that a new generation of critical historians, anthropologists and curators started to interrogate the politics behind museum exhibitions. They asked questions about the basis upon which certain objects, people, events and stories, rather than others, were selected for display. As Vergo (1988) notes in his introduction to the influential UK volume, *The New Museology*, this reflected a new recognition that every curatorial decision, every selection and every excision, every ordering of objects and information within museums drew upon interpretations of history, and what counted as history, that were inevitably partial and ideological. This realization inaugurated a gradual yet far-reaching rethink in museal practice which is still reverberating today. It also set in motion a still ongoing and unresolved debate (as well as a clutch of official codes and conventions) over the question of restitution of 'cultural property' to groups from whom it was looted or illegally exported (see Durrans 1988; Bal 1996).

Many of these critiques of museal display have drawn explicitly on the language of multiculturalism and the idea of the world as cultural mosaic. Bennett (1992) notes the historical tendency within museums to display only dominant forms of culture within universalizing rhetoric (in evolutionary discourse, by claiming that the culture they displayed was representative of the *entire* human achievement from the 'highest' to the 'lowest' evolutionary levels, and in nationalist rhetoric, that it represented the 'true spirit' of the *whole* nation). This pretension to universality, he argues, laid the ground for excluded groups to insist on being included. Those whose ties to national territory were both uncontrovertibly ancient as well as marginalized and unrecognized – such as indigenous groups in 'settler' societies – were thus able to use the dominant rhetoric to make their own claims for inclusion.

The key question for museums' practice of cultural representation is this: does 'multicultural' and 'postcolonial' display mean accepting and propagating the idea that marginal cultures have unitary identities, thus reflecting the cultural mosaic model, or does it mean setting out deliberately to undermine that idea by attempting to portray the differences, conflicts and contingencies of cultural identity? This question immediately brings into play the politics of culture, and it is one with which museums are currently struggling to come to terms. The tendency in responding to multi-culturalism has been simply to include a wider range of 'cultures' within the museum's ambit. This simply multiplies the number of cultures on view whilst continuing to obscure the role of the museum itself in mediating the power relations between those who exhibit and those who are exhibited. An alternative is to try to expose the faultlines in the cultural mosaic, and to show the contradictions and complexities underlying the various identity-claims that emerge under conditions of global capitalism. This kind of exhibitionary project is difficult to achieve, however, and can slide into incoherence or fail to 'make sense' to visitors. Perhaps an easier solution is for museums to try to show up the 'constructedness' of their exhibitions, in an effort to foreground and critique their own mediating role in defining other places and people. Yet, as we shall see later on, that strategy, too, brings its own problems.

The danger is always that museums' attempts to include subaltern voices may end up reproducing cultural difference as a natural category rather than revealing its historicity and politics. This is not a question that is internal to museums. On the contrary, it is part and parcel of the paradoxes of cultural particularism and the idea of the cultural mosaic. Although ideals of multiculturalism uphold the virtues of pluralism and the celebration of difference, insisting that any one identity – including dominant ones – is particular rather than universal, constructed rather than natural, voices that lay claim to any one particular identity *within* the mosaic often use the universalizing language of essentialism to do so. For this reason, Coombes (1991) sees the 'banner of multiculturalism' as itself a problem, since it provides an easy and unchallenging means for exhibitions to celebrate cultural diversity as a 'scopic feast' and a 'contented global village'. Under this banner, they can avoid engaging with the realities of racist and unequal relationships between ex-colonial and ex-colonized countries, and between genders and classes. In other words, displaying difference can make it into a fetish that serves to conceal the political interests at stake in its production and maintenance.

The complexity of the political interests potentially involved is well illustrated in Tunbridge and Ashworth's (1996) detailed discussion of Canada's heritage and museums policies. They show how the federal state has been determined to integrate the country's diverse minorities into a vision of the Confederation as cultural mosaic, as part of Canada's ongoing search for national identity. The representation of Canada's First Nation peoples is undertaken at the Canadian Museum of Civilisation in Hull, Quebec – a city linked into the federal capital Ottawa by a deliberate heritage development plan (designed to cement Quebec's federal belonging). This museum attempts to perform a balancing act among the competing claims of Canada's different minority groups. Here, a hall of 'native culture' shows, among other things, the museum's spectacular collection of totem poles from the West Coast. In the History Hall, there is a series of tableaux of streetscapes and lifestyle reconstructions showing the different linear 'stages' of Canada's history, from early Norse settlement to the present day. Throughout, the emphasis is on showing how Canada is an integrated community and 'ritual space', its unity made up of – and not troubled by – its various minorities (Delaney 1992).

The problem with such exhibitions is that, in invoking cultural difference, they then subsume it into an overarching story of a wider identity (in this case, a national identity). This wider identity is represented simply as a container for internal differences, obscuring the ways in which the Canadian nation itself was forged through racial exclusions and inequalities. As Hageman (1991) puts it in her insightful discussion of the US Smithsonian's permanent exhibition, A Nation of Nations, which also tries to celebrate cultural diversity, such exhibitions end up reproducing a 'weak' version of ethnicity. They suggest that all cultures (whether Jewish, White, Black, Italian or Hispanic) are equivalent components of the US cultural mosaic, united by an underlying national experience common to them all (in this case, through a shared history of consumer products).

Out of the cultural mosaic?

If the idea of the cultural mosaic is an enduring one in national museums' narratives of their 'home' nations, it has been more obviously open to attack in representations of other cultures. Many exhibitions now consciously avoid the 'living tableau' view of 'ethnic' culture by trying to show how so-called traditional cultures have changed in relation to global conditions. This may involve foregrounding, for example, the 'post-contact' relations between indigenous populations and the West, and highlighting ongoing processes of assimilation, resistance and/or adaptation within the culture. For example, in an analysis of Paradise, an exhibition of the Waghi New Guinea highlanders at the British Museum's Museum of Mankind, objects were deliberately included that showed signs of the population's contact with capitalism (such as beer bottles and coke cans). Further, the curator consciously tried to show up the stereotypes and devices of conventional museal display. However, Clifford (1995) points out that no matter how much the anthropologist/curator tried reflexively to acknowledge his (in this case) representational power, the fact remains that the

Waghi were not present in the exhibition – 'they' were over 'there', and their actual voices were little represented in the exhibition (see also Lidchi 1997). It could also be argued that showing processes of assimilation achieve little on their own, for they often serve simply to insinuate the inevitability, and thus the apolitical nature, of change and modernization on the Western model (Coombes 1991).

Many colonial-era museums, stuck with colonialist collections, have mounted temporary exhibitions which deliberately try to subvert racist stereotypes. In another Canadian example, Riegel (1996) contrasts the Royal Ontario Museum exhibition of 1989–90, *Into the Heart of Africa*, with a 1991–92 one called *Fluffs and Feathers*. In her analysis, the former failed in its claim to subvert Western-centric constructions of Africa because it limited its critique to a gentle verbal irony conveyed in wall panels. The verbal irony was too distant and restrained to counteract the powerful stereotypes that inevitably surrounded the ethnographic objects on display. The latter exhibition, on Canadian Native peoples, managed to challenge conventional standpoints more effectively by organizing the whole exhibition itinerary around a journey that gradually led the visitor to dismantle the conventional images that white Canadians hold of Native groups.

The difficulties of challenging long-internalized stereotypes and received ideas about history are not simply a museal issue. They arise not only through the politics of representation and exhibition but through the continuing unequal relations between centres of power, populations and groups outside the museum's walls. Museums can hardly be asked to 'sort out' on their own the impossible knots of the colonial inheritance, as though such unravelling were simply a textual and exhibitionary task. If the power relations which uphold and sustain exhibitionary categories (of self/other, us/them, here/now) remain in place 'outside', museums will both struggle to change and be less relevant in doing so (Coombes 1991). A glance at attempts to change undertaken at a much more consciously populist and visitor-oriented museum, Colonial Williamsburg in Virginia, US, shows the enduring nature of racist discourse and the virtual impossibility of making the museum into its solution.

This famous antebellum heritage site established by Rockefeller Jr. in the 1930s, found itself by the 1960s the target of growing criticism from historians' outraged at its utter neglect of the area's black slave history (Gable 1996). Gable shows how interpreters employed at the site's African-American interpretation department, set up in the late 1970s to try and respond to these concerns, tried to get black history 'mainstreamed' at all the site buildings and attractions in order to reflect the fact that almost half of the town's population in the eighteenth century were slaves. Getting the story of 'the other half' into the mainstream, mainly white-led guided tours and talks of the site, proved a difficult endeavour, however. This was because the guides were schooled and trained only to make historical statements and offer interpretations if these were based on 'well-documented fact'. As a result, much of the history of slaves' daily lives remains marginalized or neglected at Colonial Williamsburg because key aspects of it, such as the topic of miscegenation and its consequences for individual lives, have not been 'well-documented' outside (due to the secrecy and denial of white slavers, as well as the topic's political sensitivity). Consequently, the museum continues, in Gable's (1996) view, to deliver a history that takes for granted 'the fundamental impermeability of racial boundaries' (Gable 1996: 198). This suggests that fundamental changes have to occur in both scholarship and public education more broadly if there is to be a corresponding shift in public sites of display.

Art, ethnicity and identity

Art museums might seem to ride above much of these intensely political debates. After all, art is art, not life, and whereas other museums have to grapple with the question 'what is life?', art museums simply answer the question 'what is art?' A piece of machinery placed in a science museum, one could argue, refers us to the social world of inventions and discoveries, in an art gallery, it invites appreciation of its aesthetic form. So, art is about aesthetics, or culture in the hierarchical sense, and it is other museums that deal with culture in the anthropological sense. However, Bal (1996) questions the validity of this distinction, by pointing to the predominance of certain widely dispersed norms of artistic value in art museums the world over. These values are capable, in the same way as ethnocentric ideas of cultural modernity, of consigning anomalous forms to the category of 'ethnic' or 'primitive' art. Thus, the very category of 'ethnic' art refers us back to the self/other, here/there, West/rest dichotomies we have been examining. MacCannell (1992: 121–2) has pointed out in this regard that powerful groups invariably assign the label 'ethnic' to the culture of others, whilst reserving the idea of 'normal' or 'standard' for their own. Indeed, artefacts from non-Western cultures exhibited in the West are often read ambivalently as both art and ethnographic document, suggesting there is always something 'else', i.e. an ethnic identity, to which they refer.

Ethnographic objects become reconfigured as collectable artworks through markets of display which create scarcity and transform them into an object of the gaze (Kirshenblatt-Gimblett 1998). These markets are not separate from the discourses of orientalism and cultural 'otherness' which also structure the ethnographic exhibition. Returning to our example of Canada, Nemiroff (1996) shows how the cultural products of Native Canadians were first treated exclusively in the national art gallery as ethnographic specimens, and only in 1927 was the first exhibition of 'Indian art' held, juxtaposing the artefacts with those from Western artists. These shows of Native art helped to instigate a 'myth of primitivism' that has, since then, provided virtually the only point of entry for Native/First Peoples artists to exhibit in the mainstream museums of North America. In the early exhibitions, Native art was usually displayed without the names of the artists, mobilizing static images of a generalized 'otherness'. From the late 1980s on, First Nation peoples in Australia, Canada and the US, who were making some strides in national political representation (e.g. in Canada's Assembly of First Nations) began to get their work shown in more mainstream galleries. However, Nemiroff (1996) notes the ongoing difficulties these artists face in penetrating the artworld mainstream, where their work is often valued only for its encapsulation of so-called 'Indian culture'. If they try to escape this compartmentalism by innovating, they find themselves facing charges of assimilation and loss of authenticity. Thus, in subtle but far-reaching ways, colonial perspectives continue to structure access to the artworld, producing the dilemma of 'how to sustain cultural difference while contesting marginality' (Nemiroff 1996: 432).

Indeed, the idea of the cultural mosaic seems to be alive and well in global art markets, where certain kinds of 'ethnic' art have become very collectable. This is the case with Latin American art, for instance, as Ramirez (1996) shows in her insightful analysis of the links between markets and the idea of the cultural mosaic. She describes how the economic valorization of cultural difference has created a new transnational artistic and administrative group of entrepreneurs whose exhibitions are financed by big business. Their links with the real locations of artistic production on which the traded cultural symbols depend are minimal. They are dependent on a powerful new breed of curators-turned-interpreters who mediate between local artists and collectors, helping to establish and perpetuate the kinds of styles the market requires. These markets tend to deal in instantly recognizable mythic tropes centred on well-rehearsed images of 'otherness' and difference, homogenizing in the process all artists of Latin American or Latino origin. Identity 'on the ground', by contrast, works to show up the differences both within and among these groups (for example the differences between a few high-profile, successful Latin American artists and clusters of lesser known artists in various Latin American countries). Thus, the 'democratic aperture' opened up by multiculturalism's appreciation of marginal art-forms is compromised when it becomes locked onto the interests of transnational capital, which seek to integrate and consolidate markets through generalized promotional-symbolic systems (Ramirez 1996: 34).

The folk, the people and the 'other within'

If the myth of primitivism has been fundamental in producing ethnicity and identity as categories of artistic and commodity value, so we can see a corresponding myth – the myth of the folk – as another foundational value of museum display. This figure brings us to the other 'other' with which museums have long been concerned – the vanishing, domestic 'other within'. Kahn (1995) talks about the myth of peasantism which has haunted the artistic and literary imagination in Europe ever since modern Europeans first started to destroy their own peasant cultures. Museums began with the ethnographic specimens of foreign cultures, as we have seen. But by the middle of the twentieth century, the West's own indigenous 'others' were also on display in the new folk museums. Although Sweden produced the world's first, pioneering folk museum in 1891, at Skansen, most European and American folk museums were a product of the 1930s and 1940s, an era when these societies were rapidly losing their rural, small-scale agricultural economies. In the US, for example, Henry Ford established his famous Greenfield Village in the 1930s, and a wealthy business-person called Albert B. Wells opened Old Sturbridge Village in 1946, which put on display the handicraft system of New Englanders. Such folk museums elaborate a fully-fleshed-out homology between place and culture, by turning a piece of the cultural mosaic into a realized, traversable, visitable environment, complete with reconstructed dwellings, streets, workplaces and, of course, shops. This open-air, material site summons up place quite literally – in a way the traditional museum label, painted backdrop or even diorama could never achieve.

The folk museum is an umbrella concept, and the general model that underlies it has produced different outcomes in different countries. In what follows, I discuss two different adaptations of the folk museum model, one in Wales and one in France. In the Welsh case, the folk museum concept became atrophied and hackneyed, occupying a merely exhibitionary role in presenting 'the folk' for the tourist gaze. The Welsh museum has tried to adjust to new times, by changing its name and becoming active in buttressing the Welsh language movement and other contemporary issues, but still struggles to seem relevant to today's changed social realities. In the

French case, by contrast, museums of this nature have developed in tandem with a dynamic social movement based on peasant rights. There is some basis for suggesting that the French 'eco-museum' movement has allowed the image of the rural worker to seem more engaged, political and contemporary than the romantic and static image of the 'folk' in the anglophone countries.

The Welsh Folk Museum, opened in 1948 (now called the Museum of Welsh Life), followed the same principles as Skansen. It aimed to replace the traditional museum focus on objects in cases with a whole, reconstructed environment displaying the life of 'the folk'. Constructed in the grounds of St Fagan's Castle, which had been donated to the Museum by the Earl of Plymouth, The Welsh Folk Museum established an open-air setting for reconstructed rural buildings displaying craft and farming traditions. Iorweth Peate, its founding curator, wanted 'not to create a museum which preserved the dead past under glass but one which uses the past to link up with the present' (Peate 1948: 13). He hoped that to his museum would come 'school-children for tuition, architects, artists and craftsmen for inspiration, country men and women "to cross the bridge of memories", colliers and quarrymen to view anew their wider heritage and townsfolk to discover the permanence of Welsh life' (Peate 1948: 61). Peate was aiming thereby to inspire the reinvigoration of rural Welsh communities, not as aestheticized objects of the tourist gaze but as models for localist, craft-based utopian alternatives to what he saw as the tyranny of industrialism (Gruffudd 1995). He did this by identifying a collection of surviving farmhouses and buildings typical of key traditions and periods in rural Wales, demolishing them and carefully reconstructing them stone by stone in a village arrangement. In this way, he brought the *gwerin* (the Welsh word that straddles the English terms 'people' and 'folk') into the grounds of the Earl's castle.

Meanwhile, in France, a similar folk-museum movement had also been pursuing a project of displaying rural crafts and traditions, initiated by Georges-Henri Riviere and his National Museum of Popular Arts and Traditions (here I am indebted to Poulot 1994). In France, the movement was oriented around the construct of the peasant and the rural worker, rather than the folk, but, in fact, this movement seems to have had much in common with Peate's Welsh folk movement. In both traditions, the emphasis was on displaying rural ways of life as active, relevant and vigorous, not as a vanished and anachronistic dead world. Both hitched the idea of displaying rural life to national mythologies which depended on images of the land. The Welsh *gwerin*, as Gruffudd (1999:151) points out, were mythologized in Wales as 'rural, Nonconformist, moralized and

Welsh-speaking; an idea that would be used in opposition to Anglicisation and to the imposition of an urban-industrial Britishness on Wales' (see also Morgan 1986). In France, the figure of the peasant was used during the Vichy regime as a means of bolstering its 'back to the land' ideology. This was mirrored in Nazi Germany through the *Heimatmuseums* movement. The Welsh nationalist vision of the links between land and *gwerin* – always a means of countering the political and economic dominance of England within British national identity – cannot, of course, be aligned with the national-Fascist images deployed by strong centralized governments in France and Germany in the 1930s and 1940s. Nevertheless, both visions were 'of their time', in that they used folk display to picture the nation as a 'community of communities' – both national and localized at the same time.

In spite of the ideological commitment within both the Welsh and French folk museum movements to promote rural communities as active, vigorous contributors to the national identity, it was only in the French case that this developed into a vibrant museum movement with political relevance for the post-1960s. Peate's technological-arcadian vision never materialized. This can perhaps be explained by the fact that France had a continuing and active peasant movement, which was also able to influence a central government (through both informal peasant choruses and the National Peasant Corporation), whilst in the UK, no such peasant movement existed,[1] and Wales had no government of its own. The Welsh *gwerin* construct became atrophied (as perhaps it always had been), seeming to offer a vision of the Welsh-self which slid into a mythification of the 'vanishing other'. Thus, contrary to Peate's original aims, the museum seemed to be stuck with a romantic vision of a timeless, unchanging folk, not dissimilar in its ideological effects to the displays of the 'other' in ethnographic collection museums (see Francis 1981; Smith 1990/91). Eventually, the term 'folk' became unsustainable, and in the 1980s, the museum changed its name to the Museum of Welsh Life. It also acquired some industrial-era buildings, such as a row of miners' cottages and a miners' institute, in order to reflect, belatedly, the socially and economically important history of industrial Wales.

In the French case, by contrast, the peasant museum movement developed into a new and dynamic phase with the advent of the eco-museum in the 1970s (Poulot 1994). In the process, it became centred on industrial and de-industrialized localities rather than rural ones alone. What was innovative about the eco-museum concept was 'its orientation toward the community, expressed both in its specific geographical scope and in the emphasis placed on *participation by the inhabitants*' (Poulot 1994: 72, my emphasis). This participatory ideal, it seems, has given it a progressive edge, bringing it into the ambit of a more radical museology. Indeed, the Querrien report to the socialist Mitterand Government in 1981 recommended that 'the local population take charge of the activities of the eco-museum through an appropriate organization (typically a voluntary association) and that workers participate in its research and training programs' (quoted in Poulot 1994: 73). The museum should be skills-oriented rather than a haven for objects; the salvaging function to be replaced by one of interpreting and discovering culture. Thus, the eco-museum both offers an alternative to the museums' traditional legitimating claims as well as reconfiguring its relation with the public, substituting an emphasis on the exhibit with an emphasis on communication.

The eco-museum, as it emerges through Poulot's account, appears to present both significant continuities but also discontinuities with the new generation of heritage museums in the US, Britain, Germany and elsewhere in Europe. In its emphasis on representing local communities in terms of ordinary, working-class people and everyday life, it has affinities with industrial-heritage museums such as the Beamish Open Air Museum in the UK, or Lowell's National Historic Park in Massachusetts (on these, see Chapter 5). However, the eco-museum's project of engaging local people in exhibition research and design in order to revivify vanishing skills and a sense of collective identity suggests that it has more in common with the 'cultural centres' of the Pacific discussed in Chapter 4. For instance, the eco-museum is not, as Poulot makes clear, merely a display case for cultural identity, but a participatory forum. As such, it serves to expose the failings of many heritage museums as they are currently constituted. The focus on social utility in the eco-museum's immediate locale is rarely seen in heritage museums, which tend to provide only indirect economic benefits to the locality, such as through the generation of consumer-spend and tourism. The ideals of participatory and democratic interaction between local people and local museums has not, on the whole, been a feature of the heritage museum, in spite of its celebration of vernacular voices (see Dicks 2000b).

There are, however, pressures working in the direction of greater public participation in museums. In the UK, for example, local history museums are now obliged to formulate policies for working with, and attracting 'users' from, local communities. As many local museums struggle to survive in a protracted period of funding-crisis, their other roles and justifications may come more to the fore, now talked about under the banner of 'social inclusion'.[2] This includes their role as educators, community oral-history facilitators and community 'outreachers'. Of the two major publics that history museums engage, namely their financial revenue-providers (states, governments, corporations, agencies, trusts and museum visitors, who tend to be from upper-/middle-class backgrounds) and their 'originating populations' (namely the people(s), frequently of lower class, whose histories are displayed in museums), museums can no longer be deaf to the interests and demands of the latter (Ames 1992: 12). For instance, there are now examples of a new kind of 'people's museum', trying to chart a course away from the perceived failings of the heritage and folk models. So-called 'people's museums' are usually museums of place (e.g. The People's Story in Edinburgh, UK), minority groups (such as the National Museum of the American Indian in New York) or diasporas (such as The Museum of Chinese in the Americas in New York's Chinatown). These are more involved in providing a focus for local community involvement and renewal than in providing a spectacular tourist experience. They may provide both display-space and work-space for local art and crafts, as well as acting as a meeting-place for local groups and organizations.

Desperately seeking visitors

The question of broadening out museums' roles so that they can both appear more relevant and potentially find new justifications for public funding, brings us to the question of their relationship with visitors. This relationship is underscored by a particular tension, and one which has become heightened in recent years due to increasing market pressures – namely, the tension between museums' leisure-oriented and educational functions. Many sites of cultural display discussed in this book, including museums, have tried to resolve this tension through marrying the two into a discourse of 'edutainment', or have themselves emerged as solutions to this tension by embodying edutainment as their *raison d'être*. These moves have naturally caused considerable contention and ferment in the museum world, which, of all the sites of display discussed in this book, is the most clearly located at the 'serious', educational end of the spectrum. However, it is this 'serious' image itself which has prevented museums, it has been argued, from properly fulfilling their public educational role.

Museums, education and class

Study after study has shown that museums appeal mainly to those with high educational credentials. Beginning with Bourdieu and Darbel's pioneering work in the 1960s, there has been much evidence to suggest, as well as a widely-held perception, that museums do not cater for most ordinary, working-class visitors and their families. In Bourdieu and Darbel's analysis (based on various large-scale surveys in France in the 1960s), it is suggested that working-class visitors to art museums experience them as a test – which they fail – of their cultural capital, and hence they learn to devalue their own taste (Bourdieu and Darbel 1991). This links into Bourdieu's wider project of showing how cultural institutions of various kinds, including schools and museums, conceal the arbitrariness of taste by presenting elite taste as universal (Bourdieu 1984, 1993). Thus, it has been argued that, whilst claiming to represent universal knowledge, museums actually represent the interests of a dominant patron class (see Duncan and Wallach 1980).

Recent surveys have tended to confirm this picture, although there are important gaps in the research base. The Henley Centre's 1995 survey (see Selwood *et al.* 1995) showed that 34 per cent of ABs (those in professional, high-status occupations) and 23 per cent of C1s (in skilled, non-manual occupations) visited museums in 1993/94 as opposed to only 14 per cent of C2s (skilled manual) and 10 per cent of DEs (unskilled and unemployed). However, a major difficulty of museums surveys is that the term 'museum' embraces a wide range of diverse attractions, covering both art galleries at one end of the spectrum and heritage-theme parks at the other. Recent trends such as the incorporation of themed and interactive elements into museums and the boom in heritage centres offering simulated experiences rather than displayed collections show how the blurring of boundaries makes the umbrella term 'museum' increasingly unhelpful. Certainly, the appeal of local, living-history, industrial museums and metropolitan art galleries might be expected to differ quite markedly. Unfortunately, the necessary research here has not been done, although several small-scale studies have found evidence of a higher percentage of visitors from the skilled, manual classes to industrial heritage sites (Light and Prentice 1994; Divall 1998).

Proving their educational value has become a key issue for museums today. As governments have increasingly championed the cause of widening access to education, so grants and public monies for museums have become conditional upon their establishing educational programmes in order to justify their status as public institutions. By claiming that they provide a service to the community, museums can also argue for exemption from certain taxes and for grants to assist with capital expenditures (Zolberg 1994). As we have seen, the kinds of knowledge museums propagated and the methods they used for displaying it went largely uncritiqued for most of their first century of existence. However, as educational curricula and pedagogy started to become objects of critical attention from the 1960s on, both the subject matters and the exhibitionary strategies of museums were opened up to critical scrutiny. Therefore, it is not only their increasing consumer-leisure functions which have impelled museums towards more hybrid sites and modes of display, it is also a general commitment in current political orthodoxies to the values of interactive, learner-centred education and public access to culture.

Widening access

Art museums have registered these pressures particularly starkly, due to their role as custodians of 'high' art. Whilst science, history and natural history museums have always been more oriented to the general public than to professional scientists or historians, art museums have historically courted more specialist audiences such as art critics, art historians, collectors, artists and highly educated sections of the public (Zolberg 1994). Art appreciation has been seen as a matter of individual taste rather than the social distribution of cultural knowledge. Internally, the exhibition curator has been a much more highly esteemed museum position than the museum educator. It was, for instance, as a response to the marginalized role of education in art museums that the Centre Pompidou (the Beaubourg) in Paris was opened, which has a deliberate commitment to widening public access to art. It departed from the model of the grand gallery and substituted a 'supermarket' approach, with a variety of different events, exhibition spaces and consumption outlets displaying more popular forms as well as high art. However, there is some evidence to suggest that visitors use the different museum spaces just as they would 'outside', in that the high art gallery is visited by those with the highest cultural capital, while others approach the museum primarily as a playful space of consumption (Heinich 1988; see also Zolberg 1994).

Certainly, museums are now highly aware of their 'accessibility problem', particularly since their funding is increasingly competitive and based on being able to demonstrate healthy visitor numbers. Indeed, there has been a wholesale change in museums' entire approach to their visitors over the past 10 to 15 years. This is typified by the new breed of heritage centre, which is fully focused on strategies for attracting support:

> Managing a heritage attraction is about much more than traditional museological concerns like conservation, interpretation, education and access. It is about managing a shop, a catering operation, a wedding venue. It is about commissioning market research, choosing design agencies, preparing conservation plans, project managing, buying

computer systems, applying to the Heritage Lottery Fund, persuading people to join a Friends scheme, writing business plans, lobbying politicians, organising special events that bring in more money than they cost, and so on and so forth.

(Geddes 2001: 318)

The traditional tasks of collection museums prioritized several functions other than display. A typical pre-1980s museums policy comprised 'collecting/acquiring, conserving/restoring, securing in safety, registering and documenting, and, only in fifth place, displaying' (Tunbridge and Ashworth 1996: 36). Visitors were an afterthought, a necessary encumbrance which had to be carefully managed so as to avoid interfering with these other more important functions. At the same time, there was general agreement as to what was considered collectable, why it should be collected, how it was to be classified and how displayed.

This consensus began to be replaced by fragmentation and conflict during the 1980s (Hooper-Greenhill 1992). Much of the disagreement focused on how museums should respond to the market pressures to which they were increasingly being subjected. In art museums, curators became more under the sway of the artist/dealer/collector triad, which meant that their decision-making was increasingly ensnared in market forces (Alloway 1996). The curator's role also became much more specialized, focusing more than ever before on the design of exhibitions – which was traditionally seen as the least important of the curator's functions (Heinich and Pollak 1996). By the 1990s, the staging of temporary exhibitions had become absolutely key to an art museum's revenue-raising and profile-raising activities, since it offered greater returns in both senses than the permanent collections. This reflects a tendency for art exhibitions to be much more glossily staged, with an enhanced attention to site architecture, scenography, wall colourings, lighting and the production of sophisticated accompanying texts in the form of brochures, catalogues and videos. Thus, exhibitions are now consciously constructed in order to show the public 'what the work cannot reveal on its own' (Heinrich and Pollak 1996: 237). Installation and interpretation have become central to the exhibition's appeal.

Art museums are setting out to attract much higher volumes of visitors, and to manage them in new leisure-focused ways. The phenomenon of the past ten years has been the 'blockbuster' arts show, which draws record-breaking audiences by showing the work of extremely high-profile artists. Blockbusters are increasingly essential to museums' financial planning, allowing them to clear deficits accrued by smaller and more obscure exhibitions, or even just to mend the roof. An early UK example was the British

Museums' famous Tutankhamun exhibition of 1972, which drew 1.75 million visitors. In 1984, New York's Metropolititan Museum staged the hugely expensive blockbuster, Van Gogh in Arles, which generated knock-on financial returns to Manhattan amounting to 50 times the entire initial outlay of the show. In the 1990s, London's Tate Gallery attracted 406,000 visitors to its Cezanne exhition in 1996, 813,000 attended the mammoth Monet exhibition at the Royal Academy in 1999, and half a million came to see the Tate Modern's Matisse-Picasso event of 2002.[3] The Matisse-Picasso show travelled on to Paris's Grand Palais, and from there to New York's Museum of Modern Art in February 2003. Visitors to the show in London did not have to queue but could buy timed tickets instead, and, while they waited their turn, listen to live jazz music over a glass of absinthe and a talk by George Melly.

This development is symptomatic of the focus on attracting the popular tourist/spectator gaze – as opposed to the minority gaze of art critics and art-lovers – which is a central feature of cultural display today. If visitors won't come to the museum, the museum will come to the visitor. Thus, museum exhibitions, increasingly, are moving out into non-traditional display-spaces (as we saw in Chapter 4). The UK government, for example, has recently suggested museums put collections in shops, schools and even pubs. The Museum of London already has objects on display in 'London Bridge railway station, in offices, in schools, in the Royal Opera House – it's only a question of how daring you can be'.[4]

Museums and malls

Souvenir mugs and other merchandising at London's Matisse-Picasso exhibition of 2002 greatly added to the direct revenue from ticket sales. In the 1980s, many museums embraced shopping as a key element in their efforts to transform their image in the public's mind (Macdonald 1998). At the same time, this was a response to a changing relationship with the state, wherein public financial support was dwindling. Macdonald notes that 'museums came to foreground the question of what the public would "buy"; and talk was increasingly of "packaging" exhibitions as "products" or "brands", of identifying "unique selling points", and of the importance of "corporate image" and "market niche"' (Macdonald 1998: 118). She calls this the 'supermarket model' of exhibition-making.

The traditional museum model limited shopping to the gift shop near the exit, where goods on display were carefully selected to reflect the museum subject-matter (such as souvenirs of the collections, or crafts). New generation museums, by contrast, integrate shopping and dining space into the very fabric of the building. Manchester's grandly refurbished Museum of Science and Industry, for instance, has replaced its small restaurant with a vast open-plan contemporary structure which can seat 200 diners. The Louvre's recent renovations have given it a new wing with 8300 square metres of subterranean shopping mall, through which visitors can enter the museum and avoid the queues through the glass pyramid above (McTavish 1998). The Victoria and Albert Museum in London was declared by its director Sir Roy Strong to be capable of becoming the 'Laura Ashley' of the 1990s, and it attempted (unsuccessfully) to revive its flagging visitor numbers with the slogan, 'An ace café with quite a nice museum attached'.

New approaches to display: from objects to experiences

Museums today, then, are no longer repositories of objects but are in the business of attracting visitors. They promise to take them on journeys of discovery and not to subject them to corridors of dusty glass cases. They offer them the sights and sounds of people's lives and communities instead of shooshing them around collections of revered objects. Many museums have, as a result, become highly sensory environments: packed full of things not only to see but also to hear, touch, smell and – in the case of 'living history' – to talk to and interact with. New museal display exploits the image just as much as the object (Kirshenblatt-Gimblett 1998). Interactives allow visitors to gain responses and 'feedback' from exhibits, rather than being confronted by the implacable silence of objects. Visitors can perform tasks, challenges and games, such as tracing their own family genealogies. To some extent, at least, the ideal of the contemplative gaze has been disrupted (Ward 1996).

The word 'experience' has become central to today's museum and, in this, exhibition-designers using the traditional indoor gallery-spaces of museums have learnt lessons from the open-air 'living history' museums discussed in the last chapter. Various kinds of media are now in evidence – including theatre and performance art, photographs, audio-visual films on small screens or big screens, audio voice-overs via head-sets, interactive touch-screen programs on computer monitors, as well as more traditional museal media such as wall displays and glass cases. There are, however, two different principles of display (discussed usefully by Kirshenblatt-Gimblett 1998) upon which exhibitions may draw. The first of these ('in-situ' display) uses the principles of simulation and/or reconstruction to provide a glimpse of the larger reality that surrounds the object, or events in a wider story that is being told. It seeks to immerse the visitor in a wrap-around staging of a human situation illustrating the use or significance of objects and customs. Some museums use reconstructed streets, shops and houses (aping the living-history and folk museum) or include miniature reconstructions and scenic dioramas situated inside walk-through galleries. These techniques have been around for some time, and there is now a trend within in-situ display towards more sophisticated screen, light and sur-round-sound technologies, replacing the older reliance on life-size models in static dioramas and tableaux.

However, more formal kinds of display (what Kirshenblatt-Gimblett calls 'in-context' as opposed to 'in-situ' display), are still in evidence in museums today. Here, objects are arranged, usually in classic wall-display and glass-case techniques, according to the formal relationships among them, i.e. in taxonomies or sequences of knowledge. Examples of in-context displays would be collections of jewellery, costume or weaponry arranged chronologically, so as to illustrate their historical development, or geo-graphically, so as to illustrate the styles of particular regions. Increasingly, in-context displays are combined with new technology, such as display cases that activate voice-overs delivered via visitors' head sets. Many of these use in-situ techniques. At the Zaanse Schans museum in Holland, for example, as visitors gaze at the cases of costumes and artefacts of the region's historical inhabitants, electronic sensors activate head-set record-ings of period conversations dramatized by actors. In fact, dramatic, in-situ representations like this are becoming increasingly common in museum galleries, part of the tendency we have been noting towards providing objects with 'real' human stories, and allowing these to be directly accessed through media technology.

Many have argued that the use of dramatic, experience-centred modes of display, especially so-called 'interactives', rely on producing sensation to the detriment of knowledge and understanding. Macdonald (1995, 1998), for example, argues of the Science Museum's Food for Thought exhibition, which majored on hands-on exhibits, that the exercise bike that shows the effort required to burn off one calorie, the distorting mirrors that offer reflections of one's self-perceptions, the 'smellerama' that invites visitors to guess the smell, simply provide sensory experiences rather than facts or principles which the visitor can apply elsewhere. This suggests that inter-activity alone does not produce knowledge if there is insufficient input from the exhibition itself. Although the topic of visitor decoding is not one that I can attempt to cover adequately here, my own research at a living-history museum suggests that visitors came away with quite an in-depth under-standing of the issues presented (see Dicks 2000a). Rather than objects or gadgets, this museum used information-intensive communication strategies through a mixture of audio-visual films, lit-up, speaking diorama figures and live, guided tours with ex-miners. These strategies produce a highly elaborated, even didactic form of communication, rich with words and images, which enables quite complex and detailed stories to be told.

The refusal of interpretation

Such techniques, heavily reliant on explicit narratives, clear interpretation and unambiguous reconstructions, contrast quite strikingly with more 'postmodern' and aestheticized approaches to display. Techniques of bricolage, pastiche, montage, quotation, and so forth represent a different tendency to that of simulation. They are designed to ask questions about the nature of representation rather than answering ones about the interpretation of history. For example, the Museum of Sydney features a large display case containing hundreds of pottery fragments and rural machinery from the city's past, ordered aesthetically, rather than intellectually, to look visually appealing (see Marcus 2000). No text informs us of their origins, significance or uses: instead, textual quotations are offered with no attempt at synthesis. According to Marcus, the exhibition seeks to display the impossibility of clearly and definitively describing the founding of Sydney. This is a politically troubled question, due to the tensions still reverberating between Aboriginal and colonialist interpretations of that history. The effect of the aesthetic techniques, argues Marcus (2000), is to side-step political engagement with the complexities of the subject by substituting a baffling fragmentation that fails to tell the viewer anything much about either Aboriginal or colonialist interpretations of history. The displays comment on the impossibility of representation rather than on the history they are ostensibly 'about' (see also Coombes 1991).

The rejection of fixed visitor itineraries can present similar fragmenting effects. Increasingly, museums use gallery spaces rather than interlinked rooms so that museum visitors can make their own choices about how they move around and what they decide to look at. Giving visitors choices and 'freedoms' is seen as important. Barriers and cordons are now avoided unless strictly necessary. Thus, a 'pick'n'mix' approach to museum space is encouraged, offering a variety of different spectacles in different media form which the visitor can select. In the above-mentioned Food for Thought exhibition, for example, there is no single storyline, but rather a collection of 'themed areas, rather as supermarkets have shelves and counters devoted to particular products' (Macdonald 1998: 123). Visitors are thus segmented into lifestyle niches just as consumers are. Macdonald finds that the visitors to Food for Thought are 'so caught up with making choices and participating that there is little opportunity to ponder the politics of what is on offer' (1998: 128).

Knowledge ends up being reduced to snippets of information from which visitors pick and choose. Rather than having an unfolding meta-narrative which steers visitors towards 'a body of accumulating truths', it becomes 'segmented and localised' (Macdonald 1998: 130). These strategies, ostensibly democratizing and accessible, may instead simply forestall critical engagement with the exhibition's subject-matter.

We can see from the afore-going discussion that museums are currently being pulled in a number of different directions. The drive to increase visitor numbers in an increasingly marketized climate represents one source of pressures. A second is to meet the demands of marginalized groups who wish 'their' culture to be included in the public display-case. Another challenge, potentially in conflict with the first two, is that of responding to critiques of cultural essentialism that have emerged through post-coloni-alism and 'post-paradigm' anthropology. This last involves struggling to represent complexities that may not be obviously amenable to the tourist gaze. To begin to formulate exhibitionary approaches that both pull in visitors and deal with the challenges of representing culture constitutes, for museums, a most difficult task ahead.

Notes

1   It is worth noting that the English peasantry, at least, had been destroyed much earlier than the French one, so that Raymond Williams (1973) was able to describe the role of the countryside in English literary imagination as long dominated by pastoral, labour-less, history-less visions of happy 'folk' rather than peasant-workers.
2   See Nightingale, J. (2000) The people's show, *Guardian*, 18 October.
3   Statistics reported in *The Times*, 20 August 2002: 3.
4   Director of London Museum, quoted in Maev Kennedy (2000) Dust off fusty image, museums told, *Guardian*, 19 January.

Further reading

Bennett, T. (1995) *The Birth of the Museum: History, Theory, Politics*. London: Routledge.
Coombes, A.E. (1994) *Reinventing Africa: Museums, Material Culture and Popular Imagination in Late Victorian and Edwardian England*. London: Yale University Press.

Macdonald, S. (ed.) (1998) *The Politics of Display: Museums, Science, Culture.* London: Routledge

Macdonald, S. and Fyfe G. (eds) (1996) *Theorising Museums*. Oxford: Blackwell.

Greenberg, R., Ferguson, B.W. and Nairne, S. (eds) (1996) *Thinking about Exhibitions*. London: Routledge

Poulot, D. (1994) Identity as Self-Discovery: the Eco-Museum in France in D.J. Sherman and I. Rogoff (eds) *Museum Culture: Histories, Discourses, Spectacles*. London: Routledge.

7 │ VIRTUAL DESTINATIONS

Imagine being able to walk down the streets of Paris, seeing the sights and hearing the sounds around you, without leaving your home. You are able to converse with a friend who is also online, and the two of you decide to fly to Tahiti together. As you travel around the globe, you stop momentarily at places of interest to view three-dimensional (3D) representations of local structures, learn about representative works of art, browse historical information for the area, or view real-time video and audio feeds of local events.

(from Virtual Terrain Project website)

Visiting culture no longer requires the physical presence of visitors at geographical locations. With the advent of the World Wide Web, computer users suddenly find a world at their fingertips. Back in 1985, Feifer had already noted the touristic possibilities afforded by both old and new media:

> The passive functions of tourism (i.e. seeing) can be performed right at home with video, books, records, and TV. Now there is even the Sony Walkman, the portable tapedeck: with headphones to enable the anti-tourist to remain in a place of his choice mentally while he is physically travelling around.
>
> (Feifer 1985: 269)

How old fashioned this statement seems in the era of the web, and yet the point is the same – through communications technology, one can be physically located in one place, and mentally in quite another. With the advent of the web, the possibilities for armchair travel have suddenly multiplied. Millions of websites and thousands of messaging systems give us glimpses of other people and places all over the world. 'Travel' on the web may be undertaken by clicking one's way around multiple sites of display (in a consumption-oriented model), or by connecting to sites of synchronous communication, such as chat-rooms (in an interaction-oriented model). Both suggest affinities with off-line travel, in the emphasis on cultural discovery, visual exploration and managed inter-personal encounters. Yet there are still important differences between bodily travel and its digital counterpart. Tourism receipts are multiplying all the time, in spite of the technological transportation offered by television, film, personal stereos, mobile phones and computer networks. Some of these differences and contrasts will be discussed in this chapter.

Advances in digital representation, always achieving ever-greater mimetic powers, have made the world of creative software design a particularly high-profile one. It is a world that has provided the inspiration for many of the developments in cultural display discussed in these chapters. Some of the key characteristics of contemporary cultural display we have discussed exhibit features epitomized by digital environments – such as accessibility, legibility, interactivity, visual condensation and intensity, the fantasy of immersion, substitution for the real world and the achievement of 'presence through distance'. Networked computer screens (at home, at work, at school, in high streets, in cafés), whose content changes according to our input, which connect us up to absent others and which give us instant feedback, have become a mundane element of daily life in the affluent West. Successful websites deploy a range of communicative devices to keep the user's attention. They have rapidly become live, pulsating nodes that are highly iconographic, easily readable, mobile and ever-changing. They have also, arguably, provided a blueprint for similar trends in 'off-line' cultural display – towards greater interactivity, feedback and simulation, for example. In this sense, web design is a major laboratory for design-solutions dedicated to enhancing visitability – in both virtual and material environments.

The Internet as visitable space

In spite of Feifer's (1985) comments, there is some justification for seeing computer networks as more in tune with the tourist gaze than earlier electronic media. Like the new interactive museums, the Internet offers feedback-loops rather than a one-way flow of communication. It is also inherently flexible. Broadcasting, by contrast, is tied – for the time being at least – to a fixed schedule of short-duration programmes controlled and delivered from a central station. The web presents a potentially limitless universe of individually managed and enduring (if not permanent) sites that can be visited at the user's will. It simply 'sits' there, waiting for the user to click their way around it in their own time. The user *activates* the web, while she or he can only *access* the television schedule. Further, television programmes follow sequentially on from each other in channels, and, no matter how much these have multiplied in recent years, the viewer can still only flick among different sequentially delivered schedules. By contrast, hypertext on the web allows a labyrinthine (or to use Landow's (1997) term, 'rhizomatic') experience of infinite branching from site to site, pro- ducing a continual sense of ever-present yet unknown destinations lying in wait just a click away. The path that a user traces through this labyrinth is not pre-mapped: it is both unique and exploratory in a way that television viewing can never be.

Such differences suggest that the web is inherently a more 'visitable' and 'travellable' medium than television or film. In Chapter 1, I discussed the ways in which simulation-rich themed environments and interactive museums respond to and overcome some of the representational limitations of camera technology. Their materiality means they offer various kinds of supplemental authenticity (or 'aura', in Benjamin's (1973) terms). For example, rather than the 'illusion' of the movies, living history museums provide the experience of immersion in a three-dimensional, wrap-around world of 'total theatre' (Eco 1986: 45). Networked computers overcome the camera's limitations in similar ways, although without the materiality. Watching television involves gazing at a pre-constituted and finished world. Even in live TV, what we see on the screen is managed and controlled by the professional apparatus of broadcasting. By contrast, the web seems capable of bringing other people directly into one's home on their own terms. One can 'step through the looking glass' and find others there (Turkle 1997: 9). As a many-to-many communication medium (as against the few-to-many domains of television, films, newspapers and books), some accordingly have seen the Internet as a new democratic 'knowledge space' that ignites the possibility of direct, person-to-person interactions on a mass scale (see, for example, Levy 2001).

A culture of digital mediation

Yet, I would argue, digital displays of culture also close off as much as they communicate. In cyberspace, screened behind computer terminals and separated by potentially vast distances, virtual actions are protected from actual responses (Reid 1995: 174). This is something it has in common with most of the material venues of cultural display explored in this book. In Chapter 2, tourism was discussed as a system that provides access to otherness (such as the exotic, the far-away or the past) within conditions of sameness (in the form of contemporary Western comforts). In order to achieve this, the system generates numerous technologically enhanced sites of mediation, such as tourist enclaves, museums, theme parks and heritage sites, that handle this contradictory situation by representing other cultures in consumable form. By positioning themselves between the tourist and the life-world she or he wants to access, they claim to substitute for it. Tourism thereby strives to deliver 'gain with no pain'.

In relation to virtual tourism, we can see the Internet as the ultimate promise of pain-free travel. It is another mediating agency, this time in the form of a screen, which interposes itself between the tourist and the 'offline world' and claims to facilitate and safeguard his or her access to it. By offering an escape from the embodied nature of reality, its imaginary space allows the user to feel safe and in control. Screens, as Bauman (1993: 178) reminds us, however, mean we can gaze openly and without fear of reprisal at strangers, who become 'infinitely close as objects but doomed to remain, happily, remote as subjects of action'. It should be remembered that, rather than face-to-face encounters, the computer simply provides an *inter*-face, which makes its form of communication very different from that of direct, unmediated interaction (see Thompson 1995).

A culture of digital simulation

Computer interfaces are, by definition, pre-programmed. As Turkle (1999: 296) notes, recent trajectories have impelled computer technology away from its initial, science-led 'culture of calculation' into a new, design-led 'culture of simulation'. Current programming developments focus on the refinement of its *usability*, through advances in graphical interfaces, inter-activity and navigation. To avoid being alienating or perplexing, many digital environments shy away from the experimental or the daring, and instead depend on a selection of familiar, real-world scenarios. Ever more sophisticated graphical user interfaces (GUIs) mediate between the user and the computer's programming language, representing the latter in the form of familiar life-settings. The Windows interface mimics the paper-based office-domain. Websites represent options in terms of directed journeys, through arrows and forward/back options. For this reason, Stallabrass (1999: 110) suggests that computer graphics design 'throws an analogue cloak over digital operations' by creating a highly legible, user-friendly and routinized iconographic environment.

This is a lesson that has been taken up by material-world urban designers, whose blueprints for improving street legibility conceive cities as giant communication nodes (discussed in Chapter 4). Urban design seeks to make the city as accessible and user-friendly as a website. Computer interface design, accordingly, offers a second-order realm of display feeding off the first-order one, but also feeding back *into* it. The material world becomes more interactive; the interactive domain more material world-like. Virtual reality offers the fantasy of constructing in digital form the very same sensory environments that are found in the material world (see below). And these sensory environments are themselves being reconstructed through principles of networking, interactivity and legibility. Indeed, there seem to be more and more resonances, and skills-transferrals, emerging between the online and the offline world. The net effect, it could be argued, is to produce increasingly familiar, formulaic and standardized environments – both in the virtual and the material world (see the discussion of urban standardization in Chapter 3).

Four kinds of virtual tourism

Computer networks seem to contain within them the fantasy of perfect visitability. But what does the idea of virtual travel mean, and can it really offer a substitute for the 'real thing'? As we shall discuss below, it is important to consider what kind of an experience tourism is in its traditional, material mode. I shall suggest that it is not capable of replication through digital simulation. Before examining these issues further, we should consider what is the nature of the relationship between computer networks and tourism. I suggest here four principal ways in which they are intertwined.

1   **E-commerce.** The web allows a network of communication to be established between potential tourists and suppliers. Online booking was expected to rise from $2 billion in 1998 to $17 billion in 2003 (see Buhalis 2001). Online communication makes targeted marketing available to smaller organizations as well as larger ones, thus increasing the proliferation of more specialized, flexible, mix'n'match tourist products. Recent developments include the introduction of sites (such as priceline.com) organizing the auctioning of unsold tickets and last-minute packages, where customers suggest their own prices. More airlines and companies can also sell direct to customers instead of relying so heavily on intermediaries. We are thus seeing the emergence not only of the 'paperless travel agency' (Urry 2002) and the virtual travel agency, but also perhaps the increasing redundancy of the travel agency itself.

2 **Place-promotion**. Virtually every local tourism organization one can think of now has its own website. And most local councils' tourism and recreation departments host websites dedicated to promoting the tourism potential of their region. These vary in sophistication from a few simple pages describing the area, to fully clickable interactive sites showing various images and layers of information. Some city websites operate as very sophisticated marketing tools, aimed at conference organizers and inward-investing firms (Graham 1999). Others are mainly aimed at tourists and visitors. These sites limit the website's role to that of information, promotion and appetite whetting; the point is to persuade people to leave their computer screens and go there in person. By contrast, the next two uses pinpoint what is potentially more radical and novel about the idea of virtual tourism – the possibility of computer-mediated communication supplementing, or even substituting for, the touristic experience itself.

3 **Non-corporeal travel**. The web itself comprises a navigable universe offering destinations in the form of interesting websites. The experience of 'moving' from site to site and following links within sites can be likened to the experience of travelling. This is one sense in which we can talk of virtual travel or tourism. For example, metaphors frequently describe web-use in terms of a journey: visiting, navigating, finding, surfing, searching, etc. Websites can be virtual venues of cultural display, allowing groups with computer access but without great material resources to exhibit their culture, in the hope that people will come visiting. In this way, one can find out about other cultural identities on display with the click of a mouse (for example, the Native American Virtual Cultural Centre pages are 'dedicated to promoting, preserving and protecting traditional and contemporary arts by Native American Peoples' – see their website)

4 **Virtual destinations**. In a more radical sense, one can think of emergent technologies that allow an experience of 'being there' which might be said to substitute for tourism and to satisfy the touristic desire to gaze upon the 'other'. This potentially includes all those uses which are set up to provide spectacle in and of themselves – such as web-cams and virtual reality. Here, although the technology is still primitive, there are signs of an emergent, alternative, touristic imaginary. I am going to limit my discussion here to the last two of these forms of digital tourism.

Internet use as non-corporeal travel

First, as a means of non-corporeal travel, the Internet offers the virtual tourist a multitude of destinations without moving from his or her chair. In what Robins and Webster (1999), following Serres (1995), call a 'Pantopian ideal', the net promises to overcome the tyranny of spatial and temporal distance. It can transport the computer-user instantly from place to place and time to time, irrespective of where she or he is located. Of course, all that really happens is that a computer modem sends a bunch of coded squawks over the phone to another computer modem and receives more squawks back, but it can do this so quickly that they can be converted into a viewable picture in the space of a few seconds (Holderness 1998). The web thus provides the illusion of being transported somewhere. While we dispatch an email as if it were a speeded-up letter going off into the unknown, we expect a clickable hyperlink to give us an instantaneous screenful of new data. In this way, we experience 'presence at a distance' through what appears to be 'instant travel' and the achievement of synchronicity (Robins and Webster 1999). With its millions of instant arrivals, the web eliminates the 'dead space' of material world travel (Chapter 4).

Using the Internet invites us to follow our noses and go where the next interesting-sounding link takes us. Unhindered by baggage or timetables, we can set off on an infinitely branching journey. Multiple search engines and gateways have appeared to help us 'find our way' and avoid getting 'lost'. Websites acting as gateways provide access, in the form of hyperlinks, to hundreds of other websites. They are a kind of virtual tourist office, offering routes to tours and experiences beyond their doors. For example, Virtual Sites offers eight gateways, ranging from a Virtual Tours gateway to a Virtual Shopping Mall. Virtual Tours invites us to:

> Travel and visit the Smithsonian to museums in Paris and St. Petersburg all in one day. The interactive exposure, the sights and sounds will leave you with a rich memorable experience. What you could only imagine five years ago, today you can actualize while you travel with a virtual passport throughout the World Wide Web.
>
> (from Virtual Sites website)

Selecting the World Tours option brings the promise that by clicking on each country or city icon, 'you'll be sent on an exciting interactive journey'. The reality, however, is rather more mundane. Activating the links actually delivers one directly into the pages of old-fashioned print media in the familiar form of the *Lonely Planet Guide*, or the US city *BestRead Guide*. Alternatively you may find yourself dispatched off to online tourist agencies, other gateways or other companies' 'tours' consisting of hypertext accompanied by online photographs. What you don't find is the destination offered as an experience in its own right. It is only 'there' in the form of reports, pictures and information which talk *about* it.

Another example is Virtual Tourist.com, a commercial online tourist agency that provides information – primarily for US users – on a large number of destinations around the world. The information it provides about each destination takes the form of emails from travellers and residents, so that the website operates as a vast online notice board (neatly allowing the company to avoid the resource costs of having to compile any information itself). For example, people with inside, personal knowledge of a particular destination post travel tips, send messages, provide photos and make recommendations about hotels, restaurants, and such like, so that one is able to access the experiences of people who have *really* been there (one trusts). The site promises that 'coming soon' is the facility to group together all information pertaining to a chosen destination and to print it out into one's own virtual tourism guide. All of these virtual tourism sites seem to offer information rather than experiences, second-hand reports rather than direct representations of the places mentioned. In this sense, non-corporeal travel resembles a never-ending process of preparing for a trip rather than a simulation of the trip itself.

Virtual destinations

This brings us to a potentially more radical form of net tourism – the creation of virtual destinations. This involves providing a computer-mediated experience which is capable of standing alone – to be the touristic experience itself. The web as it currently stands is not really suited to such a project, since what it does in the main is provide clickable pages of hypertext and hypermedia. However, the possibilities implicit in two web-deliverable technologies, namely MUDs (multi-user domains) and web-cams, may well provide evolving models for virtual tourism experiences. What they do is to put on display a digital destination where others can be seen to reside. Although very different from each other (web-cams providing a consumption-oriented, and MUDs an interaction-oriented experience), they both reflect the fantasy of reconstructing the life-world in representational form. In this, they take the principle of the world-as-exhibition, discussed in earlier chapters, and turn it into an environment through which one can move at will. This idea of the strollable exhibitionary environment takes material form in the themed and festival-retailing zones discussed in Chapter 3. It takes its ultimate virtual form in the idea of virtual reality, which is also discussed below.

Video games

The major precursors of the idea of the virtual destination are video and computer games. Still immensely popular amongst children, teenagers and many (predominantly male) adults, computer games vary enormously: from the 'hectic and immediate', to the 'deep, complex and time-consuming' (Carr 2003). Nintendo games, for example, endlessly repeat the same simplistic plot sequences, but the player's interest is always maintained by the promise of gaining entry into the next space, of 'mastering these little worlds and making them your own playground' (Fuller and Jenkins 1995: 62). Many invite the player to explore a plethora of spectacular spaces, immersing them in gorgeous scenery that is superfluous to the actual action. In Streetfighter II, for example, a choice of different global locations for a kickboxing tournament is on offer: a Chinese street market, a Soviet factory, a Brazilian dock, a Las Vegas show palace. Part of the game's allure is the programmers' attention to simulating spatial details – a tap dripping, an elephant trunk swaying – which are largely irrelevant to the action, but essential to the pleasures of visual excess, or 'eye candy' (Fuller and Jenkins 1995: 62). In this way, the ability to interact with displays of place and culture recognizable from the offline world is a central element of the pleasure afforded by these games.

The fascination of these scenic details seems to lie in the display of technology's ability to mimic and to let us play with a world we already recognize. As in theme parks and interactive museums, the appeal lies both in the simulation and the mastery of reality – the one being enabled by the other. In simulation-oriented games, such as SimCity 4, the sense of mastery is produced by the ability to customize a simulated life-world in accordance with the user's imagination. Beginning with a patch of undeveloped land, the player can proceed to construct an entire city, complete with residential and commercial districts and a full infrastructure of roads, power lines, hospitals, airports and the rest. Players are rewarded for developing strategies to make their city grow, both economically and physically. The game's promotional literature claims it provides the pleasure of 'exploring the worlds you create out of your own imagination [where] you're rewarded for creativity, experimentation, and understanding, with a healthy, thriving universe to call your own' (Maxis Software toys catalogue, quoted in Friedman 1995: 81).

Being able to create and control a world 'to call your own' suggests a new kind of highly managed, quasi-touristic space that can be both explored and manipulated. The freedom to discover, however, is simply an effect of pre-programmed options. The gamer feels in control of a malleable universe full of surprises, but succeeding at the game actually involves discovering the rules of the program. Once these are learnt, the game's interest typically fades. With the new generation of networked multi-player games, this task-centred and focused experience of 'discovery' becomes something more socially interactive. Online games bring thousands of players together into a live game-world in which they participate via avatars. This world represents shared terrain rather than the individual universes of the solo gamer. Multi-player games reintroduce live unpredictability through the multiple inter-ventions of other human actors. This 'live' quality underlies their appeal.

MUDs and MOOs

This brings us to other forms of simultaneous, web-based multi-party communication such as MUDs (multi-user domains) and chat-rooms. These present intriguing opportunities for virtual encounters with the 'other'. In networked communication systems, one can talk directly with others located in distant places. This communication can be asynchronous as in email, bulletin boards and conferencing systems, such as Usenet (where users request saved messages about a selected topic and then send in their own contributions). Synchronous communication, by contrast, allows the real-time exchange of messages. Chat-rooms, such as Internet Relay Chat, provide interfaces which allow for the text sent by one user to be separated on the screen from that sent by another. On the screen, one sees someone else's written text appearing line by line, to which one can respond immediately with one's own typed message. Different channels offer dif-ferent topics and groupings. It is thus possible to have a group discussion on a live, many-to-many basis.

MUDs take the idea of synchronous communication further by simu-lating a setting or environment within which it takes place. Text-based MUDs limit the screen environment to the written word but MUDs using graphical user interfaces, also known as MOOs (multi-user object-oriented domains) display simulated locations (such as mansions, dungeons, castles or whatever) in which users can 'appear' in the form of avatars. Whilst many MUDs are simply multi-player games, the new generation of 'social MUDs' allows users to join a 'community' housed in a particular setting within which they can build friendships, meet new people and establish collective norms of behaviour (see Smith and Kollock 1999). A generic term for graphical MUDs is collaborative virtual environments (CVEs). As virtual reality imaging technology develops, the graphical environments available for interaction are becoming more and more convincing, including the use of 3-D domains. We can imagine eventually being able to enter and explore a 3-D town square, encounter others there and talk to them. MUDs and CVEs – especially when they become deliverable via mobile phone – represent the possibility of cross-cultural communication via virtual sites of display that potentially obviate the need for travel. I shall return to this issue below.

Web-cams

Web-cams are remote video cameras connected up to the Internet. By connecting to one, it is possible to view real-time images of distant others on one's own home computer screen. Current state of the art is far from inspiring. First, it is rather difficult to find web-cams not aimed at the pornography market. Secondly, at currently standard modem speed and bandwidth levels, video footage often ends up becoming a series of still images. For example, through the Virtual Sites Asia gateway, one can view Chaweng Beach in Thailand and see rather shadowy images of people sitting in a café overlooking what is clearly a delightful beach. Every few minutes a new picture shows that the people you are watching have moved. This reminds one that the picture is live and real, and that these people are 'actually' there now, presumably unaware that they are being watched by someone sitting at a desk thousands of miles away in Wales. Quite aside from the ethical problems raised by such covert forms of observation, the problem with web-cams offering this kind of view is that most are visually uninteresting after a couple of minutes' perusal. They simply record whatever is going on in front of a fixed lens, and – as this is usually positioned at a fixed distance, and often at a great height (e.g. from towers, bridges, tall buildings, etc.) – there is actually very little to be seen in terms of meaningful social action. It seems those who install them have yet to learn the lesson learnt long ago by visual ethnographers and film-makers: you cannot simply point a camera at an environment and expect meaning to emerge.

Some web-cams can be operated remotely over the Internet connection so that they point to different views. Through the Virtual Sites Europe gateway, for example, one can manoeuvre and zoom a web-cam situated on the top of the Finnish Broadcasting Company's transmission tower in Helsinki. However, even though the camera is moveable, this remains yet another great panoramic vista that offers no detail or meaningful cultural interaction. In terms of a tourism experience it is rather like spending one's holiday standing on top of the Eiffel tower. The moveable web-cam does, however, suggest potentially more interesting applications of web-cams combined with telerobotics. For example, a cooperative community project set up at the University of Southern California called Tele-Garden created a minia-ture indoors garden in the 'real' (offline) world which could be accessed via an Internet connection. It allowed net users who had signed up to the cooperative by email to explore *and tend* the living garden, by remotely operating a robot, via their Internet connection, to which a web-cam was attached. On a first-come, first-served basis, they could get the robot to perform simple requests such as watering, planting and viewing the garden. They could also communicate with other members by entering 'the village square', a virtual chat-room.

This application was not intended as a touristic experience, and indeed the environment itself – a miniature laboratory garden – was not a very stimulating one from the perspective of the tourist gaze. However, one can imagine a more engaging, interactive experience being provided if the environment had been a fully realized, large-scale, visually rich garden constructed outdoors, with paths and mazes and interesting nooks and crannies. What is novel about such experiments is their intertwining of virtual cultural display (what one sees on the screen) with the offline, material world (where one's remote-controlled digital actions 'take place'). Networked telerobotics thus presents the rather scary prospect of lots of geographically separated people being able to change a distant environment physically, while sitting miles away at their computer terminals.

Perhaps in the future we will be able to control cameras remotely at a range of different sites, enabling us to view and listen to distant environ-ments without leaving our seats. For example, the idea of 'ubiquitous telepresence', discussed by Doherty *et al.* (1997), would enable any Internet user to control remotely a web-cam attached to a robotic device installed in a display environment such as an art museum, and command it to move around the collection. This would deliver a completely customized 'virtual tour' to the user. The user would connect to the museum server, check out and pay for a device, and start moving it around the museum, examining the entire collection at whatever degree of resolution the video camera provided. Alternatively, every interesting artefact or sight at a museum or other cultural display could have its own web-cam attached to it to enable networked virtual gazing. Pondering these possibilities forces one to think, if access were to become so easy (with no queues, crowds or fatigue), why not stay home and be a virtual visitor forever?

Virtual environments

A fourth type of application, still in its infancy regarding Internet access, is virtual reality. Whereas web-cams rely on the positioning of cameras in the material world, virtual reality software aims to reconstruct it digitally through techniques of computer simulation. The term 'virtual reality' refers both to the technology of creating virtual worlds as well as the experience of being immersed in them. For this reason, the term 'virtual environment' (VE) is often preferred, since this refers to the 3-D computer-generated realms that virtual technology permits (Hillis 1999). VEs are 'immersive' in that they use iconographics to try and simulate the appearance of the 'real world', or the appearance of a fantasy world which is convincing in its use of perspective, geometry, etc. They are usually experienced through a head-mounted display, often with a joystick added to provide the sensation of touch as well as sight and sound. VEs make cyberspace visible and touchable by giving it an environmental, place-based form.

Some very basic VEs have been set up on the web which can be accessed by a plug-in (a device that interacts with a web browser) capable of decoding virtual reality mark-up language (VRML). So far, their uses have been largely educational. For example, the Theban Mapping Project, based at the American University in Cairo has an educational interactive website that provides 3-D computer models of the tombs in the pyramids in Egypt's Valley of the Kings. One can 'enter' a 3-D graphical plan of each tomb and listen to audio voice-overs giving information about the artefacts and wall decorations found there. With its reliance on computer graphics and cartoon-image maps, however, it does not offer a convincing or mimetic simulation of reality. In theme parks, by contrast, stand-alone VEs using head-mounted displays are already on offer, allowing the experience of walking within a fully fleshed out digital world.

Indeed, there are efforts being made to enable the whole world to be representable in virtual form. For example, the goal of the Virtual Terrain Project is 'to foster the creation of tools for easily constructing any part of the real world in interactive, 3D digital form' (from the Virtual Terrain Project website). On their website, they quote US ex-Vice President, Al Gore, whose enthusiasm for cyberspace is well-known: 'I believe we need … a multi-resolution, three-dimensional representation of the planet, into which we can embed vast quantities of geo-referenced data'. It is possible that we shall soon see virtual reality mapping projects which will allow any part of the earth's terrain to be examined in 3-D via a computer screen, both in aerial view and in high-resolution close-up. This could be done either through digital simulation techniques or through satellite video images. This is a scenario that echoes the J.L. Borges fable cited by Baudrillard (1983), in which the emperor orders the cartographers to produce a perfect map of the empire. They respond by creating one that exactly and completely covers all the imperial territory itself. Baudrillard uses this story to describe contemporary powers of simulation, wherein (according to him) the boundary between reality and representation has dissolved.

Virtual mapping suggests that the world could be explored in two forms, as material matter (atoms) and digital simulation (bytes). Whilst the major applications of such a project would probably be scientific or governmental (such as geological, military and environmental modelling), it is inconceivable that its touristic possibilities would remain unexploited for long. Indeed, companies specializing in developing VR (virtual reality) software invariably name tourism as one of their potential markets. A virtually mapped world would correspond to the idea of a 'third nature', or 'cybersphere' (see Luke 1999). In this conspectus, 'first nature' is the earth in its natural state – the 'ecological biosphere' – while 'second nature' is the built/constructed environment, or the 'technosphere'. Third nature is simply another constructed setting within which life – and travel – can take place. If the VE gaze can travel everywhere, and if hearing, touch and smell (even taste?) can come along for the ride, what 'advantage' is retained by the material world itself, whether biosphere or technosphere?

Mimetic, kinetic VR is still too bandwidth-hungry for Internet delivery at current capacities, and technologies of VR simulation are still in their infancy. Whilst we wait to see how the technology shapes up, a more prosaic VR experience is available in the form of interactive panoramic virtual reality images. These 360-degree still images are deliverable over the Internet via imaging applications such as Apple's QuickTime player. To view these images, no helmet or joystick is required. One simply downloads the image and can then click on any part of it to 'turn' the image around 360-degrees and see the panorama from any point (one can even inspect the ceiling or the sky if desired). There are numerous sites offering panoramic images ranging from classic tourist sights, such as New York's Times Square (on Apple's own QuickTime website) to Andrew Nemeth's images of anonymous MacDonalds diners in Sydney, Australia (www.4020.net/). However, the experience of slowly downloading such an image is frustrating, it is difficult to see much in the way of detail on the small computer screen, and the ability to examine a photograph from 360-degrees is not particularly illuminating after the first couple of minutes. Although the viewer's perspective can be moved around, which is at least of minimal interest, it ultimately remains just a still image rather than anything that might be thought of as a virtual world.

Virtual museums

The Australian Maritime Museum in Sydney uses 360-degree virtual panaoramas in its interactive website, which offers five virtual tours of its exhibitions. This experiment indicates the extent to which museums are increasingly taking advantage of computer technology. The UK Tate Gallery website, for example, now receives an incredible 200,000 hits a day, while the Museum of the History of Science in Oxford attracts 100,000 individual virtual visits a year, compared to 35,000 physical ones.[1] The '24 hour museum' (www.24hourmuseum.org.uk) is a gateway to virtual museum sites in the UK which received 1.5 million hits in its first month up and running. Museums have, in fact, been the pioneers of virtual access to culture. This might seem less surprising when one considers museums' critical relations with space and visitability. First, visitors can access a digital museum from home and as many times as they wish for as long as they wish, thus potentially increasing museums' accessibility. Secondly, all museums that house collections have to grow continually, and so confront the problem of finding new space both for archived artefacts and for displays. Digitization, the ultimate compact storage method, is unlikely to replace the keeping of material artefacts. However, museums might, in future, keep their physical space for material collections and hold their exhibitions in virtual form. Alternatively, museums are being set up that are entirely digital and have no physical existence (see the Alternative Museum or the Digital Art Museum).

Thirdly, digitization can enhance interpretation by providing objects with more contextualization – through, for example, links to histories, specialist papers, information about the temporal and spatial provenance of objects, and so on. Digital images of artefacts could also be animated, showing how objects are used (such as a clay urn being filled with water) and how they change over time (as it is worn away). Such possibilities raise the spectre of images substituting for objects and historical speculations being presented as fully realized facts. Does digital display represent the down-grading of material 'aura' – such as the physical imprints left on an object by its history (showing wear and tear, for example, or damage, or just the patina of use over time), as well as its connection back to its makers'/users' physical labour? This reflects some of the concerns about cultural 'authenticity' discussed in earlier chapters. In Chapter 1, for example, I emphasized how museums remain distinctive precisely because of their promise to safeguard objects' material aura. Now that they are capable of providing virtual, public mirrors of their entire collections, these auratic functions may slip further from view.

Virtual display does, however, allow 'ordinary' people to display their culture without costly built exhibition space. For those many small and under-resourced groups who lack extensive artefactual and archival records, the web makes display feasible for the first time. For example, the Saskatchewan Indian Cultural Centre in Canada hosts the Virtual Keeping House Museum, a website which allows users to view two-dimensional images of artefacts and artworks produced by First Nations artists. These artworks are being produced anyway, but without the website their display would be both costly and less easily accessed. And it is not only through websites that museums can make use of digitization to enhance participation. A novel interactive museum installation recently exhibited at the (material) Pompidou Centre in Paris, was called Pockets Full of Memories (see Legrady 2002). It invited visitors to select an object they were carrying on their person, and then to scan this into digital form (via a custom-built scanning kiosk) and to input data about its characteristics and personal significance. The results were stored in a database and a special algorithm then positioned the objects in ever-changing map views projected onto the gallery walls. Almost 20,000 visitors contributed over 3300 objects, including many of their own scanned heads, hands and feet – bits of themselves they wanted to leave behind. Such virtual display technologies exploit to the full the tendencies we have been noting in visitable environments, towards the display of 'ordinary' people's, 'living' stories, allowing an easily managed form of popular, interactive participation. Visitors were invited to leave *their* imprint on the museum, rather than being left with only its imprint on them.

The digital image is not a substitute for the real object, nor is it the real object in a different form. In fact, it is not material at all but rather a metaphor for the real (we have learned to naturalize this metaphor by coming to accept that bytes can stand for atoms). The public's appetite for seeing the 'real' Mona Lisa at first hand is not diminished by the millions of reproductions that are available (Anderson 1999). Thus, the material–digital divide is not in danger of collapsing. Further, it is clear that the digital image and the material object are read in very different ways. Computers do not afford value-free reflections of the world, but pre-programmed perspectives (see Wallace 1995). So we should be wary of arguments that suggest digitization enables direct, unmediated access to objects by the public, thus somehow rendering curatorial perspectives and exhibition design redundant. Digital representation is not neutral – whether through web-cams or VR – and in many ways it adds yet another mediating layer in relation to the object itself (which is already interpreted by virtue of having been collected and displayed). This suggests a descent into multiple levels of representational distancing going under the guise of direct, virtual replication.

A digital alternative to tourism?

This reminder of the distancing properties of computer technology brings us back to the question of whether and how digital 'third nature' might be able to offer visitable domains of cultural display that can compete with those in the material world. As environments which are richly symbol-laden, and as scenic locations for the visitor's self-presentation, we can see the clear affinities between graphical MUDs and MOOs, in particular, and other, offline sites of cultural display. Both graphical MUDs and material-world cultural tours/performances, for instance, offer cross-cultural communication a real-life context – in the first case, through interactive simulated backdrops, and in the second case, through 'living' cultural 'front regions' (MacCannell 1976). As video and audio delivery over the net improves, we can envisage a new form of cross-cultural meeting-place emerging. For example, streams of real-time video footage of Florence's Piazza Signoria could provide a backdrop for virtual encounters with real Florentines. Perhaps we will be able to see and speak to a live tour guide who can give us our own personalized tour around the Uffizi Gallery without leaving our seats.

However, MUDs set up self–other relations that differ from physical sites of cultural display such as museums. First, physical museal exhibitions are the product of a central, organizing perspective. Secondly, they consist of substitute worlds, i.e. 'dead' representations that stand for 'living' (or ex-living) things which are absent. MUDs, by contrast, construct a symbolic environment in order to serve as a spontaneous meeting place with others, not to act as a substitute. These others may be physically absent, but they are 'communicatively' present. In Chapter 2, I discussed tourism as a system that mediates between the visitor and the visited by setting up constructed sites and enclaves of cultural display. This is not a reciprocal system, due to the subject/object relations set up by the mobile tourist gaze and the static sight. One gazes, the other is gazed at. Is it possible to detect, in networked interactive environments like MUDs a more egalitarian alternative, a mediating forum for cross-cultural encounters that allows direct and meaningful communication between users who are *all* – equally – visitors?

In order to tackle such a question, we need to step back and consider whether there is any meaningful comparison to be made between virtual, non-corporeal tourism and the 'real' thing. Answering this means thinking through what 'real' tourism means, and what kinds of pleasure(s) it affords.

There are several features of offline tourism which clearly cannot be replicated in digital form. First, when we travel offline, we take our bodies with us. Virtual travel, on the other hand, is travel in the head. Only bytes travel in cyberspace; atoms stay put. Interestingly, it is in the digital era that writers on tourism have come to recognize the implications of the body in shaping the tourist experience. As a counterpoint to (although clearly influenced by) the classic focus on the tourist gaze instigated by Urry's (1990) work and drawing on Foucauldian perspectives, writers on tourism have recently emphasized the embodied nature of travel. The differences between non-corporeal and corporeal travel suggest that encounters in digital form lack many of the dimensions of potentially transformative interaction with people, places and time that make up the real-world journey (see Kaplan 1994; Edensor 1998).

A second feature of 'real' tourism is the desire for spectacle and sensation. But what kinds of spectacle and sensation? As Urry (1990, 2002) has argued, tourism is not simply a means of consuming environments; it is a form of pleasure that derives from its contrast to the everyday. No matter how sanitized and managed through the package-tour system, tourism still brings with it the promise of an altered psychological state. This difference is not only a matter of what we gaze upon, but of bodily participation and some (at least) perception of risks and the unknown. In this regard, MacCannell (2001) identifies two forms of the tourist gaze. The first is content with the apparatus of conventional touristic representation, recognizing it as a construction. The second is more restless, searching for unexpected and idiosynchratic details that do not conform to received stereotypes. It seems unlikely that electronic travel – a necessarily pre-programmed construct – could substitute for this second gaze. Even in terms of the convention-bound first gaze, the non-corporeal, safe and sedentary nature of digital interaction makes it a different experience to its physical counterpart.

Thirdly, and relatedly, 'real' tourism involves disorder, difference and the ever-present potential for cultural misunderstanding and even conflict. The tourist buys a package or constructs an itinerary with certain preconceptions in his or her head, but physically going there means these are vulnerable to challenges of all kinds from the destination itself. The lifeworld awaiting at the end of the journey is, to a greater or lesser degree, unknowable in advance. Real life is in constant flux: even the most standardized repeat package tour can never replicate the exact same conditions for every visit. In cyberspace, however, digital environments, as the product of programmed sequences, exist in order to be manipulated and controlled by the visitor/user. This provision of mastery means that virtual environments are lacking in the basic qualities of unpredictability that characterize the offline world. Even in the most sophisticated computer game, one eventually learns the means of achieving victory or success; indeed, the goal of unravelling the programmer's vision is the key to the game's pleasure just as its attainment means 'game over' (Friedman 1995).

Users of MUDs and chat-rooms would, of course, protest that human interaction over the Internet can be just as unpredictable and challenging as offline communication. It is true that, in contrast to virtual reality, bulletin boards or websites, synchronous, multi-user virtual communication offers more of the qualities of offline interaction. Indeed, it could be argued that it brings people into contact who would never 'normally' know of each other's existence. MUDs and chat-rooms are thus a means of effecting virtual encounters with strangers as well as friends. Perhaps, then, they can bring the net-traveller into more immediate and sustainable relationships with other people than the other mediating sites of cultural display discussed in earlier chapters.

At first glance, MUDs and chat-rooms seem to remove the inhibitions of physical co-presence, and thus to get beyond the constraining norms of politeness and wariness that usually structure interaction with strangers (Reid 1995). Yet what is interesting about these kinds of anonymous multi-party communication spaces is that, in spite of this freedom, they appear to act as meeting-places for like minds, where relations of mutuality and common interest are affirmed. Social MUDs, for instance, frequently take the form of virtual communities, housed in virtual buildings, where the interaction is focused on establishing intimacies and behavioural norms. Pursuing these relationships over a period of time constitutes the main pleasure afforded by the environment. When users become hostile or aggressive this is seen as breaking the rules and dealt with accordingly, in a variety of ways (Reid 1999). Thus, both deviance and conformity are constitutive aspects of the MUD world, which is an enactment of mutuality rather than difference. In other words, the MUD or chat-room itself mediates the encounter with the other by providing a convention-bound stage to bridge the self–other gap. As Reid (1999: 112) observes, there is 'no moment on a MUD in which users are not enmeshed within a web of social rules and expectations'.

In this sense, MUDs act as sites of cultural mediation which translate the unknown into familiar form. In other words, otherness is tamed and managed by established conventions and codes which enable users to feel they are operating in a known and familiar world. In fact, as Robins and Webster (1999) argue about cyberspace as a whole, it is an apparatus dedicated to the fostering of affinities and order rather than differences and disorder. Thus, although social interaction may be disinhibited with regard to certain offline norms, MUDs operate through imposing other norms in the form of social restraints and even censorship. This seems to extend to respecting offline social identities, in spite of the arguments of utopian cyberspace proponents that social positionings such as race and gender can be circumscribed and even supplanted online. Against this, there is evidence to suggest that both actually continue to be identified and reproduced in chat-rooms and MUDs (see Burkhalter 1999), and even that gender is reproduced online in more conservative, stereotypical and rigid ways than in embodied, face-to-face interaction (see O'Brien 1999). It would seem that much of the communication that takes place in online meeting places is oriented to the creation of community rather than the discovery of difference (Robins and Webster 1999). Whereas offline travel and tourism is always haunted by the possibility of disruption, the completely sealed off digital world encourages the fantasy of endless mutuality. Material sites of cultural display may claim to substitute for the 'other', but they can never shut it out altogether.

Of course, not all virtual networks aspire to be homogeneous communities. Nor does every participant take the activities of membership seriously. Many participate in these networks in order to perform and play with different identities rather than to build relationships where professed identities can be trusted to be real. Some may genuinely wish to meet other 'real' selves and exchange knowledge which derives from truthfulness about offline identity, and thus, potentially, to pursue relations of difference and 'otherness'. Others are more committed to experimentation, and are seeking liberation from the real contexts of their offline lives and interests (see Reid 1999 for a discussion). This is not to suggest that authentic cross-cultural communication on the net can only take place on the basis of truthfulness (or that offline communication is characterized by such). Rather, it suggests that there is no more likelihood of securing 'authentic' relations with and knowledge about the 'other' online than there is offline.

In many ways, the activity of 'community building' on the net is a heartening idea. It seeks to transcend distance and strangeness by establishing ongoing, live and routine communicative contact with distant others. This is not, by any stretch of the imagination, a 'bad' thing. By staging these contacts in graphic virtual environments, they are rendered more situated, more akin to the local material life-world. As Tomlinson (1999) points out, this kind of personalizing and familiarizing strategy, which allows otherness to be 'brought home' to us, may be necessary for establishing the grounds for meaningful moral engagement with distant life-worlds. But there is a danger of seeing screen-mediated relationships with others as intimate, direct and transparent, through the impression of spontaneous reciprocity. Tomlinson (1999) reminds us that, as well as facilitating communication by overcoming time and distance, mediation also intervenes between the phenomenological world and our senses. We perceive the world *through* the medium. Media of all kinds thus transform communication through the operation of various codes. This means the computer screen cannot give us direct access to distant places and people as though they were actually standing in front of us and sharing our life-world.

Dreams of perfect, net-based cross-cultural communication are punctured in other ways too. In Chapter 2, it was proposed that offline travel tends to delimit encounters between tourists and locals in particular ways so that most tourists have little or no contact with most locals. In computer-mediated encounters, these barriers are even more extensive and concrete – even though the technology appears to promise total accessibility. The only people one can meet on the web are those with access to a computer, a modem, an Internet service provider, a functioning phoneline and a reliable supply of electricity (Holderness 1998). In the world's top 40 developed economies in 1994, only approximately half had more than three telephone lines for every ten inhabitants (Holderness 1998). That number dropped to one in ten for the bottom quarter. India, ranked 39, had only 1.1 telephone lines and 0.1 PCs for every 100 inhabitants. Those economies not included in the top 40, such as virtually all the African countries, are clearly excluded altogether for all intents and purposes from the network communications revolution. And even those, like India, who do have national communications links to the World Wide Web, have such low bandwidth that participation in MUDs and chat-rooms is virtually impossible. Many are limited to 'store-and-forward' low cost email systems such as FIDOnet.

Just as developing countries manage step by step to upgrade their *entire* Internet connectivity, so new virtual reality applications are invented which require the same bandwidth capacity per *household* (Holderness 1998). Moreover, even where connectivity exists in the developing world, it is most likely to be available only to those who live in cities, where most telephone lines are located, and then only to those few who can pay the (very) expensive subscription charges. The effect of these considerable inequalities in distribution mean that most networked communication occurs between users from wealthy nations, possibly extending to a small elite from less developed countries composed of 'expats', academics and professionals employed in large companies, universities and governments. It is indeed a plausible scenario that the net itself will become increasingly segmented, with its free public portion slow and poorly resourced, left behind by private, limited-access, high-speed intranets (Sassen 1999). Considerations of gender, too, suggest that the offline world is exclusionary, since it is disproportionately populated by men. Users of the novel and innovative digital city set up in Amsterdam, Digitale Stad, for example, are estimated to be 90 per cent male (Bergman and van Zoonen 1999).

Conclusion

For Turkle (1997) and others (e.g. Rheingold 1994; Negroponte 1995; Levy 2001), virtualization has potential for progressive human interaction, enshrined in the cyberspace promise of a more communitarian, open, democratic space of communication. This vast electronic network brings into being a universe of knowledge which, in contrast to institutionally embedded knowledge in the real world, is not hierarchically organized, and to which everyone (given the resources) has equal access. However, the virtualization of knowledge is also, potentially, anti-democratic. For example, argue Robins and Webster (1999: 224), if we examine virtualization 'from the perspective of the world whose reality we are being invited to abandon', we can see that the celebration of de-territorialized, disembedded knowledge devalues knowledge which is situated in localized, material, everyday contexts. Further, if cyberspace provides a means of escaping the constraints of locally situated interaction, it does so not primarily for individuals, but in the service of a new 'extraterritorial space of enterprise' which allows corporate interests to operate as independently of political and cultural boundaries as they can get away with (1999: 225). Robins and Webster (1999), among others, argue that network space has been colonized by an emerging 'global virtual class' of highly communications-literate enterprise workers, allowing this privileged elite to become even more remote from and uninterested in the social realities and cultures that the rest of us inhabit (see also Luke 1999).

Although cyberspace facilitates relationships with distant others, these exist purely in the form of communications – as detached, disembodied verbal and image-based exchanges in the electronic network. Like television, it encourages a non-committal relation with the world, a 'zapping' domain where everything is watchable rather than graspable (Bauman 1996). Communication is not, however, the same as existence, and exchanging messages about the world is not the same as knowing it. As Hillis (1999: xxxiv) rightly points out, 'although communication is a necessary condition for people to act socially, on its own, communication can never be a sufficient guarantee that this activity will occur' (see also

Mattelart 1994, on the tendency to equate communication with emancipation). Just because on the net no one knows you're black, gay, female, disabled – or a dog (to refer to a famous newspaper cartoon lampooning the net's promise of anonymity) – this does not mean that one can escape the social disadvantage enshrined in these categories simply through talking to each other in cyberspace. We still live, eat, sleep, work and socialize in the material, offline world, and its exclusions, restrictions, hierarchies and inequalities are still dividing us from each other in the age of the Internet. The allure of being connected to a vast network brings the danger of succumbing to an illusory sense of the social – to a 'new monasticism' which encourages us to think that we can know, understand and be social with others through our lone access to the communications port of our computer or interactive TV (Haywood 1998).

Virtual culture, argue Robins and Webster (1999: 239), is 'driven by the desire to suppress the complexities, difficulties and divisions that characterize real geographies'. It encourages us to see social life in miniature form. Virtual chat-rooms, MUDs and MOOs claim to be spaces where, through talking together in virtual neighbourhoods, we can find solutions to world problems – as though the world's problems could be 'conceived in the image of the village pump or the town square' and were no more challenging than sorting out problems in a local community (Robins and Webster 1999: 230). The screen offers itself as a metaphor for the life-space, inviting us to see its small, human-scale exchanges and informal 'chats' as microcosms of the world as a whole. It thus steadfastly ignores the big, immovable structures of global capitalism which cannot be translated into screen-size interactions among persons.

We can see in cyberspace, therefore, a form of distancing which is more profound, and arguably insidious, than the other sites of cultural display I have been discussing in this book. Whereas cyberspace innovation seems to be intent on the achievement of perfect replicability, exhibitions, museums and theme-parks are still clearly recognizable as representations (in spite of some of Baudrillard's claims). Digitalization is judged to succeed where it most perfectly captures the 'real' in all its kinetic, multi-sensory intensity. As Robins' and Webster's (1999) analysis tellingly shows, however, this mimeticism is only epiphenomenal. Its replication of the real extends to the appearance and feel of reality, but not its materiality or its resistance to control. Successful digitalization depends on making us convinced of its reality (such as by making pixels invisible) in order to grant us the impression of controlling reality.

These fantasies of mastery are perhaps not dissimilar from those underpinning other, offline sites of cultural display discussed in this book. I want to argue, nevertheless, that these remain distinctive in particular ways. I have shown in other chapters how more and more space is being turned into visitable culture, and how turnstiles and boundaries around this space are increasingly being removed. And, as museums and theme parks try to enhance their mimetic powers and thus achieve greater levels of visitability, they seek to immerse us in interactive simulations of the past in ways which are not dissimilar to VR. Similarly, as shopping malls metamorphose into miniature cities, so they promise to enclose us in reconstructions that are more convenient, safe and pleasure-oriented than the real thing. And, at the same time, urban enclaves respond by turning into 'fantasy city' (Hannigan 1998). Many arguments can thus be made about the general encroachment of cultural display and simulation into the 'ordinary' corners of life, such as shops, schools, streets and scenery. Such arguments have been made quite forcefully, in fact, throughout this book. And it could certainly be further argued that, in taking the next 'logical' step – from material constructs to digital ones, from second nature to third nature – there is no real 'break' involved. Already, public space has been eroded and we have become accustomed to having everything available in consumable form. Already we are familiar with the language of the symbol and quite happy with the ubiquity of spectacle and simulacra. Already we seem used to the idea of communication in the form of feedback and push-button options. Surely virtualization is just the arrival of yet another layer that mediates, privatizes and simulates our relationship with the external world.

In one sense, virtualization *is* just another mediating channel. But where it sets itself up as a replica of reality (as in VEs, interactive telerobotics or the idea of 'ubiquitous tele-presence'), the computer's mimetic powers hide the fact that it excludes crucial aspects of human life (qualities such as physical pain, proximity and contact, embodiment, co-presence, materiality and space). VR and tele-presence seem set on dissolving the distinction between reality and representation. But, *contra* Baudrillard, this distinction is still extremely important, particularly in matters where striving for the truth is essential (such as education, science, politics and history). Where it matters less, perhaps, is in the world of leisure, consumption and play. Wandering around the city and losing oneself in an 'emporium of signs' does not necessarily endanger one's ability to go home, pick up a newspaper and settle down to make sense of the world. Nor does finding oneself surrounded by cultural display while on holiday mean that one can't look beyond it (indeed, as MacCannell (1999) argues, the very ubiquity of display itself impels one to do so).

Equally, one can switch off the computer and return to the real world, without – as techno-pessimists fear – finding that world has disappeared.

And one can hardly switch off and not notice the difference. Further, much computer-use of the synchronous/interactive or VE kind is very much a playful, leisure-oriented activity. For this reason, and for the others discussed above, I do not think that VEs or cyberspace are about to substitute for corporeal cross-cultural interaction and travel. However, digitization is certain to become more ubiquitous and taken-for-granted in the future. If we increasingly live our lives through networked screens, then material reality is reduced to an image, becoming less intrusive, disturbing or unsettling. It becomes a place from which we can always log off. And if space melts into bytes, so does a fundamental aspect of human existence – its necessary dependence on space and the production of space (see Lefebvre 1991).

As MacCannell (1976) says, we are always searching for more reality and meaningfulness under conditions in which we are increasingly denied them. The future provision of virtual holiday experiences (*Total Recall* style?) may simply intensify this search. Virtual environments can never *be* reality: bytes cannot become atoms. Thus, it seems unlikely that the placed, material dimension of visiting and tourism will disappear. Indeed, it may well intensify as the touch-screen proliferates. The material, three-dimensional places which this book has discussed will, arguably, come to look even more visitor-friendly, elaborate, mobile, interactive and sign-laden when they have to compete with the representation of the world in virtual, 3-D form.

Note

1   From Puttnam, D. (1999) Antiquity at the touch of a finger, *Guardian*, 16 June.

Further reading

Hillis, K. (1999) *Digital Sensations: Space, Identity, and Embodiment in Virtual Reality*. Minneapolis: University of Minnesota Press.
Mackay H. and O'Sullivan T. (eds) (1999) *The Media Reader: Continuity and Transformation*. London: Sage, in association with the Open University.
Miller, D. and Slater, D. (2000) *The Internet: An Ethnographic Approach*. Oxford: Berg
Robins, K. and Webster, F. (1999) *Times of the Technoculture: From the Information Society to the Virtual Life*. London: Routledge
Smith, M. A. and Kollock, P. (eds) (1999) *Communities in Cyberspace*. London: Routledge.
Turkle, S. (1997) *Life On The Screen*. New York: Simon & Schuster.

GLOSSARY OF KEY TERMS

Authenticity.   This term refers to the qualities of genuineness and originality which are often attributed to human cultures, especially those which are seen as more traditional and meaningful than late modern, Western consumer culture. The public exhibition of signs of cultural authenticity appears to underlie many sites of cultural display today, although the extent to which visitors actually see these as authentic is a matter of debate (see MacCannell 1999; Urry 2002).

Cosmopolitanism.   This term refers to the quality of being able to assimilate many different cultures, rather than being confined to local or national prejudices or limitations. As Hannerz (1990) notes, cosmopolitans are a small elite of the world's population which is financially well-off, socially and geographically mobile and culturally literate. Cosmopolitans appreciate the signs of cultural difference and authenticity, and thereby have an investment in other people staying as 'locals' in order to provide them.

Cultural imperialism.   The thesis of cultural imperialism (see Schiller 1996) suggests that the values and commodities of Americanized corporate consumerism are swamping the world's remaining distinctive local cultures through the acceleration of processes of globalization. As opposed to older models of geopolitical conquest, this new *cultural* imperialism is ruthlessly effective in incorporating all societies into a global, capitalist monoculture that works in the interests of Western, and particularly North American, political and economic interests. However, this term has been controversial; see, for a critical discussion, Tomlinson (1999).

Cultural mosaic.   This term is borrowed from Kahn (1995), and refers to a particular view of the world that sees it as comprising lots of different and distinctive cultures, each occupying a clear geographical location and/or belonging to an identifiable group of people. It is a view which is a product of cultural relativism (i.e. the belief that every culture has its own values and must be understood and judged on its own terms, rather than according to a universal set of criteria). It is a view of culture that has been rejected by writers working within a post-colonial, deconstructivist perspective.

Cultural particularism. This refers to the idea that different groups of people possess strong and well-defined cultural differences which serve to distinguish them from each other. It can be opposed to the term 'cultural universalism', which proposes that there are widely shared characteristics that serve to unite, rather than to divide, the various peoples of the world. Robertson (1992) shows how globalization both produces and is produced by the interdependence of cultural universalism and particularism (see also Barber 1995).

Deindustrialization. This term describes the processes by which national economies and regions lose their erstwhile identities as established centres of industrial (especially manufacturing and extractive) production. It is used particularly to describe the decades of industrial restructuring from the 1970s (and particularly the global oil crisis) onwards, during which many Western economies shifted from a manufacturing to a service-sector base (see Harvey 1989a).

Enframing. A term used by Mitchell (1988) to describe the processes of representation typical of the nineteenth century Western colonialist mindset. This defined and pictured places in terms of *views*, standing for values of order/disorder, discipline/anarchy, etc. It echoes the arguments of Heidegger (1951) that modern ideas of 'reality' define it as that which can be represented.

Exhibitionary complex. This term is Bennett's (1988, 1995), which he uses to describe the wide variety of novel exhibitionary venues that began to appear during the second half of the nineteenth century. These included public museums, dioramas and panoramas, international exhibitions, arcades, public gardens and department stores. They served to familiarize the public both with emergent academic disciplines (such as history, anthropology and biology) and with 'new technologies of vision' such as the camera (1988: 73). They thereby helped to inculcate a general public attitude of spectatorship and curiosity towards 'other' cultures and environments.

Expositions. These are large-scale, lavish international exhibitions, hosted in turn by different nation-states, in which the products and services of national economies are vaunted. In their Victorian heyday, they were the monopoly of the colonial powers (especially Britain and France) and were used to display the cultural customs (often via living 'ethnological villages') of the conquered nations. Later, they became more narrowly concerned with the display of commodities rather than people, but cultural display continues to be central to their function of illustrating a global 'pecking order' of nation-states and corporations (see Harvey 1996).

Globalization. This is a blanket term referring to the increasingly global reach of various distribution systems (including the media, agencies of political governance, capitalism, industry, weapons and the military, and so forth). It has been variously defined by different writers. Beck (2000: 11), for example, describes it as 'the processes through which sovereign nation-states are criss-crossed and undermined by transnational actors with varying prospects of power, orientations, identities and networks'. We can think of various axes of globalization, including its political, economic, informational and cultural varieties. See also Giddens (1991).

Heritage. In its broadest sense, heritage refers to something that is passed down from one generation to the next. As Lowenthal (1998) points out, the word always implies a 'legatee' (the person to whom the heritage 'belongs' and to whom it is passed down), and it therefore implies a present-day orientation (for the past is valued in today's terms). There has been a long-running 'heritage debate' in the UK over how to interpret the explosion in heritage sites since the 1980s (see for example, Wright 1985; Hewison 1987; Samuel 1994; Tunbridge and Ashworth 1996; Lowenthal 1998).

Identity-claims. This term refers to the ways in which groups (especially marginalized groups) may identify themselves as possessing certain unifying qualities, customs, values and/or experiences, and use these to stake their claim, through various struggles for autonomy and public recognition, to a particular cultural identity (e.g. gay identity; Native American identity; Islamic identity). This has often resulted in various public battles between dominant cultural institutions and marginalized groups. In museums, for instance, groups have demanded that their history be included in exhibitions of dominant culture (as in slave history) or that 'cultural property' appropriated by national collection museums should be restored to its original owners.

Interpretation. This refers to various techniques used to render intelligible, particularly through the use of cultural referents, environments and places that otherwise would not be particularly interesting, accessible or striking for visitors. The countryside, in particular, has been subjected to various interpretation strategies. The original proponent of interpretation was Freeman Tilden, 1957.

Living history. The use of real people, usually in costume, to act out historical scenarios and events at heritage sites, from battle re-enactments to craft demonstrations and the simple enactment of daily life.

Mimesis. The process of producing a faithful replica of reality, i.e. one that resembles, or mimics, it as closely as possible. Photo-mimesis refers to the technology of producing what appears to be a mirror-image of reality via the camera.

Otherness. The term given to the qualities of cultural difference (e.g. different customs, lifestyles, life-experiences, ways of thinking, etc.) that the West has historically ascribed to non-Western cultures. In post-colonial writing, the term is used to show up the West's dependence on binary models of thinking (such as black/white; male/female; modern/traditional; civilized/primitive) that seek to establish its own cultural and political values as dominant and natural (see Said 1978; Bhabha 1994; Gilroy 1994).

(Post)modern. Postmodernity is the term given by some social theorists to the period after the end of modernity (usually dating from the 1970s on) in which

certain profound social transformations (e.g. in information technology, in class relations, in economic production and distribution, etc.) are said to have occurred, such that the whole social and cultural order has been irrevocably altered. The prefix 'post' is often written in brackets, as here, because the term is highly controversial. Some writers (e.g. Lyotard 1979; Harvey 1989a; Bauman 1992) see it as a definite 'condition'; others refuse to identify an epochal break with modernity (e.g. Habermas 1987; Giddens 1990).

Reality TV. A genre of TV programme that became popular in the late 1990s, and which involves the televized reconstruction of various real-life situations in which actual people (rather than actors) agree to live for certain periods of time and to be filmed whilst doing so. Some take the form of game shows (such as *Big Brother* and *I'm a Celebrity (Get Me Out of Here)*). The precursors were so-called 'docusoaps' in which various categories of worker (such as traffic wardens and driving instructors) were filmed doing their job on a round-the-clock basis, and interacting with members of the public. The major characteristic is that ordinary, everyday human interactions, not performed by actors, are filmed in close-up detail.

Simulation. This is a term introduced by Baudrillard (1989) to describe contemporary sign-saturated consumer culture, in which it is no longer possible to make a distinction between signs and reality. It refers to the production of a copy for which no original exists (for example, the creation of cities in the image of theme parks). It is contrasted with the term *representation*, in which the referent (in reality) is still clearly distinguishable from its representation.

Theme parks. These are open-air venues in which a mixture of attractions, including fantasy rides and cultural reconstructions, are brought together into one (usually enclosed and pay-bounded) area. Perhaps the central characteristic of theme parks is that they do not offer merely mechanical rides and side-shows as in the traditional fair or amusement park, but use advanced technology to simulate scenes representing various cultural identities (particularly the signs and symbols of other places and times, and filmic and literary characters and celebrities).

Urban culturalization. This refers to the use of cultural display in the redevelopment of urban areas in order to make them visitable. The refurbishment and construction of new museums and exhibition venues, mixed-use waterfront developments, as well as the theming of streets and shopping plazas are all examples of initiatives that use culture (in the form of public art, lifestyle symbols, cultural references, poetry, literature, etc.) in order to fashion a clear identity for urban areas.

Viewability. I use this term to describe the ability of places to attract the gaze of consumers, visitors and tourists. To be viewable, places need to be equipped with a well-marked, coherent and legible set of views, vistas, scenes, buildings, zones, and so forth, which enable the visitor to locate the advertised cultural identity of the place easily and quickly.

Virtual tourism. I use this term to describe the potential for an experience akin to tourism through using the Internet or other kinds of computer technology such as virtual environments (VEs). The question is whether there is any meaningful sense in which the two kinds of tourism (physical/material and virtual/electronic) can be compared.

Visitability. I use this term to describe the production of visitor-friendliness in public spaces, shops and institutions. The production of visitability refers to the ways in which culture is deliberately used in these settings to attract the tourist gaze. Visitability is simultaneously an economic and a cultural phenomenon. Although far from new, it is something which is increasing as consumer-led display proliferates.

REFERENCES

Acland, C. (1998) Imax technology and the tourist gaze, *Cultural Studies*, 12(3): 429–45.

Adams, V. (1992) Tourism and Sherpas, Nepal: reconstruction of reciprocity, *Annals of Tourism Research*, 19: 234–49.

Adorno, T. and Horkheimer, T. (1979) *Dialectic of Enlightenment*. London: Verso.

Agnew, J. and Duncan, J. (1989) (eds) *The Power of Place*. Boston: Unwin Hyman.

Alloway, L. (1996) The great curatorial dim-out, in R. Greenberg, B.W. Ferguson and S. Nairne (eds) *Thinking about Exhibitions*. London: Routledge.

AlSayaad, N. (2001) Global norms and urban forms in the age of tourism: manufacturing heritage, consuming tradition, in N. AlSayaad (ed.) *Consuming Tradition, Manufacturing Heritage*. London: Routledge.

Ames, M. (1992) *Cannibal Tours and Glass Boxes: The Anthropology of Museums*. Vancouver: UBC Press.

Anderson, B. (1991) *Imagined Communities*, 2nd edn. London: Verso.

Anderson, M.L. (1999) Museums of the future: the impact of technology on museum practices, *Daedalus* 128(3): 129–62.

Appadurai, A. (1990) Disjuncture and difference in the global cultural economy, in M. Featherstone (ed.) *Global Culture: Nationalism, Globalisation and Modernity*. London: Sage.

Appadurai, A. and Breckenbridge, C.A. (1999) Museums are good to think: heritage on view in India, in D. Boswell and J. Evans (eds) *Representing the Nation: A Reader*. London: Routledge.

Archer, K. (1997) The limits to the imagineered city: socio-spatial polarization in Orlando, *Economic Geography* 73(3): 322–36.

Arnold, M. ([1869] 1932) *Culture and Anarchy*. Cambridge: Cambridge University Press.

Ashworth, G.J. (1992) Heritage and tourism: an argument, two problems and three solutions, in C.A.M. Fleischer van Rooijen (ed.) *Spatial Implications of Tourism*. Groningen: Geo Pers.

Augé, M. (1995) *Non-places: Introduction to the Anthropology of Supermodernity*. London: Verso.

Aziz, H. (1995) Understanding attacks on tourists in Egypt, *Tourism Management*, 16(2): 91–5.

Bagguley, P., Mark-Lawson, J., Shapiro, D. *et al.* (1990) *Restructuring: Place, Class and Gender*. London: Sage.

Bal, M. (1996) The discourse of the museum, in R. Greenberg, B.W. Ferguson and S. Nairne (eds) *Thinking about Exhibitions*. London: Routledge.

Baldwin, J. and Williams, H. (1988) *Active Learning*. Oxford: Blackwell Education.

Barber, B.R. (1995) *Jihad vs. McWorld*. New York: Random House.

Barke, M. and Harrop, K. (1994) Selling the industrial town: identity, image and illusion, in J.R. Gold and S.V. Ward (eds) *Place Promotion: The Use of Publicity and Marketing to Sell Towns and Regions*. Chichester: John Wiley and Sons.

Barry, A. (1998) On interactivity, in S. Macdonald (ed.) *The Politics of Display: Museums, Science, Culture*. London: Routledge.

Baudrillard, J. (1983) *Simulations*. New York: Semiotext(e).

Baudrillard, J. (1989) *Selected Writings*, M. Poster (ed.). Cambridge: Polity Press.

Baudrillard, J. (1994) *Simulacra and Simulation*. Translated by S.F. Glaser. Ann Arbor: University of Michigan Press.

Bauman, Z. (1987) *Legislators and Interpreters: On Modernity, Post-modernity and Intellectuals*. Cambridge: Polity Press.

Bauman, Z. (1992) *Intimations of Postmodernity*. London: Routledge.

Bauman, Z. (1993) Postmodern Ethics. Oxford: Blackwell.

Bauman, Z. (1996) From pilgrim to tourist – or a short history of identity, in S. Hall and P. Du Gay (eds) *Questions of Cultural Identity*. London: Sage.

Beardsworth, A. and Bryman, A. (1999) Late modernity and the dynamics of quasification: the case of the themed restaurant, *The Sociological Review*, 47(2): 228–57.

Beck, U. (2000) *What is Globalization?* Cambridge: Polity Press.

Beckett, A. (1994) Take a walk on the safe side, *Independent on Sunday*, 27 February, pp. 10–12. Also collected in Pile, S., Brook, C. and Mooney, G. (eds) (1999) *Unruly Cities*. London: Routledge.

Benjamin, W. (1973) The work of art in the age of mechanical production, *Illuminations*, H. Zohn (trans.), H. Hannah Arendt (ed.). London: Fontana.

Bennett, T. (1988) The exhibitionary complex, *New Formations*, 4: 73–102.

Bennett, T. (1992) Useful Culture, *Cultural Studies*, 6(3): 395–408.

Bennett, T. (1995) *The Birth of the Museum: History, Theory, Politics*. London: Routledge.

Bergman, S. and van Zoonen, L. (1999) Fishing with false teeth: women, gender and the Internet, in J. Downey and J. McGuigan (eds) *Technocities*. London: Sage.

Berman, M. (1982) *All that is Solid Melts into Air*. New York: Simon & Schuster.

Bhabha, H. (1994) The other question, *The Location of Culture*. London: Routledge.

Bianchini, F. (1993) Remaking European cities: the role of cultural politics, in F. Bianchini and M. Parkinson (eds) *Cultural Policy and Urban Regeneration: The West European Experience*. Manchester: Manchester University Press.

Bianchini, F. (1995) Night cultures, night economies, *Planning Practice and Research*, 10(2): 121–6.

Bianchini, F. and Schwengel, H. (1991) Re-imagining the city in J. Corner and S. Harvey (eds) *Enterprise and Heritage: Crosscurrents of National Culture*. London: Routledge.

Boissevain, J. (1992) (ed.) *Revitalizing European Rituals*. London: Routledge.

Bommes, M. and Wright, P. (1982), Charms of residence: the public and the past, in R. Johnson, G. McLenon, W. Schwartz and D. Sutton (eds) *Making Histories*. London: Hutchinson.

Boniface, P. (1998) Tourism culture, *Annals of Tourism Research*, 25(3): 746–9.

Boorstin, D. ([1961] 1992) *The Image: A Guide to Pseudo-events in America*. New York: Vintage Books.

Bourdieu, P. (1984) *Distinction: A Social Critique of the Judgement of Taste*. London: Routledge and Kegan Paul.

Bourdieu, P. (1993) *The Field of Cultural Production*. Oxford: Polity Press.

Bourdieu, P. and Darbel, A. (1991) *The Love of Art: European Art Museums and their Public*. Oxford: Polity Press.

Boyer, M.C. (1992) Cities for sale: merchandising history at South Street Seaport, in M. Sorkin (ed.) *Variations on a Theme Park: The New American City and the End of Public Space*. New York: Hill and Wang.

Brannen, M.Y. (1993) Bwana Mickey: Constructing cultural consumption at Tokyo Disneyland, in A. Kaplan and D.E. Pease (eds) *Cultures of United States Imperialism*. Durham: Duke University Press.

Bryman, A. (1995) *Disney and his Worlds*. London: Routledge.

Bryman, A. (1999) The Disneyization of society, *The Sociological Review*, 47: 25–47.

Brown, A., O'Connor, J. and Cohen, S. (2000) Local music policies within a global music industry: cultural quarters in Manchester and Sheffield, *Geoforum* 31(4): 437–51.

Buhalis, D. (2001) Tourism and cyberspace: conference report, *Annals of Tourism Research*, 28(1): 232–235.

Burkhalter, B. (1999) Reading race online: discovering racial identity in Usenet discussions, in M.A. Smith and P. Kollock (eds) *Communities in Cyberspace*. London: Routledge.

Burns, P. M. (1999) *An Introduction to Tourism and Anthropology*. London: Routledge.

Carr, D. (2003) Game on: the culture and history of videogames, *Visual Communication*, 2(2): 163–6.

Castells, M. (1994) European cities, the informational society and the global economy, *New Left Review*, 204: 18–32.

Cheong, S. and Miller, M. (2000) Power and tourism: a Foucauldian perspective, *Annals of Tourism Research*, 27(2): 371–90.

Clifford, J. (1986) On ethnographic allegory, in J. Clifford and G. Marcus (eds) *Writing Culture: The Poetics and Politics of Ethnography*. Berkeley: University of California Press.

Clifford, J. (1992) Travelling cultures, in L. Grossberg, C. Nelson and P. Treichler (eds) *Cultural Studies*. London: Routledge.

Clifford, J. (1995) Paradise, *Visual Anthropology Review*, 11(1): 92–117.

Cooke, P. (ed.) (1989) *Localities*. London: Unwin Hyman.

Cooke, P. (1990) *Back to the Future*. London: Unwin Hyman.

Coombes, A.E. (1991) Inventing the 'postcolonial': hybridity and constituency in contemporary curating, *New Formations*, 18, Winter: 39–52.

Coombes, A.E. (1994) *Reinventing Africa: Museums, Material Culture and Popular Imagination in Late Victorian and Edwardian England*. London: Yale University Press.

Corner, J. and Harvey, S. (1991) Mediating Tradition and Modernity, in J. Corner and S. Harvey (eds) *Enterprise and Heritage: Crosscurrents of National Culture*. London: Routledge.

Cowell, R. and Thomas, H. (2002) Managing nature and narratives of dispossession: reclaiming territory in Cardiff Bay, *Urban Studies*, 39(7) 1241–60.

Craik, J. (1997) The culture of tourism, in C. Rojek and J. Urry (eds) *Touring Cultures: Transformations in Leisure and Theory*. London: Routledge.

Crang, M. (1994) On the heritage trail: maps of and journeys to olde England, *Environment and Planning D: Society and Space*, 12: 341–55.

Crang, M. (1996) Magic kingdom or a quixotic quest for authenticity? *Annals of Tourism Research*, 23(2): 415–31.

Crawford, M. (1992) The world in a shopping mall, in M. Sorkin (ed.) *Variations on a Theme Park*. New York: Noonday Press.

Crawshaw, C. and Urry, J. (1997) Tourism and the photographic eye, in C. Rojek and J. Urry (eds) *Touring Cultures: Transformations of Travel and Theory*. London: Routledge.

Curtis, B. and Pajaczkowska, C. (1994) Getting there: travel, time and narrative, in G. Robertson, M. Mash, L. Tickner *et al.* (eds) *Travelers' Tales: Narratives of Home and Displacement*. London: Routledge.

Davis, F. (1979) *Yearning for Yesterday*. New York: The Free Press.

Davis, M. (1990) *City of Quartz: Excavating the Future in Los Angeles*. New York: Vintage Books.

Davis, S. G. (1996) The theme park: global industry and cultural form, *Media, Culture and Society*, 18: 399–422.

Dear, M. and Flusty, S. (1999) The postmodern urban condition, in M. Featherstone and S. Lash (eds) *Space and Culture: City – Nation – World*. London: Sage.

Delaney, J. (1992) Ritual space in the Canadian Museum of Civilisation, in R. Shields (ed.) *Lifestyle Shopping: The Subject of Consumption*. London: Routledge.

Dicks, B. (1999) The view of our town from the hill: communities on display as local heritage, *International Journal of Cultural Studies*, 2(3): 349–68.

Dicks, B. (2000a) Encoding and decoding the people: circuits of communication at a local heritage museum, *European Journal of Communication*, 15(1): 61–78.

Dicks, B. (2000b) *Heritage, Place and Community*. Cardiff: University of Wales Press.

Divall, C. (1998) Transports of delight? Making and consuming histories at the National Railway Museum, in J. Arnold, K. Davies and S. Ditchfield (eds) *History and Heritage: Consuming the Past in Contemporary Culture*. Shaftesbury: Donhead.

Doherty, M., Greene, M., Keaton, D. *et al.* (1997) Programmable Ubiquitous Telerobotic Devices, *Proceedings of SPIE Telemanipulator and Telepresence Technologies IV*, vol. 3206. Pittsburgh, PA: SPIE.

Douglas, M. and Isherwood, B. (1980) *The World of Goods: Towards an Anthropology of Consumption*. Harmondsworth: Penguin.

Duncan, C. and Wallach, A. (1980) The universal survey museum, *Art History*, 3(4): 448–69.

Durrans, B. (1988) The future of the other: changing cultures on display in ethnographic museums, in R. Lumley (ed.) *The Museum Time Machine*. London: Routledge/Comedia.

Eagleton, T. (1983) *Literary Theory: An Introduction*. Oxford: Blackwell.

Eco, U. (1986) *Travels in Hyperreality*. London: Picador.

Edensor, T. (1998) *Tourists at the Taj*. London: Routledge.

Edwards, T. (2000) *Contradictions of Consumption*. Buckingham: Open University Press.

Fabian, J. (1983) *Time and the Other*. New York: Columbia University Press.

Featherstone, M. (1991) *Consumer Culture and Postmodernism*. London: Sage.

Feifer, M. (1985) *Going Places*. London: Macmillan.

Fine, B. and Leopold, E. (1993) *The World of Consumption*. London: Routledge.

Fjellman, S.M. (1992) *Vinyl Leaves: Walt Disney World and America*. Boulder, SA: Westview Press.

Foucault, M. (1970) *The Order of Things: An Archaeology of the Human Sciences*. London: Tavistock Publications.

Francis, H. (1981) A nation of museum attendants, *Arcade*, 16 January: 8–9.

Franklin, A. and Crang, M. (2001) The trouble with tourism and travel theory? *Tourist Studies*, 1(1): 5–22.

Fretter, A.D. (1993) Place marketing: a local authority perspective, in G. Kearns and C. Philo (eds) *Selling Places*. Oxford: Pergamon Press.

Friedberg, A. (1993) *Window Shopping: Cinema and the Postmodern*. Berkeley, CA: University of California Press.

Friedman, T. (1995) Making sense of software: computer games and interactive textuality, in S.G. Jones (ed) *CyberSociety*. London: Sage.

Frow, J. (1991) Tourism and the semiotics of nostalgia, *October*, 57: 123–57.

Fuller, M. and Jenkins, H. (1995) Nintendo and New World travel writing: a dialogue, in S.G. Jones (ed.) *CyberSociety: Computer-Mediated Communication and Community*. Thousand Oaks: Sage.

Fyfe, N.R. and Bannister, J. (1998) The eyes upon the street: closed-circuit television surveillance and the city, in N.R. Fyfe (ed.) *Images of the Street: Planning, Identity and Control in Public Space*. London: Routledge.

Fyfe, G. and Ross, M. (1996) Decoding the visitor's gaze: rethinking museum visiting, in S. Macdonald and G. Fyfe (eds) *Theorising Museums*. Oxford: Blackwell.

Gable, E. (1996) Maintaining boundaries, or 'mainstreaming' black history at a white museum, in S. Macdonald and G. Fyfe (eds.) *Theorising Museums*. Oxford: Blackwell.

Garcia Canclini, N. (1992) *Hybrid Cultures: Strategies for Entering and Leaving Modernity*. Minneapolis: University of Minnesota Press.

Geddes, D. (2001) Review of heritage visitor attractions: an operations management perspective, *Tourist Studies*, 1(3): 317–18.

Getz, D. (1994) Event tourism and the authenticity dilemma, in W.F. Theobald (ed.) *Global Tourism: The Next Decade*. Oxford: Butterworth Heinemann.

Giddens, A. (1990) *The Consequences of Modernity*. Stanford: Stanford University Press.

Giddens, A. (1991) *Modernity and Self-Identity: Self and Society in the Late Modern Age*. Cambridge: Polity Press.

Gilroy, P. (1994) *The Black Atlantic: Modernity and Double Consciousness*. London: Verso.

Gold, J.R. and Ward, S.V. (1994) (eds) *Place Promotion: The Use of Publicity and Marketing to Sell Towns and Regions*. Chichester: John Wiley and Sons.

Goodwin, M. (1993) The city as commodity: the contested spaces of urban development, in G. Kearns and C. Philo (eds) *Selling Places: The City as Cultural Capital, Past and Present*. Oxford: Pergamon Press.

Gottdiener, M. (2001) *The Theming of America: Dreams, Visions and Commercial Spaces*, 2nd edn. Boulder, CO: Westview Press.

Graham, C. (2001) Blame it on Maureen O'Hara: Ireland and the trope of authenticity, *Cultural Studies*, 15(1): 58–75.

Graham, S. (1999) Towards urban cyberspace planning: grounding the global through urban telematics policy and planning, in J. Downey and J. McGuigan (eds) *Technocities*. London: Sage.

Gregory, D. (2001) Colonial nostalgia and cultures of travel, in N. Alsayaad (ed.) *Consuming Tradition; Manufacturing Heritage*. London: Routledge.

Griffiths, R. (1998) Making sameness: place marketing and the new urban entrepreneurialism, in N. Oatley (ed.) *Cities, Economic Competition and Urban Policy*. London: Sage.

Gruffudd, P. (1995) Heritage as National Identity: Histories and Prospects of the National Pasts, in D.T. Herbert (ed.) *Heritage, Tourism and Society*. London: Pinter.

Gruffudd, P. (1999) Prospects of Wales: Contested geographical imaginators, in R. Fevre and A. Thompson (eds.) *Nation, Identity and Social Theory: Perspectives from Wales*. Cardiff: University of Wales Press.

Gupta, A. and Ferguson, J. (1992) Beyond culture: space, identity and the politics of difference, *Cultural Anthropology*, February: 6–23.

Habermas, J. (1987) *The Philosophical Discourse of Modernity*. Cambridge, MA: MIT Press.

Hageman, S. (1991) Shopping for identities: a nation of nations and the weak ethnicity of objects, *Public Culture*, 3(2): 71–92.

Halewood, C. and Hannam, K. (2001) Viking heritage tourism: authenticity and commodification, *Annals of Tourism Research*, 28(3): 565–80.

Hall, C.M. (1992) Sex-tourism in south-east Asia, in D. Harrison (ed.) *Tourism and the Less Developed Countries*. London: Belhaven Press.

Hall, S. (1980) Encoding/decoding, in S. Hall, D. Hobson, A. Lowe and P. Willis (eds) *Culture, Media, Language*. London: Hutchinson.

Hall T. and Hubbard P. (eds) (1998) *The Entrepreneurial City: Geographies of Politics, Regime and Representation*. Chichester: John Wiley and Sons.

Hanna, M. (1998) The built heritage in England: properties open to the public, visitors and visitor trends, *Cultural Trends*, 32: 37–53.

Hannerz, U. (1990) Cosmopolitans and locals in world culture, in M. Featherstone (ed.) *Global Culture: Nationalism, Globalization and Modernity*. London: Sage.

Hannigan, J. (1998) *Fantasy City: Pleasure and Profit in the Postmodern Metropolis*. London: Routledge.

Haraway, D. (1991) *Simians, Cyborgs and Women: The Reinvention of Nature*. London: Free Association Books.

Harrison, D. (1992) International tourism and the less developed countries: the background, in D. Harrison (ed.) *Tourism and the Less Developed Countries*. London: Belhaven Press.

Harvey, D. (1989a) *The Condition of Postmodernity: An Enquiry into the Origins of Cultural Change*. Oxford: Basil Blackwell.

Harvey, D. (1989b) From managerialism to entrepreneurialism: the transformation in urban governance in late capitalism, *Geografiska Annaler*, 71(1): 3–17.

Harvey, P. (1996) *Hybrids of Modernity: Anthropology, the Nation State and the Universal Exposition*. London: Routledge.

Harvey, P. (1998) Nations on display: technology and culture in EXPO 1992, in S. Macdonald (ed.) *The Politics of Display: Museums, Science, Culture*. London: Routledge.

Haug, W.F. (1986) *Critique of Commodity Aesthetics: Appearance, Sexuality and Advertising in Capitalist Society*. Minnesota: University of Minnesota Press.

Haywood, T. (1998) Global networks and the myth of equality, in B.D. Loader (ed.) *Cyberspace Divide: Equality, Agency and Policy in the Information Society*. London: Routledge.

Hegeman, S. (1991) Shopping for identities: 'A Nation of Nations' and the weak ethnicity of objects. *Public Culture* 3(2): 71–92.

Heidegger, M. (1951) The age of the world view, *Measure*, 2: 269–84.

Heinich, N. (1988) The Pompidou Centre and its public: the limits of a utopian site, in R. Lumley (ed.) *The Museum Time Machine*. London: Routledge.

Heinich, N. and Pollak, M. (1996) From museum curator to exhibition auteurs: inventing a singular position, in R. Greenberg, B.W. Ferguson and S. Nairne (eds) *Thinking about Exhibitions*. London: Routledge.

Hendry, J. (2000) *The Orient Strikes Back: A Global View of Cultural Display*. Oxford: Berg.

Herbert, D. (1995) Heritage places, leisure and tourism, in D. Herbert (ed.) *Heritage, Tourism and Society*. London: Pinter.

Hewison, R. (1987) *The Heritage Industry: Britain in a Climate of Decline*. London: Methuen.

Hewison, R. (1989) Heritage: an interpretation, in D. Uzzell (ed.) *Heritage Interpretation Volume 1: the Natural and Built Environment*. London: Belhaven Press

Hillis, K. (1999) *Digital Sensations: Space, Identity, and Embodiment in Virtual Reality*. Minneapolis: University of Minnesota Press.

Hobsbawm, E. (1999) Mass-producing traditions: Europe, 1870–1914, in D. Boswell and J. Evans (eds) *Representing the Nation: A Reader: Histories, Heritage and Museums*. London: Routledge.

Hobsbawm, E. and Ranger, T. (eds) (1983) *The Invention of Tradition*. Oxford: Blackwell.

Holcomb, B. (1993) Revisioning place: de- and re-constructing the image of the industrial city, in G. Kearns and C. Philo (eds) *Selling Places*. Oxford: Pergamon Press.

Holderness, M. (1998) Who are the world's information-poor? in B. D. Loader (ed.) *Cyberspace Divide: Equality, Agency and Policy in the Information Society*. London: Routledge.

Hooper-Greenhill, E. (1992) *Museums and the Shaping of Knowledge*. London: Routledge.

Hooper-Greenhill, E. (1994) *Museums and their Visitors*. London: Routledge.

Hubbard, P. (1998) Introduction, in T. Hall and P. Hubbard (eds) *The Entrepreneurial City: Geographies of Politics, Regime and Representation*. Chichester: John Wiley and Sons.

Hubbard, P. and Hall, T. (1998) The entrepreneurial city and the 'new urban politics' in T. Hall and P. Hubbard (eds) *The Entrepreneurial City: Geographies of Politics, Regime and Representation*. Chichester: John Wiley and Sons.

Humphreys, R. (1995) Images of Wales, in T. Herbert and G.E. Jones (eds) *Post-War Wales*. Cardiff: University of Wales Press.

Huyssen, A. (1986) *After the Great Divide*. Bloomington: Indiana University Press.

Huyssen, A. (1995) *Twilight Memories: Marking Time in a Culture of Amnesia*. London: Routledge.

Jafari, J. (1987) Tourism models: the sociocultural aspects, *Tourism Management*, 8: 151–9.

Jameson, F. (1984) Postmodernism, or the cultural logic of late capitalism, *New Left Review*, 146: 53–92.

Jameson, F. (1991) *Postmodernism: Or, the Cultural Logic of Late Capitalism*. London: Verso.

Jamison, D. (1999) Tourism and ethnicity: the brotherhood of coconuts, *Annals of Tourism Research*, 26(4): 944–67.

Jenkinson, P. (1989) Material culture, people's history and populism: where do we go from here?, in S.M. Pearce (ed.) *Museum Studies in Material Culture*. Leicester: Leicester University Press.

Johnstone, C. (1998) Your granny had one of those! How visitors use museum collections, in J. Arnold, K. Davies and S. Ditchfield (eds) *History and Heritage: Consuming the Past in Contemporary Culture*. Shaftesbury: Donhead.

Jokinev, E. and Veijola, S. (1997) The disoriented tourist, in C. Rojek and J. Urry (eds) *Touring Cultures: Transformations in Travel and Theory*. London: Routledge.

Jordan, G. and Weedon, C. (2000) When the subalterns speak, what do they say? Radical cultural politics in Cardiff docklands, in P. Gilroy, L. Grossberg and A. McRobbie (eds) *Without Guarantees: In Honour of Stuart Hall*. London: Verso.

Jordanova, L. (1989) Objects of knowledge: a historical perspective on museums, in P. Vergo (ed.) *The New Museology*. London: Reaktion Books.

Jordanova, L. (2000) History, 'otherness' and display, in E. Hallam and B.V. Street (eds) *Cultural Encounters: Representing 'Otherness'*. London: Routledge.

Julier, G. (2000) *The Culture of Design*. London: Sage Publications.

Kahn, J. S. (1995) *Culture, Multiculture, Postculture*. London: Sage.

Kaplan, C. (1994) *Questions of Travel*. Durham: Duke University Press.

Karp, I. And Kratz, C.A. (2000) Reflections on the fate of Tippoo's tiger: defining cultures through public display, in E. Hallam and B.V. Street, *Cultural Encounters: Representing 'otherness'*. London: Routledge.

Kelly, A. and Kelly, M. (2003) Building legible cities 2: making the case. Unpublished brochure, Bristol Cultural Development Partnership.

Keil, R. (1994) Global sprawl: urban form after Fordism? *Environment and Planning D: Society and Space*, 12: 131–6.

King, A. (1990) Architecture, capital and the globalization of culture, in M. Featherstone (ed.) *Global Culture: Nationalism, Globalization and Modernity*. London: Sage.

Kirshenblatt-Gimblett, B. (1998) *Destination Culture: Tourism, Museums and Heritage*. Berkeley, LA: University of California Press.

Kong, L. (2000) Cultural policy in Singapore: negotiating economic and socio-cultural agendas, *Geoforum*, 31(4) 409–24.

Lamoureux, J. (1996) The museum flat, in R. Greenberg, B.W. Ferguson and S. Nairne (eds) *Thinking about Exhibitions*. London: Routledge.

Landow, G. P. (1997) *Hypertext 2.0: The Convergence of Contemporary Critical Theory and Technology*. Baltimore, MD: John Hopkins University Press.

Lash, S. and Urry, J. (1994) *Economies of Signs and Space*. London: Sage.

Lefebvre, H. (1991) *The Production of Space*. Oxford: Blackwell.

Legrady, G. (2002) Pockets full of memories: an interactive museum installation, *Visual Communication*, 1(2), 163–70.

Lever, A. (1987) Spanish tourist migrants – the case of Lloret de Mar, *Annals of Tourism Research*, 14(4), 449–70.

Levy, P. (2001) *Cyberculture*, R. Bononno (trans.). Minneapolis: University of Minnesota Press.

Lidchi, H. (1997) The poetics and the politics of exhibiting other cultures, in S. Hall (ed.) *Representation: Cultural Representations and Signifying Practices*. London: Sage/The Open University.

Light, D. (1995) Heritage as informal education, in D. Herbert (ed.) *Heritage, Tourism and Society*. London: Pinter.

Light, D. and Prentice, R. (1994) Who consumes the heritage product? in G.J. Ashworth and P.J. Larkham (eds) *Building a New Heritage: Tourism, Culture and Identity in the New Europe*. London: Routledge.

Loftman, P. and Levin, B. (1998) Pro-growth local economic development strategies: civic promotion and local needs in Britain's second city, 1981–1996, in T. Hall and P. Hubbard (eds) *The Entrepreneurial City: Geographies of politics, regime and representation*. Chichester: John Wiley and Sons.

Lowenthal, D. (1985) *The Past is a Foreign Country*. Cambridge: Cambridge University Press.

Lowenthal, D. (1998) *The Heritage Crusade and the Spoils of History*. Cambridge: Cambridge University Press

Luke, T. W. (1999) Simulated sovereignty, telematic territoriality: the political economy of cyberspace, in M. Featherstone and S. Lash (eds) *Spaces of Culture: Cities – Nation – World*. London: Sage.

Lumley, R. (1988) Introduction, in R. Lumley (ed) *The Museum Time Machine: Putting Cultures on Display*. London: Routledge.

Lunt, P.K. and Livingstone, S.M. (1992) *Mass Consumption and Personal Identity*. Buckingham: Open University Press.

Lynch, K. (1990) *City Sense and City Design*. Boston: MIT Press.

Lyotard, J. (1979) *The Postmodern Condition: A Report on Knowledge*. Minneapolis: University of Minnesota Press.

MacCannell, D. (1976) *The Tourist: A New Theory of the Leisure Class*. London: The Macmillan Press.

MacCannell, D. (1992) *Empty Meeting Grounds: The Tourist Papers*. London: Routledge.

MacCannell, D. (1999) *The Tourist: A New Theory of the Leisure Class*, 2nd edn. Berkeley: University of California Press.

MacCannell, D. (2001) Tourist agency, *Tourist Studies*, 1(1): 23–37.

Macdonald, S. (1995) 'Consuming Science: Public Knowledge and the Dispersed Politics of Reception among Museum Visitors', *Media, Culture and Society*, 17: pp 13–29.

Macdonald, S. (1996) Theorising museums: an introduction, in S. Macdonald and G. Fyfe (eds) *Theorising Museums*. Oxford: Blackwell/The Sociological Review.

Macdonald, S. (1997) A people's story: heritage, identity and authenticity, in C. Rojek and J. Urry (eds) *Touring Cultures: Transformations of Travel and Theory*. London: Routledge.

Macdonald, S. (1998) Supermarket science? Consumers and the 'public understanding of science' in S. Macdonald (ed.) *The Politics of Display: Museums, Science, Culture*. London: Routledge.

Mackie, V. (1992) Japan and south-east Asia: the international division of labour and leisure, in D. Harrison (ed.) *Tourism and the Less Developed Countries*. London: Belhaven Press.

Macnaghten, P. and Urry, J. (1997) *Contested Natures*. London: Sage.

Marcus, J. (2000) Towards an erotics of the museum, in E. Hallan and B.V. Street (eds) *Cultural Encounters: Representing 'Otherness'*. London: Routledge.

Marcuse, H. (1968) *One Dimensional Man: The Ideology of Industrial Society*. London: Sphere Books.

Marcuse, P. (1994) Not chaos, but walls: postmodernism and the partitioned city, in S. Watson and K. Gibson (eds) *Postmodern Cities and Spaces*. Oxford: Blackwell.

Marwick, S. (1995) Learning from each other: museums and older members of the community – the People's Story, in E. Hooper-Greenhill (ed.) *Museum, Media Message*. London: Routledge.

Massey, D. (1984) *Spatial Divisions of Labour: Social Structures and the Geography of Production*. Basingstoke: Macmillan.

Massey, D. (1994) *Space, Place and Gender*. Cambridge: Polity Press.

Massey, D. (1995) Places and their pasts, *History Workshop Journal*, (39): 183–92.

Mattelart, A. (1994) *Mapping World Communication: War, Progress, Culture*. Minneapolis, MA: University of Minnesota Press.

McClintock, A. (1995) *Imperial Leather*. London: Routledge.

McGuigan, J. (1999) *Modernity and Postmodern Culture*. Buckingham: Open University Press.

McNeill, D. (1999) Globalisation and the European city, *Cities*, 16(3): 143–8.

McQuire, S. (1998) *Visions of Modernity: Representation, Memory, Time and Space in the Age of the Cinema*. London: Sage Publications.

McTavish, L. (1998) Shopping in the museum? Consumer spaces and the redefinition of the Louvre, *Cultural Studies*, 12(2) 168–92.

Mercer, C. (1999) Cultural policy: research and the government imperative, in D. Boswell and J. Evans (eds) *Representing the Nation: A Reader*. London: Routledge.

Miles, M. (1997) *Art, Space and the City*. London: Routledge.

Miles, M. (1998) A game of appearance: public art and urban development – complicity or sustainability? in T. Hall and P. Hubbard (eds) *The Entrepreneurial City: Geographies of politics, regime and representation*. Chichester: John Wiley and Sons.

Mitchell, T. (1988) *Colonising Egypt*. Cambridge: Cambridge University Press.

Moeran, B. (1983) The language of Japanese tourism, *Annals of Tourism Research*, 10(1): 93–108.

Morgan, P. (1986) Keeping the legends alive, in T. Curtis (ed.) *Wales, the Imagined Nation*. Bridgend: Poetry Wales Press.

Morley, D. and Robins, K. (1995) *Spaces of Identity: Global Media, Electronic Landscapes and Cultural Boundaries*. London: Routledge.

Mugerauer, R. (2001) Openings to each other in the technological age, in N. AlSayyad (ed.) *Consuming Tradition, Manufacturing Heritage*. London: Routledge.

Negroponte, N. (1995) *Being Digital*. London: Hodder and Stoughton.

Nemiroff D. (1996) Modernism, nationalism and beyond: a critical history of exhibitions of first Nation art, in R. Greenberg, B.W. Ferguson and S. Nairne (eds) *Thinking about Exhibitions*. London: Routledge.

Nunez, T. (1989) Touristic studies in anthropological perspective, in V. Smith (ed.) *Hosts and Guests: The Anthropology of Tourism*, 2nd edn. Philadelphia: University of Pennsylvania Press.

Oatley, N. (1998) Cities, economic competition and urban policy, in N. Oatley (ed.) *Cities, Economic Competition and Urban Policy*. London: Sage.

O'Brien, J. (1999) Writing in the body: gender (re)production in online interaction, in M.A. Smith and P. Kollock (eds) *Communities in Cyberspace*. London: Routledge.

Peate, I. (1948) *Folk Museums*. University of Wales Press.

Penberthy, D. (2001) Ducks, trucks and a pile of bricks. Paper presented to the Association for Heritage Interpretation Annual Conference, Swansea, Wales, 12–14 September.

Phillips, P. (2000) Out of order: the public art machine, in M. Miles, T. Hall and I. Boden (eds) *The City Culture Reader*. London: Routledge.

Picard, M. (1996) *Bali: Cultural Tourism and Touristic Culture*. Singapore: Archipelago Press.

Poulot, D. (1994) Identity as self-discovery: the eco-museum in France in D.J. Sherman and I. Rogoff (eds) *Museum Culture: Histories, Discourses, Spectacles*. London: Routledge.

Prentice, R. (1993) *Tourism and Heritage Attractions*. London: Routledge.

Prosler, M. (1996) Museums and globalization, in S. Macdonald and G. Fyfe (eds) *Theorizing Museums*. Oxford: Blackwell.

Raban, J. (1974) *Soft City*. London: Hamish Hamilton.

Ramirez, M. (1996) Brokering identities: art curators and the politics of cultural representation, in R. Greenberg, B.W. Ferguson and S. Nairne (eds) *Thinking about Exhibitions*. London: Routledge.

Reid, E. (1995) Virtual worlds: culture and imagination, in S.G. Jones (ed.) *CyberSociety: Computer-mediated Communication and Community*. London: Sage.

Reid, E. (1999) Hierarchy and power: social control in cyberspace, in M.A. Smith and P. Kollock (eds) *Communities in Cyberspace*. London: Routledge.

Relph, E. (1976) *Place and Placelessness*. London: Pion.

Rheingold, H. (1994) *The Virtual Community: Finding Connection in a Compu-terised World*. London: Secker and Warburg.

Richards, G. (1996) Production and consumption of European cultural tourism, *Annals of Tourism Research*, 23(2): 261–83.

Riegel, H. (1996) Into the heart of irony: ethnographic exhibitions and the politics of difference, in S. Macdonald and G. Fyfe (eds) *Theorising Museums*. Oxford: Blackwell.

Ritzer, G. (1999) *Enchanting a Disenchanted World: Revolutionising the Means of Consumption*. Thousand Oaks, CA: Pine Forge Press.

Ritzer, G. and Liska A. (1997) 'McDisneyisation' and 'Post-Tourism': com-plementary perspectives on contemporary tourism, in C. Rojek and J. Urry (eds) *Touring Cultures: Transformations of Travel and Theory*. London: Routledge.

Robertson, R. (1992) *Globalization: Social Theory and Global Culture*. London: Sage.

Robins, K. (1991) Tradition and translation: national culture in its global context, in J. Corner and S. Harvey (eds) *Enterprise and Heritage: Crosscurrents of National Culture*. London: Routledge.

Robins, K. (1995) Collective emotion and urban culture, in P. Healey, S. Cameron, S. Davoudi, S. Graham and A. Modani-Pour (eds) *Managing Cities: The New Urban Context*. Chichester: John Wiley.

Robins, K. and Webster, F. (1999) *Times of the Technoculture: From the Infor-mation Society to the Virtual Life*. London: Routledge.

Robinson, M. (2001) Tourism encounters, in N. AlSayaad (ed.) *Consuming Tra-dition, Manufacturing Heritage*. London: Routledge.

Rojek, C. (1993) *Ways of Escape: Modern Transformations in Leisure and Travel*. London: Macmillan.

Rojek, C. and Urry, J. (1997) Transformations of travel and theory, in C. Rojek and J. Urry (eds) *Touring Cultures: Transformations of Travel and Theory*. London: Routledge.

Ryan, C. (1991) *Recreational Tourism: A Social Science Perspective*. London: Routledge.

Ryan, C., Hughes, K. and Chirgwin, S. (2000) The gaze, spectacle and eco-tourism, *Annals of Tourism Research*, 27(1): 148–63.

Rydell, R. (1999) The Chicago World's Columbian Exposition of 1893: 'and was Jerusalem builded here?' in D. Boswell and J. Evans (eds) *Representing the Nation: A Reader*. London: Routledge.

Said, E. (1978) *Orientalism*. New York: Vintage.

Samuel, R. (1994) *Theatres of Memory*. London: Verso.

Samuel, R. (1998) *Island Stories: Unravelling Britain*. London: Verso.

Sandberg, M.B. (1995) Effigy and narrative: looking into the nineteenth century folk museum, in L. Charney and V.R. Schwartz (eds) *Cinema and the Invention of Modern Life*. Berkeley, LA: University of California Press.

Sassen, S. (1994) *Cities in a World Economy*. Thousand Oaks, CA: Pine Forge/Sage.

Sassen, S. (1999) Digital networks and power, in M. Featherstone and S. Lash (eds) *Spaces of Culture: City, Nation, World*. London: Sage.

Schiller, H. (1996) *Information Inequality: The Deepening Social Crisis in America*. London: Routledge.

Schouten, F.J. (1995) Heritage as historical reality, in D.T. Herbert (ed.) *Heritage, Tourism and Society*. London: Pinter.

Selwood, S., Muir, A. and Moody, D. (1995) Museums and galleries statistics: the Domus Database, *Cultural Trends*, 28. London: Policy Studies Institute.

Sennett, R. (1996) *The Uses of Disorder: Personal Identity and City Life*. London: Faber and Faber.

Serres, M. (1995) *Les messages a distance*. Montreal: Editions Fides/Musee de la Civilisation.

Shields, R. (1989) Social spatialisation and the built environment: the West Edmonton Mall, *Environment and Planning Society and Space*, 7: 147–64.

Shields, R. (1991) *Places on the Margin: Alternative Geographies of Modernity*. Routledge: London.

Short, J.R. (1989) *The Humane City: Cities as if People Matter*. Oxford: Blackwell.

Short, J.R. (1996) *The Urban Order: An introduction to Cities, Culture and Power*. Oxford: Blackwell.

Smith, A. (1990) Towards a global culture? in M. Featherstone (ed.) *Global Culture: Nationalism, Globalisation and Modernity*. London: Sage.

Smith, D. (1990/91) Labour history and heritage, *Social History Curators Group Journal*, 18: 3–6.

Smith, M.A. and Kollock, P. (eds) (1999) *Communities in Cyberspace*. London: Routledge.

Smith, V. (1988) Geographical implications of 'drifter' tourism: Borocay, Phillipines. Paper presented to the Symposium on Tourism, International Geographical Union, Christchurch, New Zealand, 13–20 August.

Smith, V. (1989) *Hosts and Guests. The Anthropology of Tourism*. Philadelphia: University of Pennsylvania Press.

Soja, E. (1989) *Postmodern Geographies*. London: Verso.

Soja, E. (1992) Inside Exopolis: scenes from Orange County, in M. Sorkin (ed.) *The New American City and the End of Public Space*. New York: Hill and Wang.

Sorenson, C. (1989) Theme parks and time machines, in P. Vergo (ed.) *The New Museology*. London: Reaktion Books.

Sorkin, M. (1992) Introduction, in M. Sorkin (ed.) *Variations on a Theme Park: The New American City and the End of Public Space*. New York: Hill and Wang.

Stallabrass, J. (1999) The ideal city and the virtual hive: modernism and emergent order in computer culture, in J. Downey and J. McGuigan (eds) *Technocities*. London: Sage.

Stanley, N. (1998) *Being Ourselves for You: The Global Display of Cultures*. London: Middlesex University Press.

Taylor, J.P. (2001) Authenticity and sincerity in tourism, *Annals of Tourism Research*, 28(1): 7–26.

The Project on Disney (1995) *Inside the Mouse: Work and Play at Disney World*. Durham: Duke University Press.

Theobold, W.F. (1994) The context, meaning and scope of tourism, in W.F. Theobold (ed.) *Global Tourism: The Next Decade*. Oxford: Butterworth-Heinemann.

Thomas, H. (2000) Europe's most exciting waterfront, *Planet*, 143.

Thomas, H. and Imrie, R. (1999) Urban policy, modernisation, and the regeneration of Cardiff Bay, in H. Thomas and R. Imrie (eds) *British Urban Policy: An Evaluation of Urban Development Corporations*, 2nd edn. London: Sage.

Thompson, J.B. (1995) *The Media and Modernity*. Cambridge: Polity Press.

Tilden, F. (1957) *Interpreting our Heritage*. Chapel Hill: University of North Carolina Press.

Tomlinson, J. (1999) *Globalization and Culture*. Cambridge: Polity Press.

Tucker, H. (1997) The ideal village: interactions through tourism in Central Anatolia, in S. Abram, J. Waldren and D.V.L. Macleod (eds) *Tourists and Tourism: Identifying with People and Places*. Oxford: Berg.

Tunbridge, J.E. and Ashworth, G.J. (1996) *Dissonant Heritage: The Management of the Past as a Resource in Conflict*. Chichester: John Wiley and Sons.

Turkle, S. (1997) *Life On The Screen*. New York: Simon & Schuster.

Turkle, S. (1999) Identity in the age of the internet, in H. Mackay and T. O'Sullivan (eds) *The Media Reader: Continuity and Transformation*. London: Sage, in association with the Open University.

Turner, L. and Ash, J. (1975) *The Golden Hordes: International Tourism and the Pleasure Periphery*. London: Constable.

Urry, J. (1990) *The Tourist Gaze: Leisure and Travel in Contemporary Societies*. London: Sage.

Urry, J. (2000) *Sociology Beyond Societies: Mobilities for the Twenty-First Century*. London: Routledge.

Urry, J. (2002) *The Tourist Gaze*, 2nd edn. London: Sage.

Van Maanen, J. (1992) Displacing Disney: some notes on the flow of culture, *Qualitative Sociology*, 15(1): 5–35.

Van Maanen, J. and Laurent, A. (1993) The flow of culture: some notes on globalization and the multinational corporation, in S. Ghohal and D.E. Westney (eds) *Organization Theory and the Multinational Corporation*. London: St. Martin's Press.

Vergo, P. (1988) Introduction, in P. Vergo (ed.) *The New Museology*. London: Reaktion Books.

Wallace, M. (1995) Changing media, changing messages, in E. Hooper-Greenhill (ed.) *Museum, Media, Message*. London: Routledge.

Wallace, M. (1996) *Mickey Mouse History and Other Essays on American Memory*. Philadephia: Temple University Press.

Wallerstein, I. (1990) Culture as the ideological battleground of the modern world-system, in M. Featherstone (ed.) *Global Culture: Nationalism, Globalization and Modernity*. London: Sage.

Walsh, K. (1992) *The Representation of the Past: Museums and Heritage in the Post-Modern World*. London: Routledge

Ward, M. (1996) What's important about the history of modern art exhibitions? in R. Greenberg, B.W. Ferguson and S. Nairne (eds) *Thinking about Exhibitions*. London: Routledge.

Ward, S.V. (1994) Time and place: key themes in place promotion in the USA, Canada and Britain since 1870, in J.R. Gold and S.V. Ward (eds) *Place Promotion: The Use of Publicity and Marketing to Sell Towns and Regions*. Chichester: John Wiley and Sons.

Warde, A. and Martens, L. (2000) *Eating Out – Social Differentiation, Consumption and Pleasure*. Cambridge: Cambridge University Press.

Welsch, W. (1999) Transculturality: the puzzling form of cultures today, in M. Featherstone and S. Lash (eds) *Space and Culture: City – Nation – World*. London: Sage.

Wernick, A. (1991) *Promotional Culture: Advertising, Ideology and Symbolic Expression*. London: Sage.

Williams, R. (1961) *The Long Revolution*. London: Penguin.

Williams, R. (1973) *The Country and the City*. London: Hogarth Press.

Williams, R. (1981) *Culture*. London: Fontana.

Wilson, A. (1992) *The Culture of Nature: North American Landscape from Disney to the Exxon Valdez*. Oxford: Blackwell.

Wright, P. (1985) *On Living in an Old Country*. London: Verso.

Wright, P. (1992) *A Journey through Ruins*. London: Paladin.

Young, I.M. (1990) *Justice and the Politics of Difference*. Princeton: Princeton University Press.

Zolberg, V. (1994) 'An elite experience for everyone': art museums, the public, and cultural literacy, in D.J. Sherman and I. Rogoff (eds) *Museum Culture: Histories, Discourses, Spectacles*. London: Routledge.

Zukin, S. (1991) *Landscapes of Power: From Detroit to Disney World*. Berkeley, LA: University of California Press.

Zukin, S. (1995) *The Cultures of Cities*. Oxford: Blackwell.

Websites

@ Bristol: www.at-bristol.org.uk
Alternative Museum: www.alternativemuseum.org
Digital Arts Museum: www.dam.org
Ducks Unlimited: www.ducks.org
Lands End: www.landsend-landmark.co.uk
Lowell National Historical Park: www.nps.gov/lowe/

Magna Science Adventure Centre: www.magnatrust.org.uk
Native American Virtual Cultural Centre: www.ableza.org
Saskatchewan Indian Cultural Centre: www.sicc.sk.ca
Techniquest: www.techniquest.org
Telegarden: telegarden.aec.at
Theban Mapping Project: www.thebanmappingproject.com
Urban Dream Capsule: www.alphalink.com-au/~surreal/
Virtual Sites: www.virtualfreesites.com
Virtual Terrain Project: www.vterrain.org
Virtual Tourist: www.virtualtourist.com/vt/
VREgypt: members.tripod.com/~AtenHotep/VRINDEX.HTM
Wildfowl and Wetlands Trust: www.wwt.org.uk/
WTO (World Tourism Organisation): www.world-tourism.org/

INDEX

CULTURAL CITIZENSHIP
Cosmopolitan Questions

Nick Stevenson

- Why has 'culture' become central to political debates?
- How might we rethink questions of citizenship in an information age?
- What is cosmopolitanism and will it become the key ideal of the future?

This readable and accessible guide links questions of identity, individualization, multiculturalism, and mediation to a politics of culture. The book draws from debates in political theory, cultural studies and sociology, and focuses on issues such as:

- The reshaping of citizenship by globalization
- New social movements
- The decline of the nation-state
- The impact of popular culture

The book argues that questions of cosmopolitanism are increasingly likely to emerge within these contexts. Whether we are discussing the destruction of the environment, issues of cultural policy, the city, or consumer culture, these questions can all be linked to cosmopolitan dimensions. Issues of rights, obligations and cultural respect are now all central to the way in which we conceive our common world. This original book asks us to rethink the kinds of politics and personhood that are suitable for an information age.

Contents
Series editor's foreword – Introduction and acknowledgements – Cultural citizenship – Cosmopolitan and multicultural citizenship: world, nation, city and self – Ecological and cultural citizenship: across the nature/culture divide – Media, cultural citizenship and the public sphere – Consumerism, cultural policy and citizenship – Cultural citizenship: a short agenda for the future – Glossary – References – Index.

192pp   0 335 20878 9 (Paperback)   0 335 20879 7 (Hardback)

openup

ideas and understanding
in social science

www.**openup**.co.uk

 Browse, search and order online

 Download detailed title information and sample chapters*

*for selected titles

www.**openup**.co.uk